Name _____ Date ____

Label each pair of lines parallel, perpendicular or intersecting.

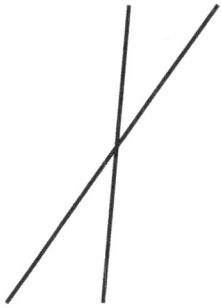  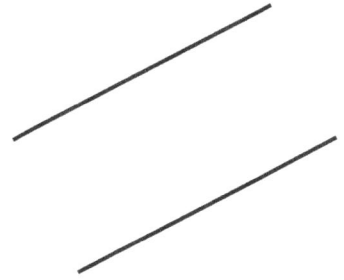

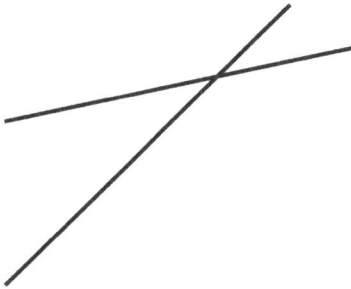 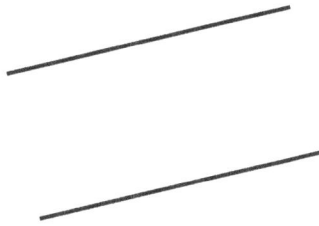 

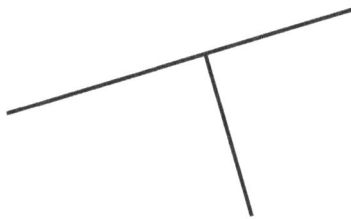 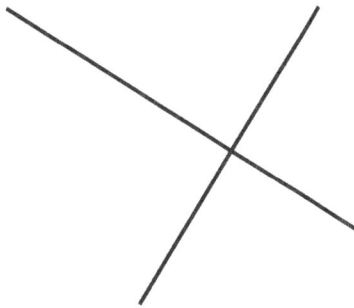 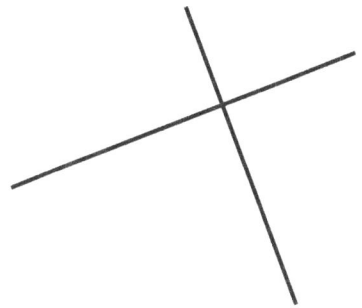

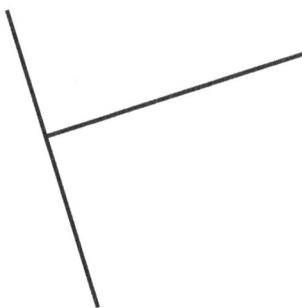  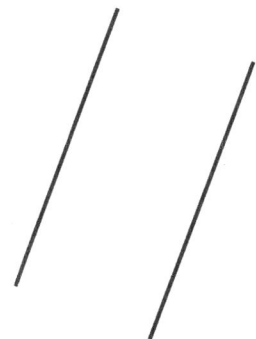

Name _____ Date _____

Label each pair of lines parallel, perpendicular or intersecting.

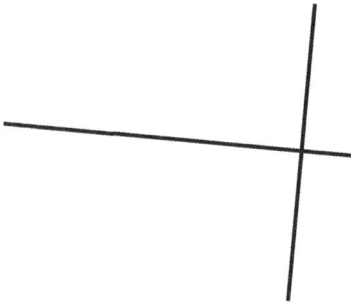

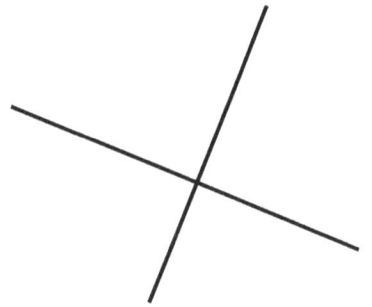

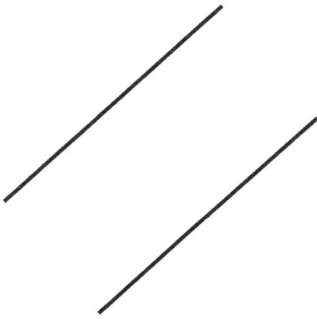

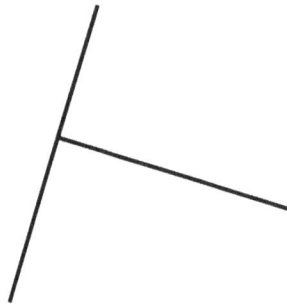

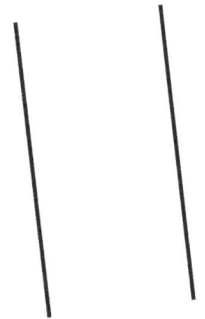

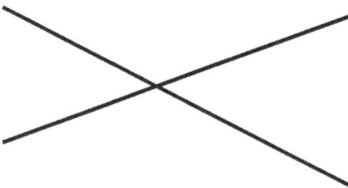

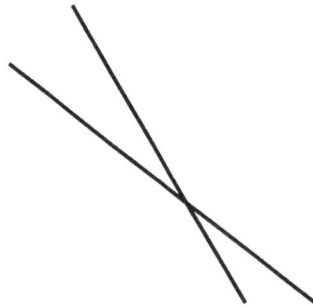

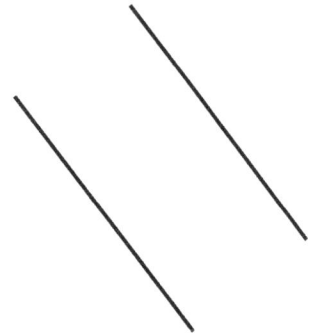

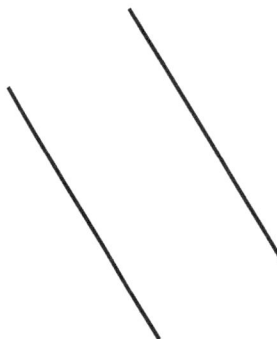

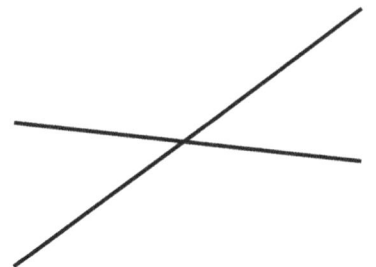

Name _____ Date _____

Label each pair of lines parallel, perpendicular or intersecting.

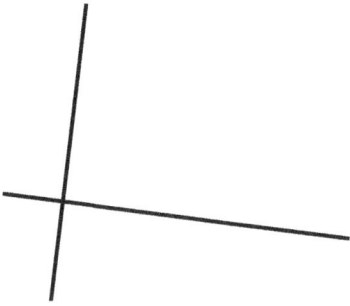

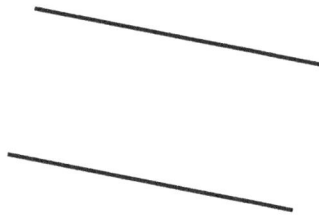

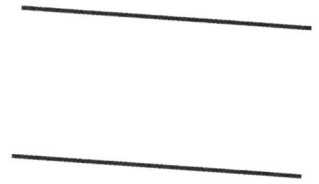

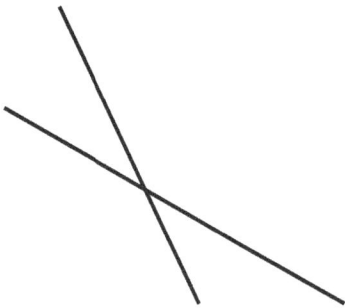

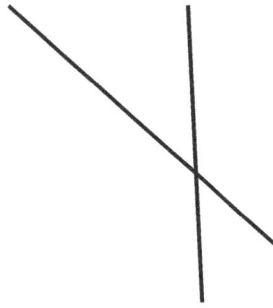

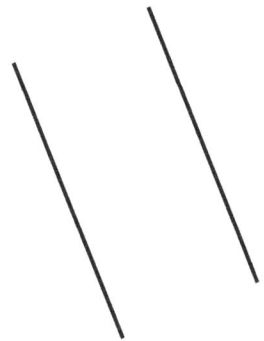

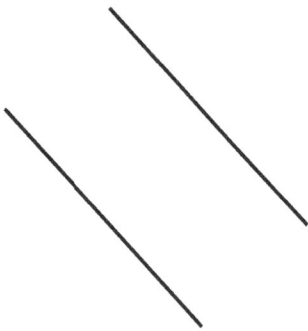

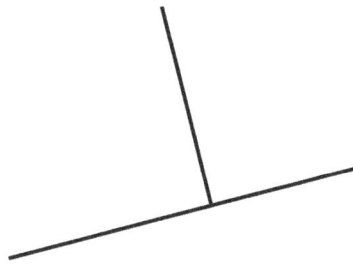

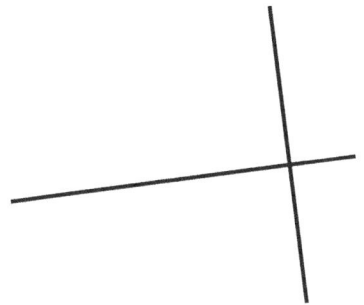

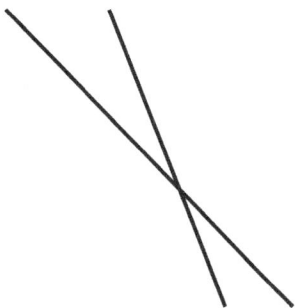

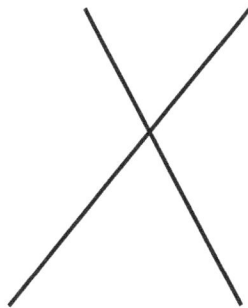

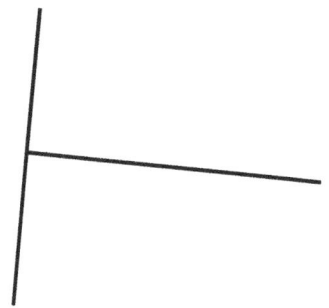

Name _____ Date _____

Label each pair of lines parallel, perpendicular or intersecting.

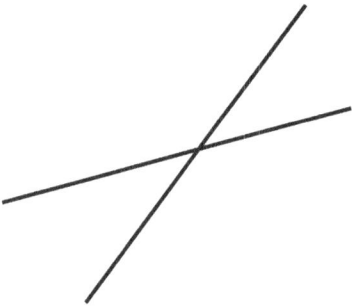

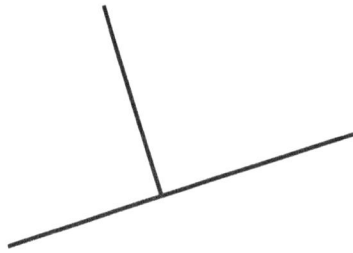

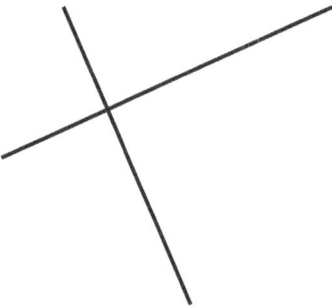

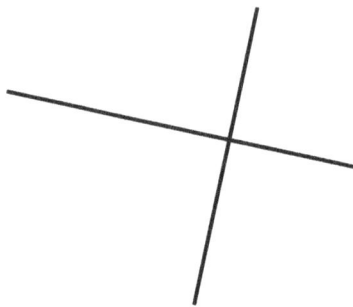

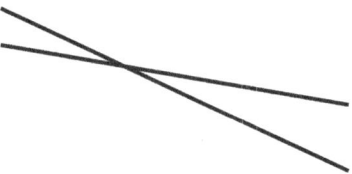

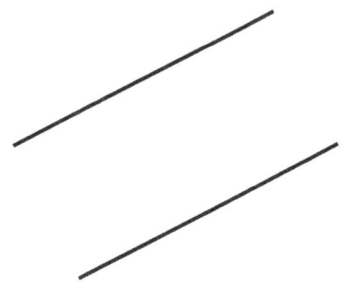

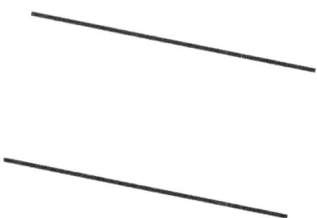

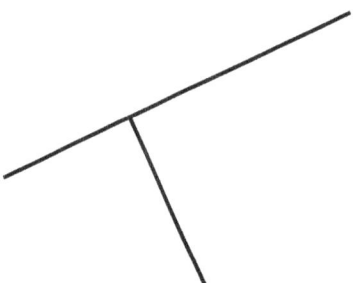

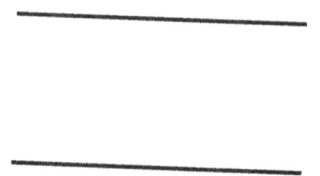

Name _____ Date _____

Label each pair of lines parallel, perpendicular or intersecting.

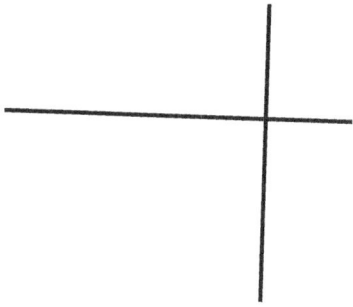

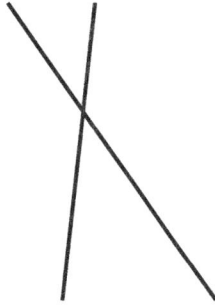

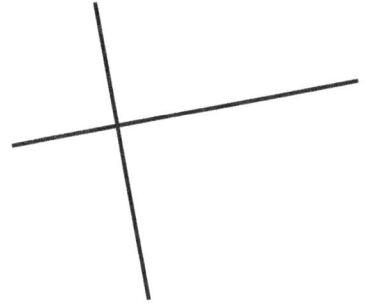

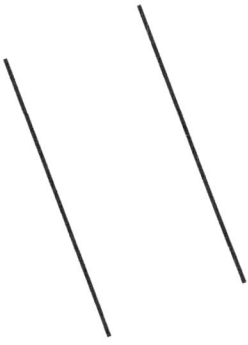

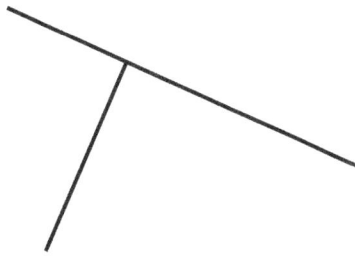

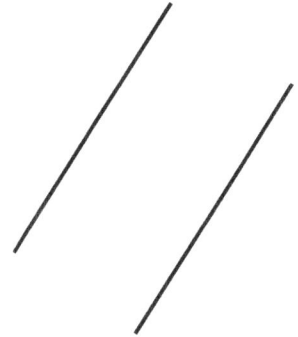

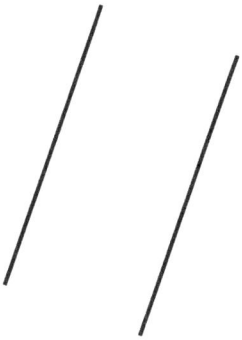

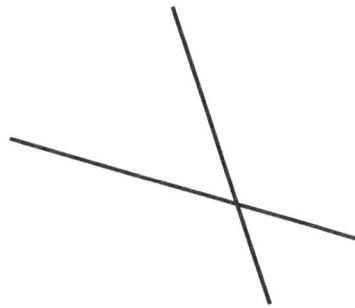

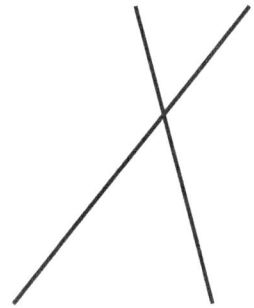

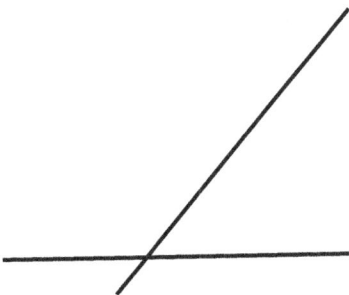

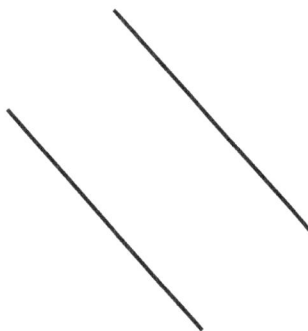

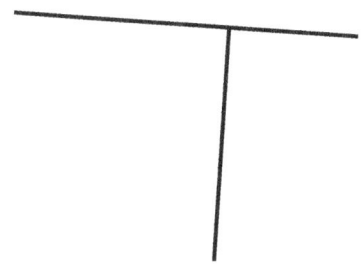

Name _____ Date _____

Label each pair of lines parallel, perpendicular or intersecting.

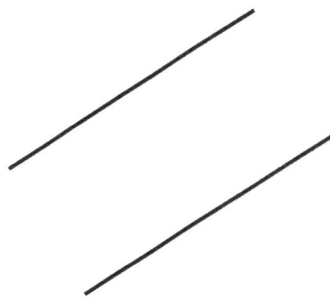

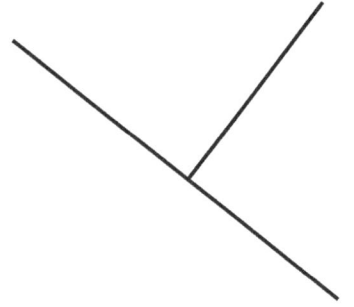

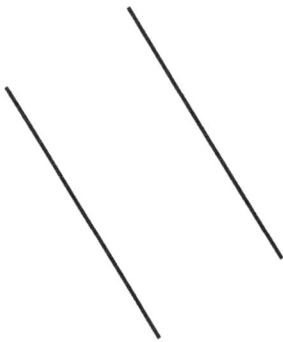

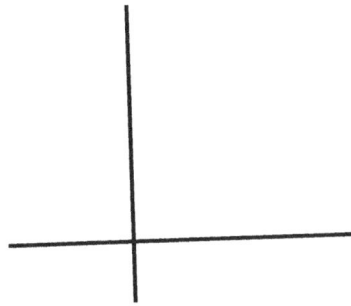

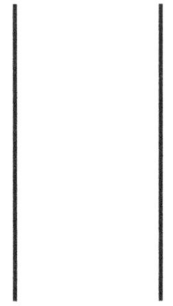

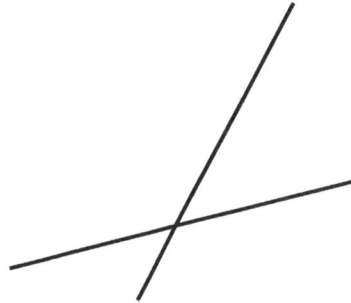

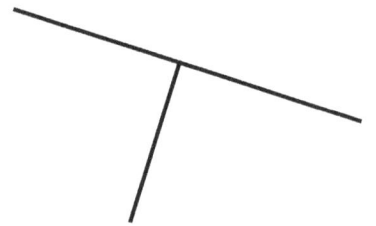

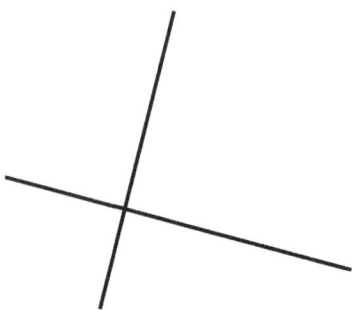

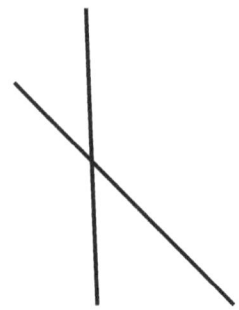

Name _____ Date _____

Label each pair of lines parallel, perpendicular or intersecting.

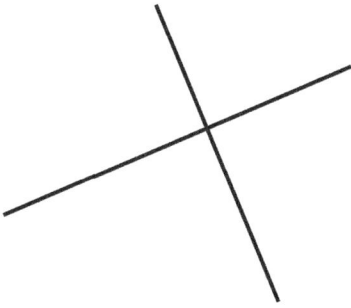

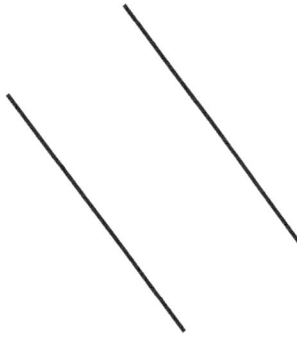

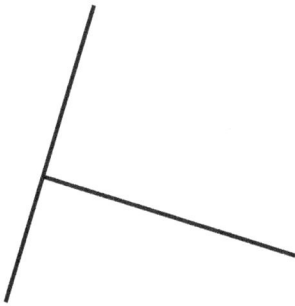

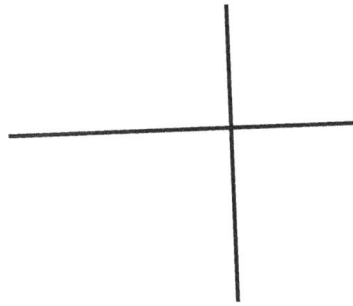

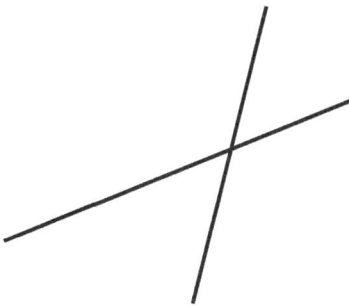

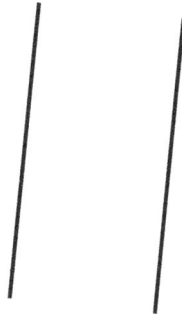

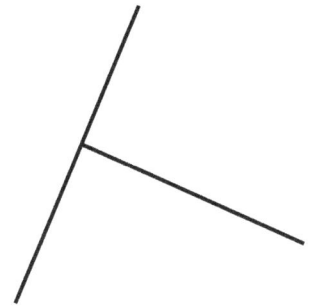

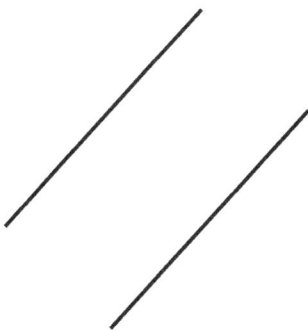

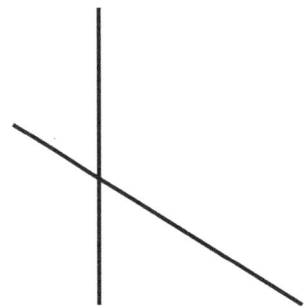

Name _____ Date _____

Label each angle acute, obtuse, right or straight.

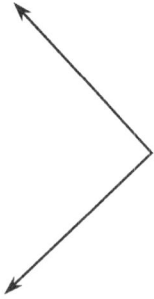 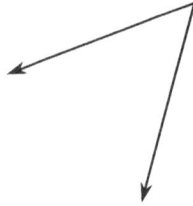 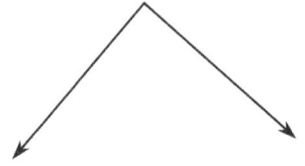

_____ _____ _____

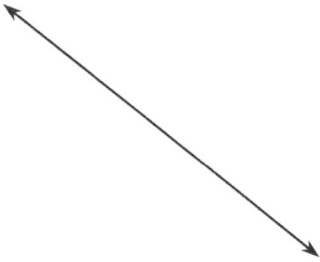 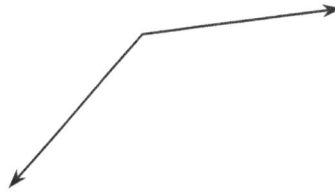 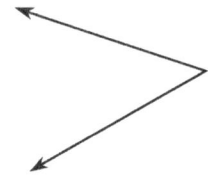

_____ _____ _____

 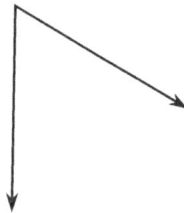 

_____ _____ _____

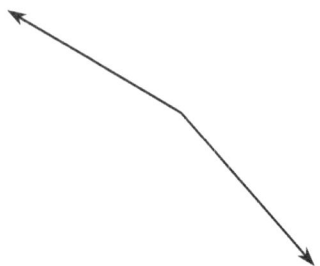 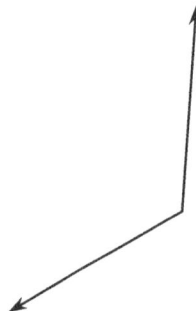 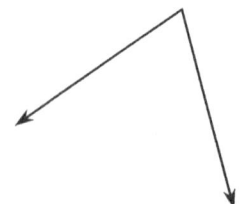

_____ _____ _____

Name _____ Date _____

Label each angle acute, obtuse, right or straight.

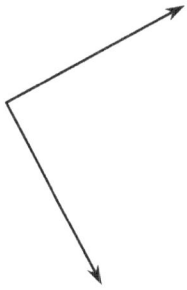

_____

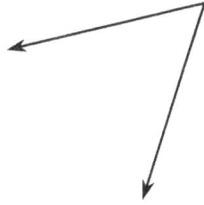

_____

_____

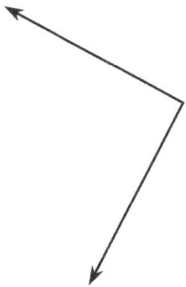

_____

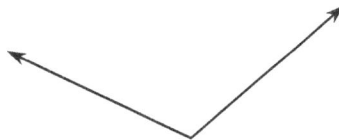

_____

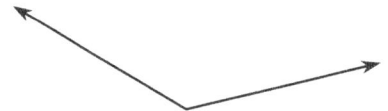

_____

_____

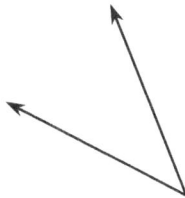

_____

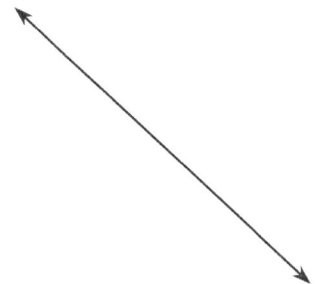

_____

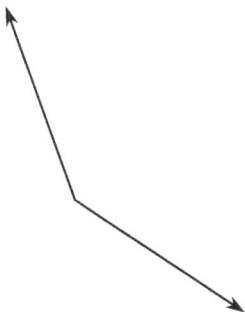

_____

_____

_____

Name _____ Date _____

Label each angle acute, obtuse, right or straight.

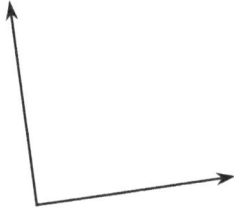

_____

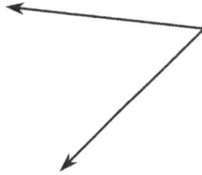

_____

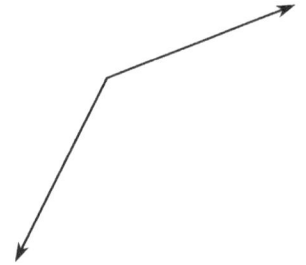

_____

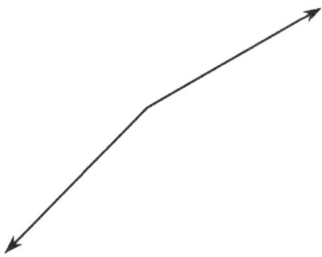

_____

_____

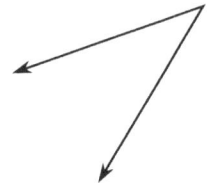

_____

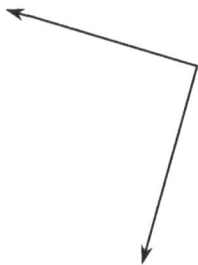

_____

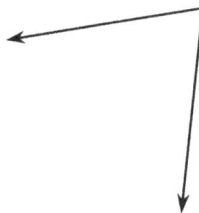

_____

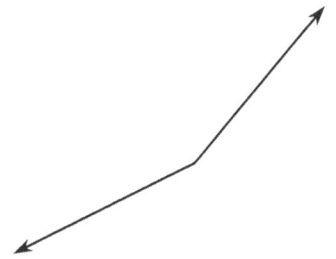

_____

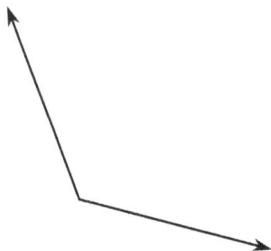

_____

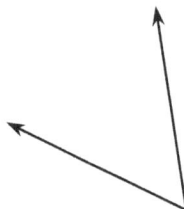

_____

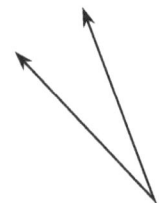

_____

Name _____ Date _____

Label each angle acute, obtuse, right or straight.

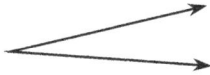

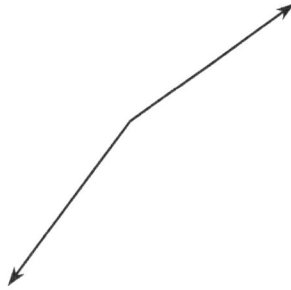

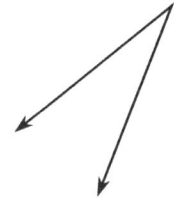

_____   _____   _____

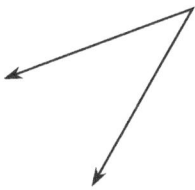

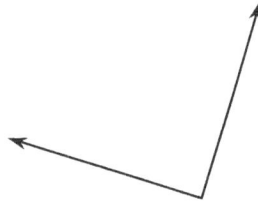

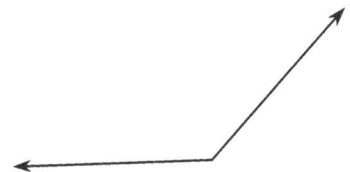

_____   _____   _____

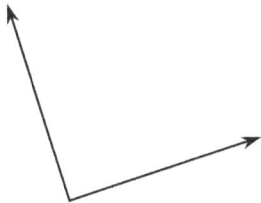

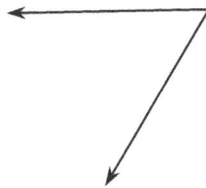

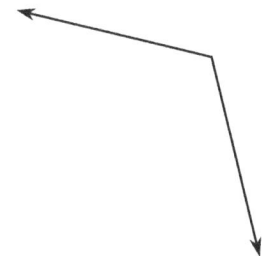

_____   _____   _____

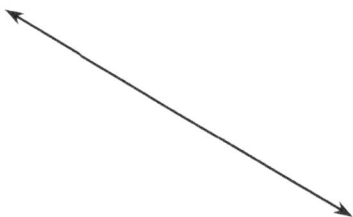

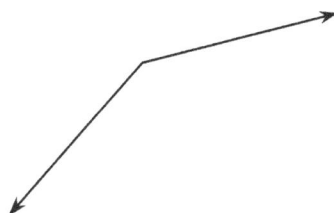

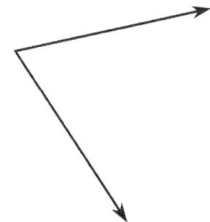

_____   _____   _____

Name _____ Date _____

Label each angle acute, obtuse, right or straight.

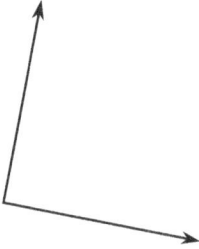

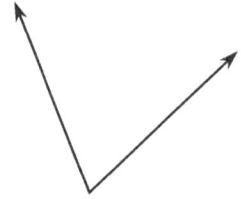

_____   _____   _____

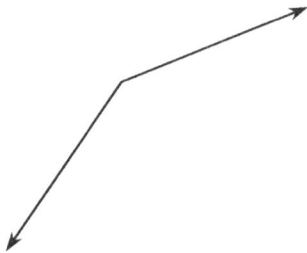

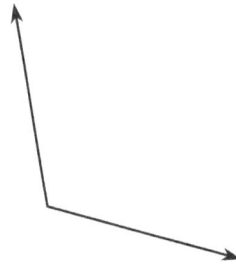

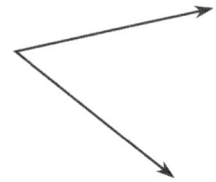

_____   _____   _____

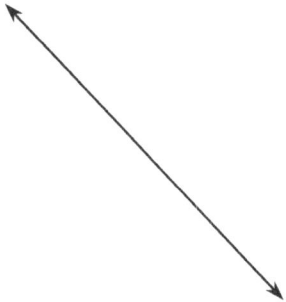

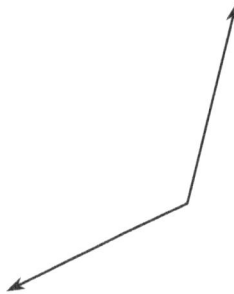

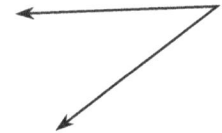

_____   _____   _____

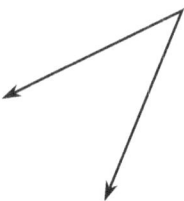

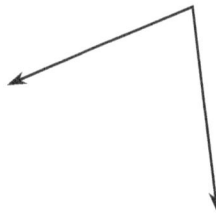

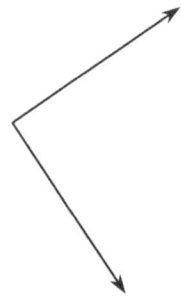

_____   _____   _____

Name _____ Date _____

Label each angle acute, obtuse, right or straight.

_____

_____

_____

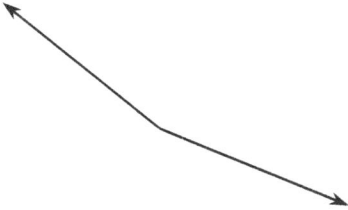

_____

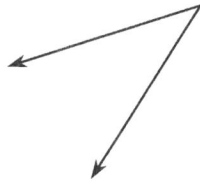

_____

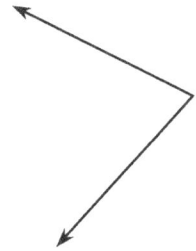

_____

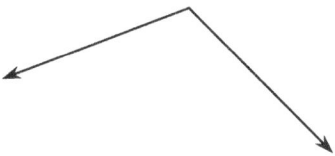

_____

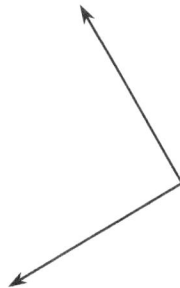

_____

_____

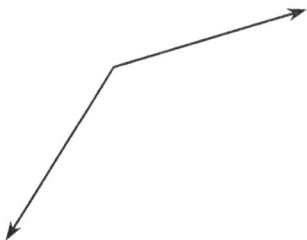

_____

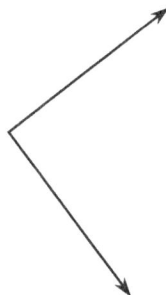

_____

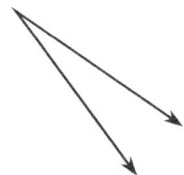

_____

Name _____ Date _____

Label each angle acute, obtuse, right or straight.

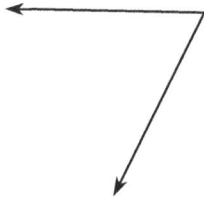

_____

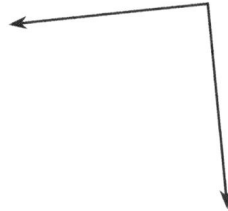

_____

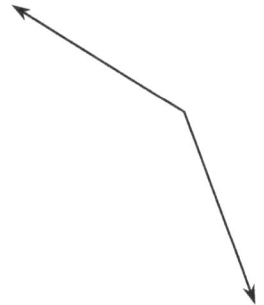

_____

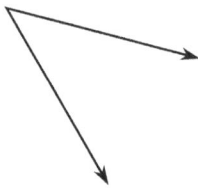

_____

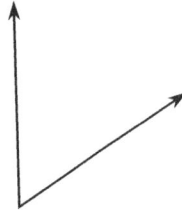

_____

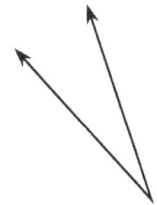

_____

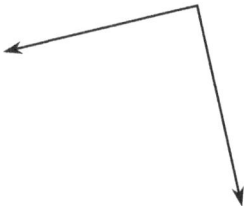

_____

_____

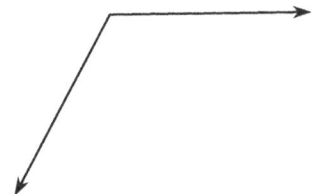

_____

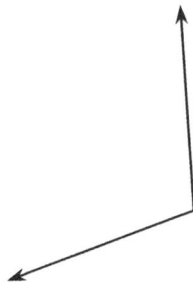

_____

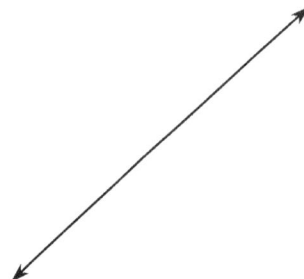

_____

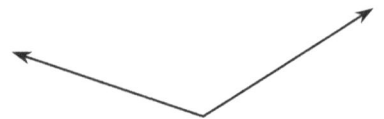

_____

Name _____ Date _____

Label each triangle scalene, isosceles or equilateral
and acute, obtuse or right.

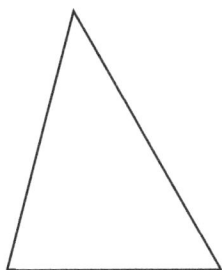

_____

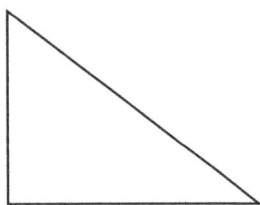

_____

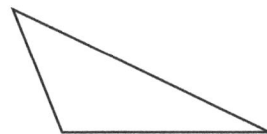

_____

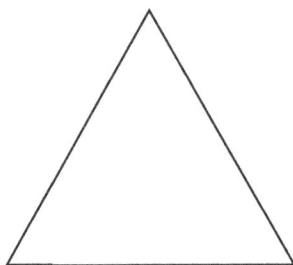

_____

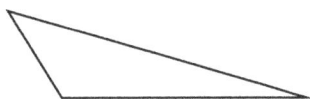

_____

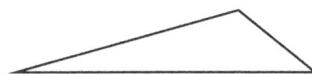

_____

_____

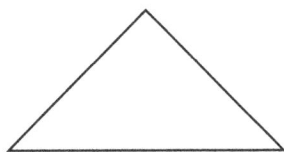

_____

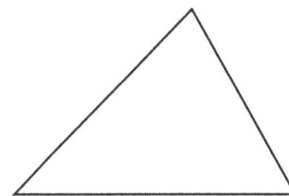

_____

_____

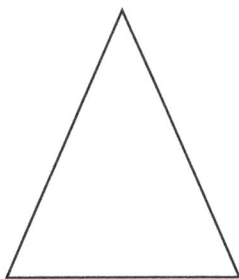

_____

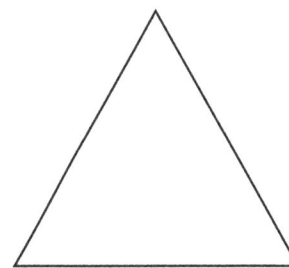

_____

Name _____ Date _____

Label each triangle scalene, isosceles or equilateral
and acute, obtuse or right.

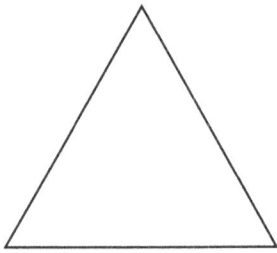   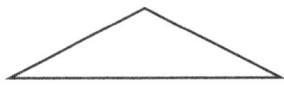   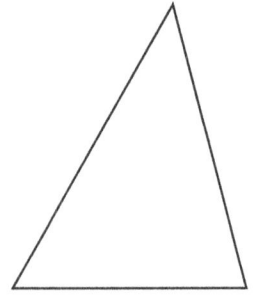

_____   _____   _____

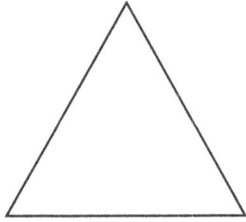   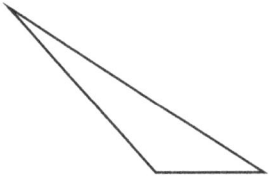   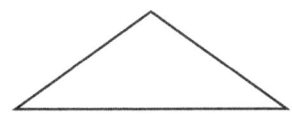

_____   _____   _____

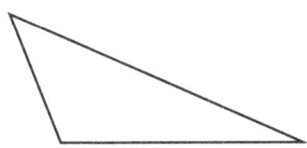   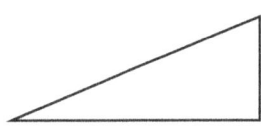   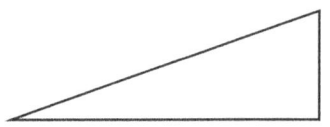

_____   _____   _____

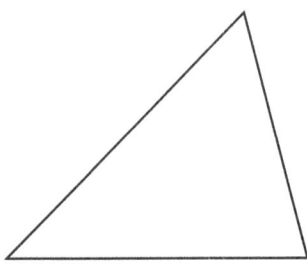   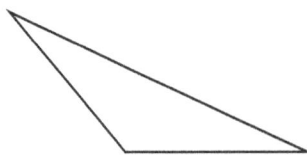   

_____   _____   _____

Name _____ Date _____

Label each triangle scalene, isosceles or equilateral
and acute, obtuse or right.

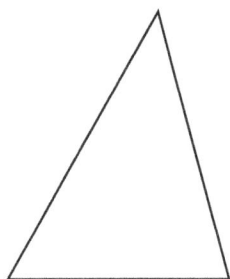

_____

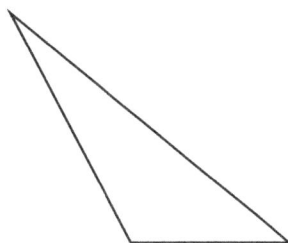

_____

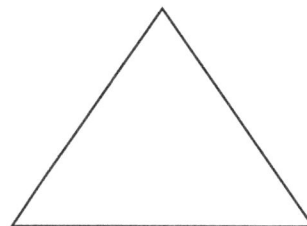

_____

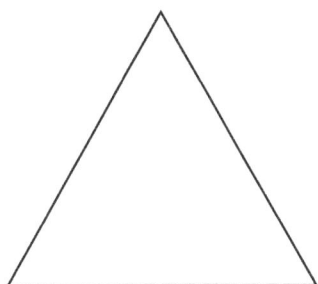

_____

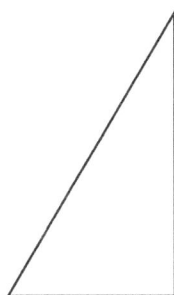

_____

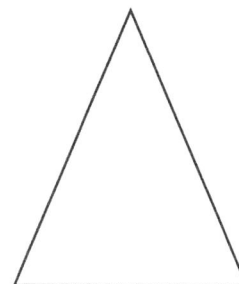

_____

_____

_____

_____

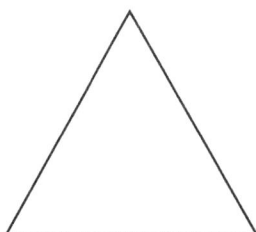

_____

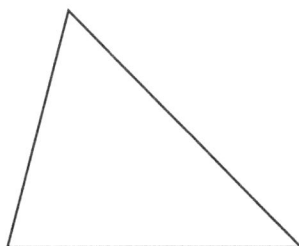

_____

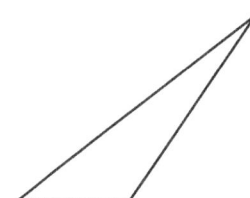

_____

Name _____ Date _____

Label each triangle scalene, isosceles or equilateral
and acute, obtuse or right.

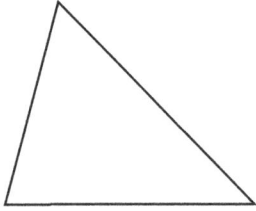

_____

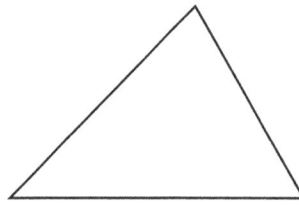

_____

_____

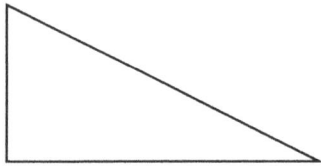

_____

_____

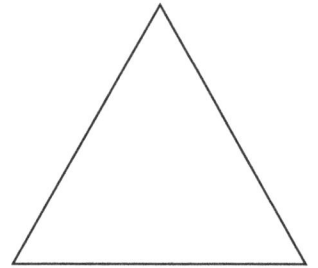

_____

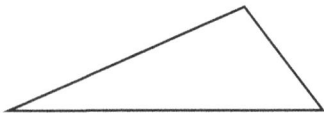

_____

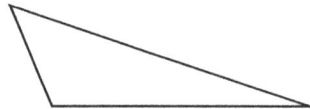

_____

_____

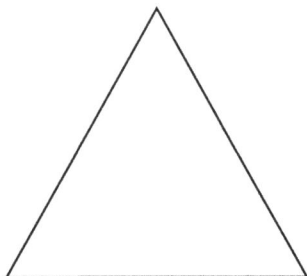

_____

_____

_____

Name _____ Date _____

Label each triangle scalene, isosceles or equilateral
and acute, obtuse or right.

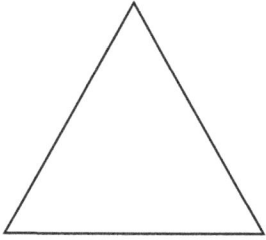

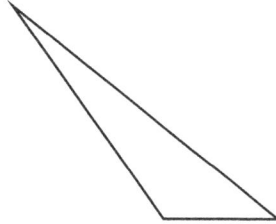

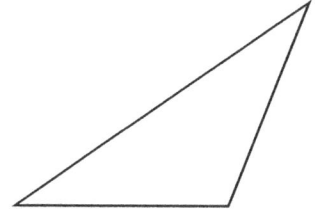

_____ _____ _____

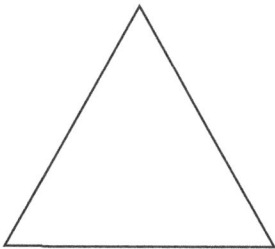

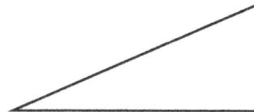

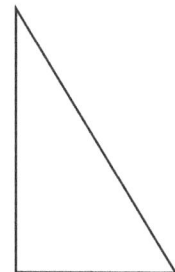

_____ _____ _____

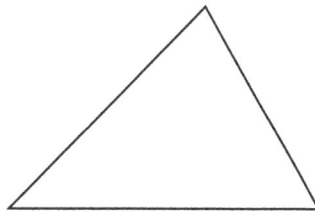

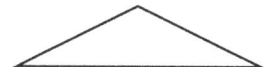

_____ _____ _____

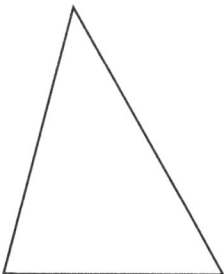

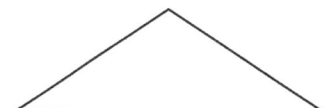

_____ _____ _____

Name _____ Date _____

Label each triangle scalene, isosceles or equilateral
and acute, obtuse or right.

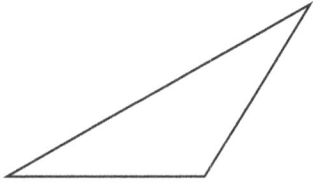      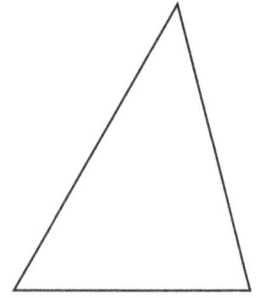

_____   _____   _____

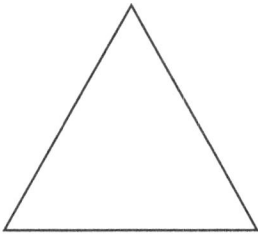   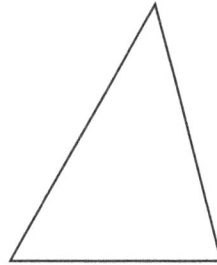   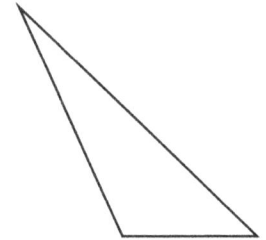

_____   _____   _____

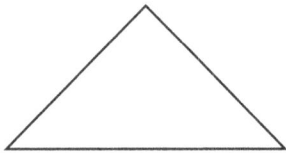   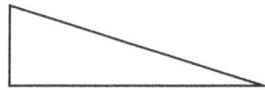   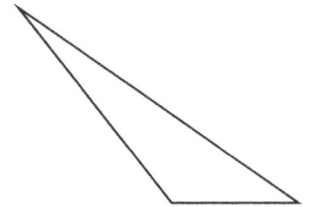

_____   _____   _____

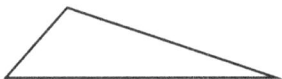   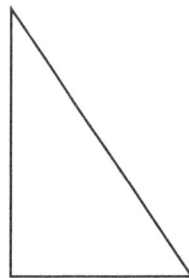   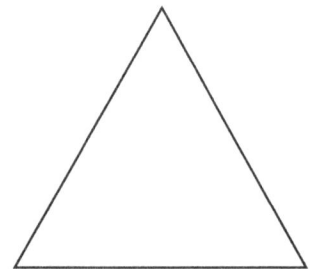

_____   _____   _____

Name _____ Date _____

Label each triangle scalene, isosceles or equilateral
and acute, obtuse or right.

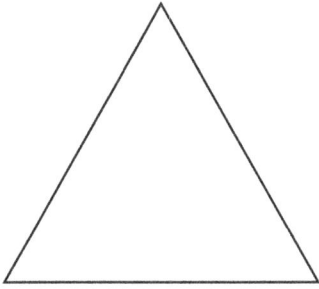   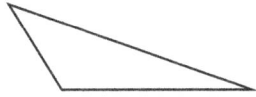   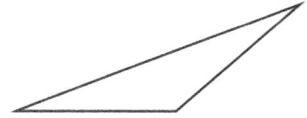

_____   _____   _____

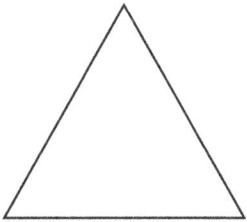   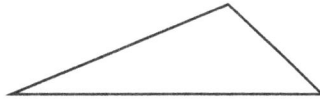   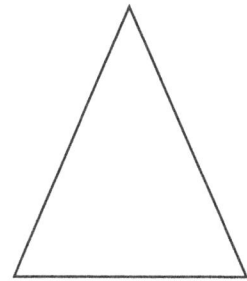

_____   _____   _____

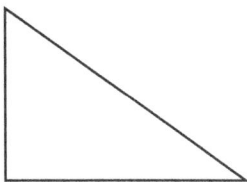   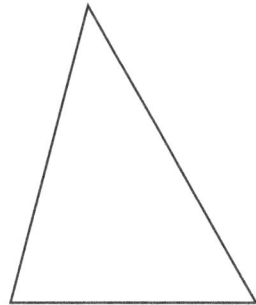   

_____   _____   _____

   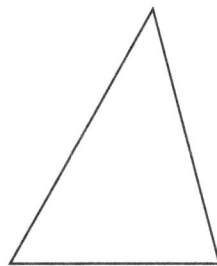   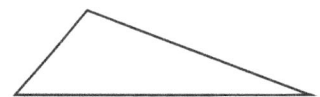

_____   _____   _____

Name _____ Date _____

Write the name of each shape.

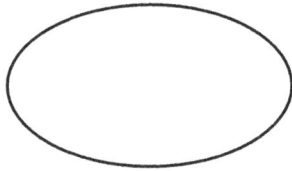

_____

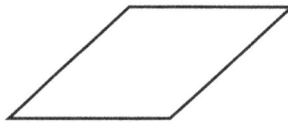

_____

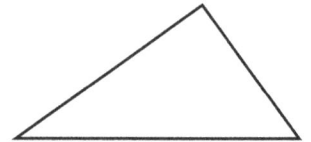

_____

_____

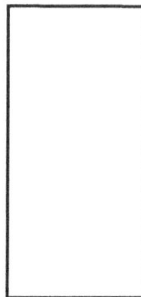

_____

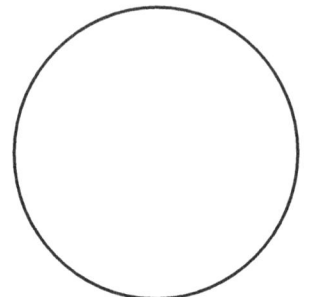

_____

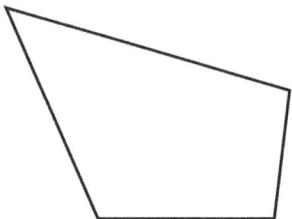

_____

_____

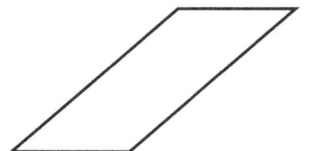

_____

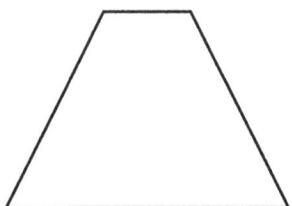

_____

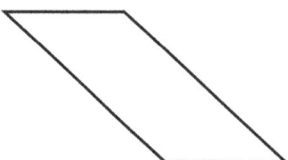

_____

_____

Name _____ Date _____

Write the name of each shape.

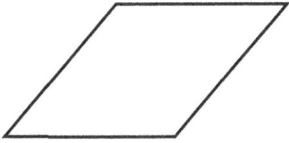 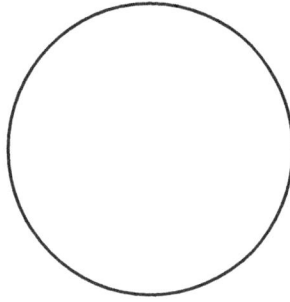 

_____ _____ _____

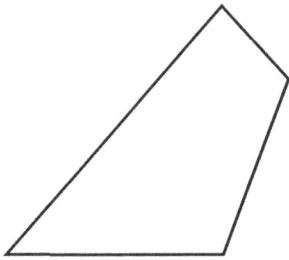  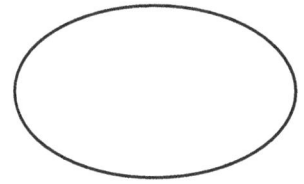

_____ _____ _____

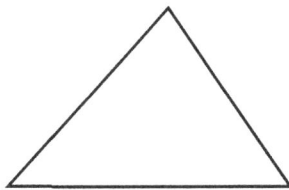  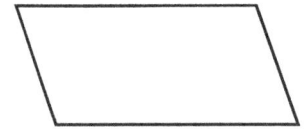

_____ _____ _____

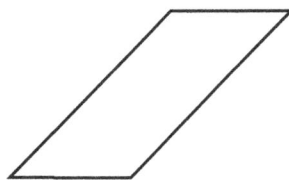 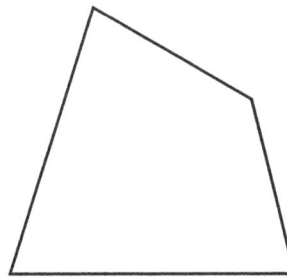 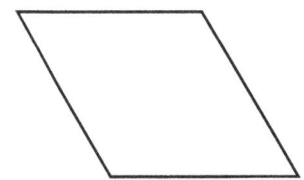

_____ _____ _____

Name _____ Date _____

Write the name of each shape.

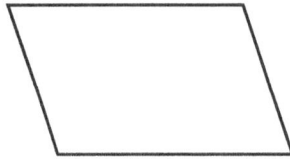

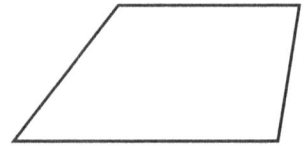

_____   _____   _____

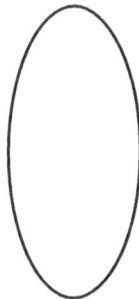

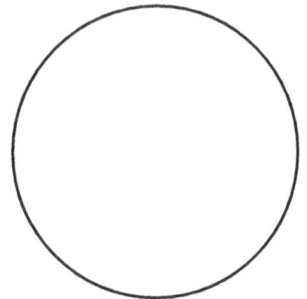

_____   _____   _____

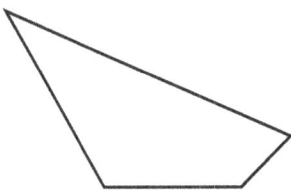

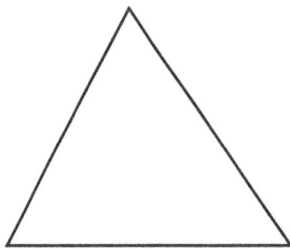

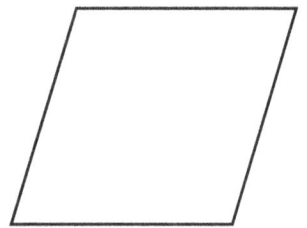

_____   _____   _____

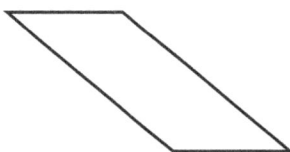

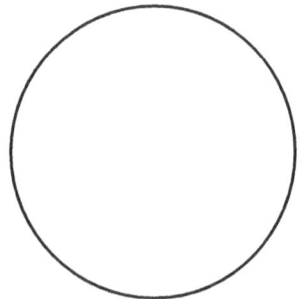

_____   _____   _____

Name _____ Date _____

Write the name of each shape.

   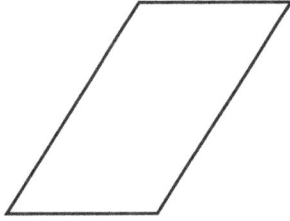   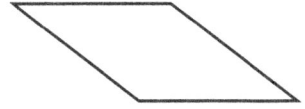

_____   _____   _____

   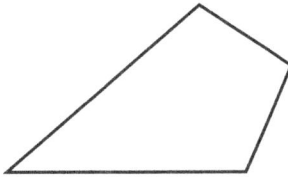   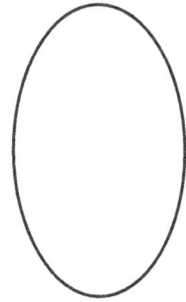

_____   _____   _____

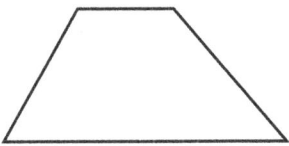   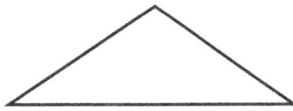   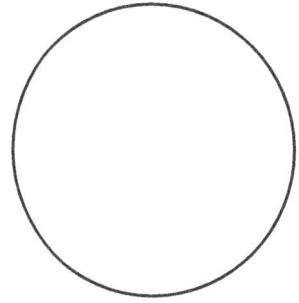

_____   _____   _____

_____   _____   _____

Name _____ Date _____

Write the name of each shape.

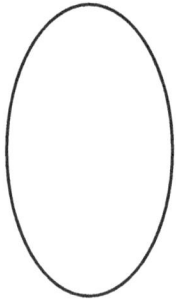

_____

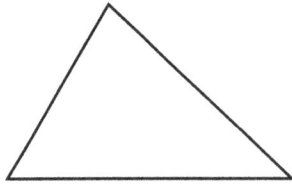

_____

_____

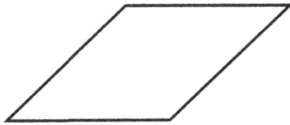

_____

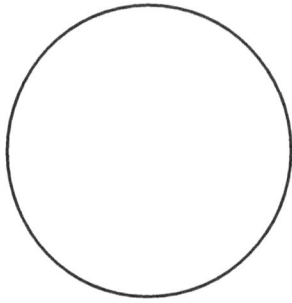

_____

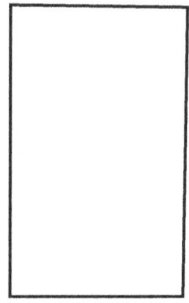

_____

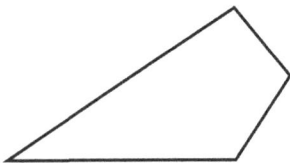

_____

_____

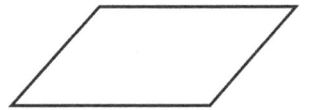

_____

_____

_____

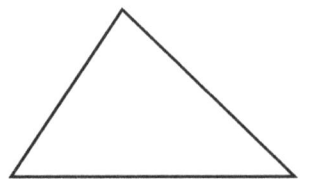

_____

Name _____ Date _____

Write the name of each shape.

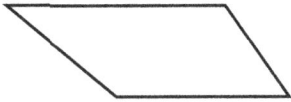
_____

_____

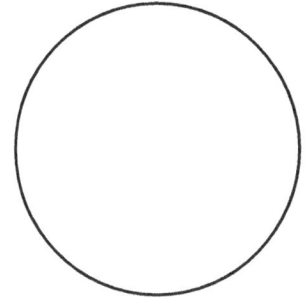
_____

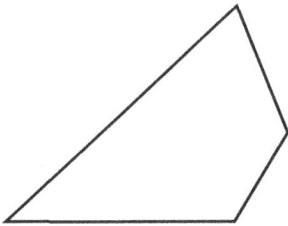
_____

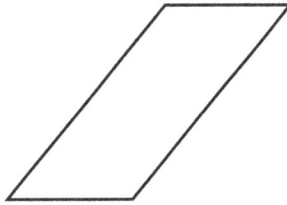
_____

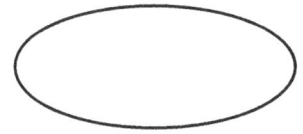
_____

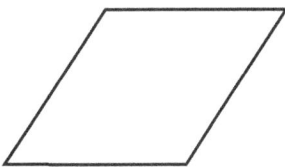
_____

_____

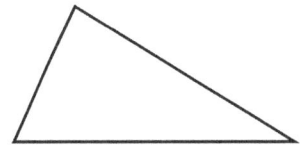
_____

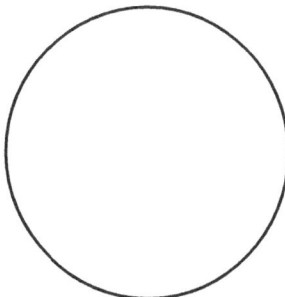
_____

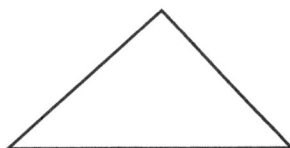
_____

_____

Name _____ Date _____

Write the name of each shape.

   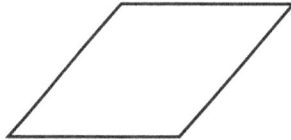   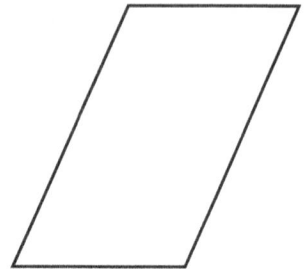

_____   _____   _____

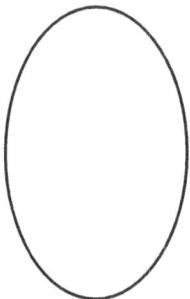   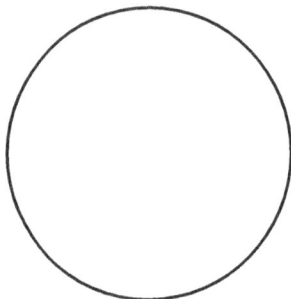   

_____   _____   _____

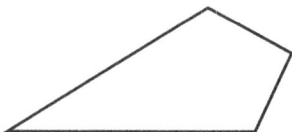      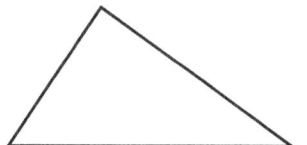

_____   _____   _____

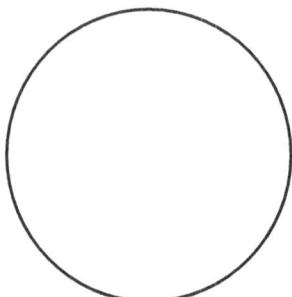      

_____   _____   _____

Name _____ Date _____

Write the name of each polygon.

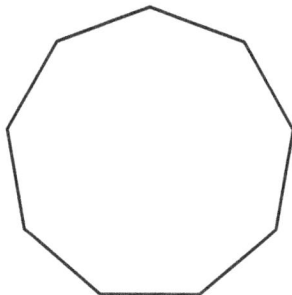

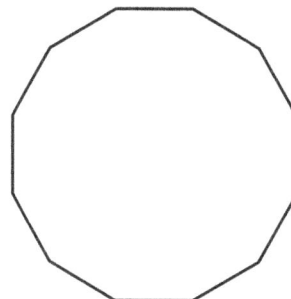

_____ _____ _____

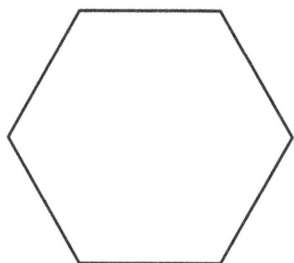

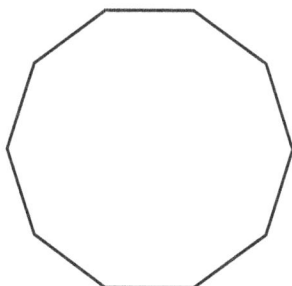

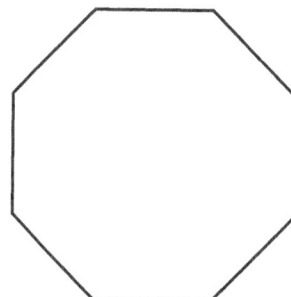

_____ _____ _____

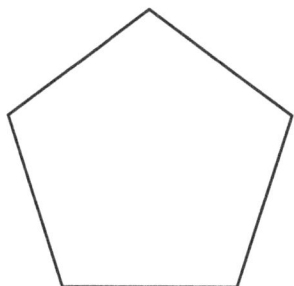

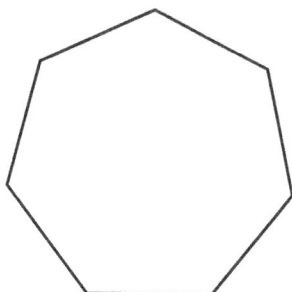

_____ _____ _____

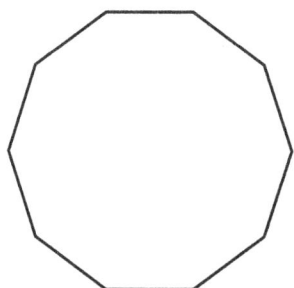

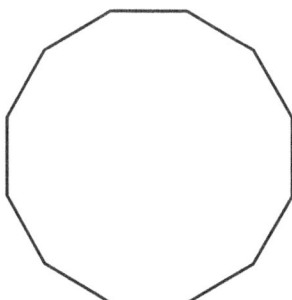

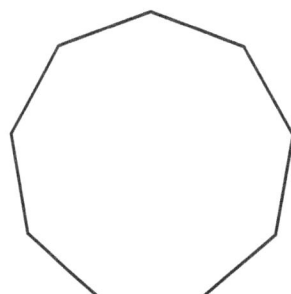

_____ _____ _____

Name _____ Date _____

Write the name of each polygon.

_____

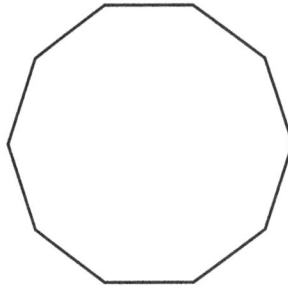

_____

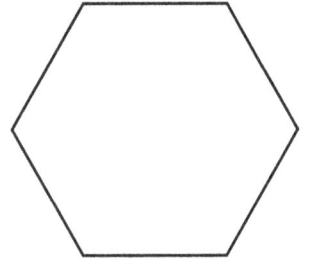

_____

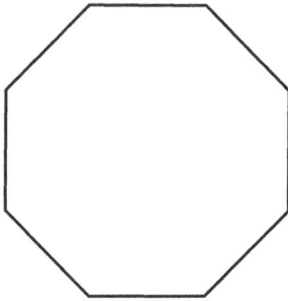

_____

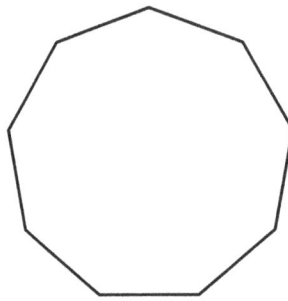

_____

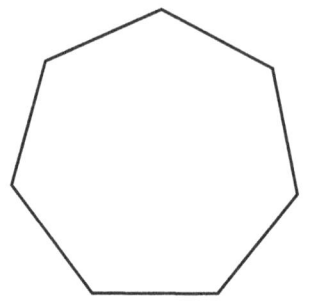

_____

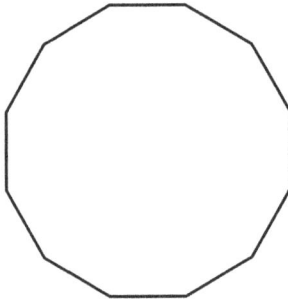

_____

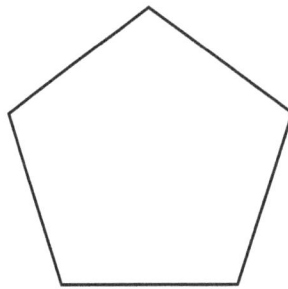

_____

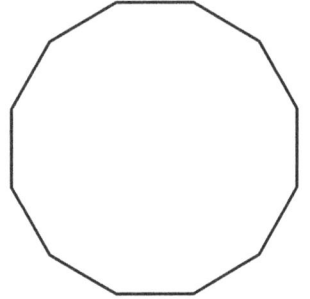

_____

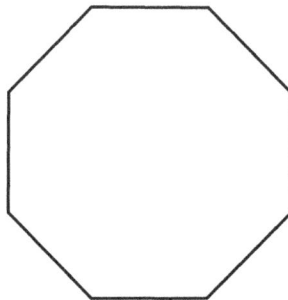

_____

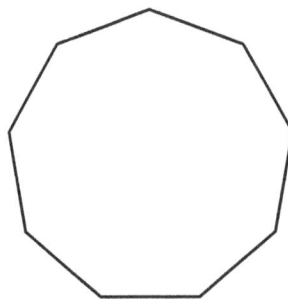

_____

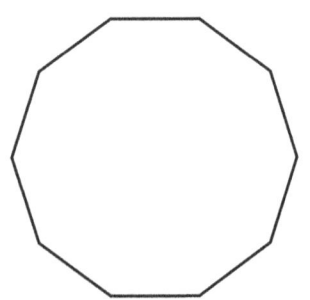

_____

Name _____ Date _____

Write the name of each polygon.

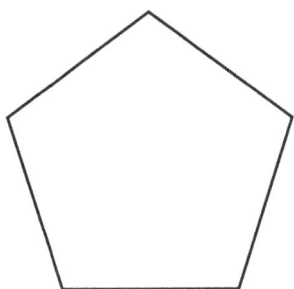

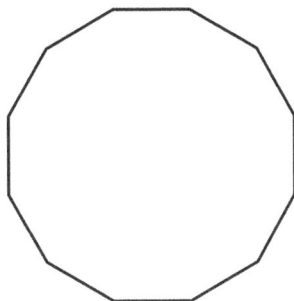

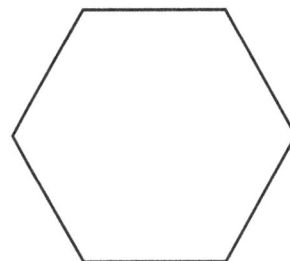

_____   _____   _____

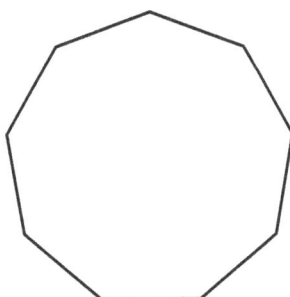

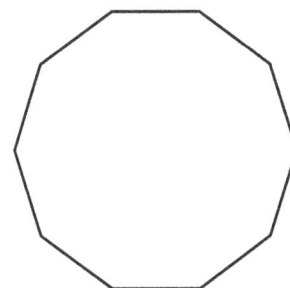

_____   _____   _____

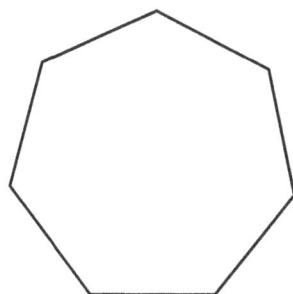

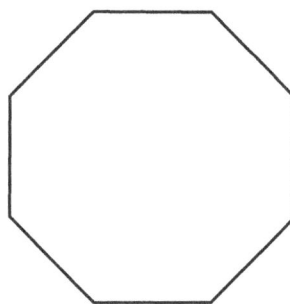

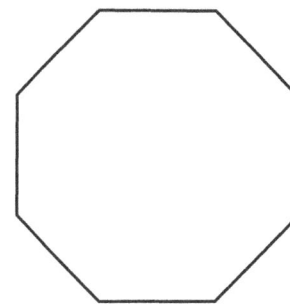

_____   _____   _____

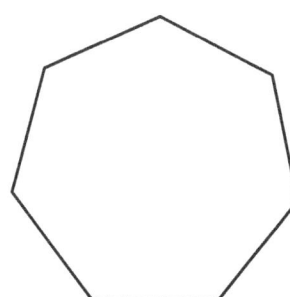

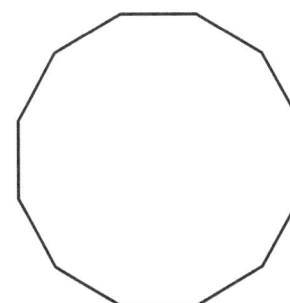

_____   _____   _____

Name _____ Date _____

Write the name of each polygon.

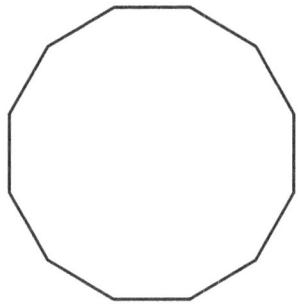

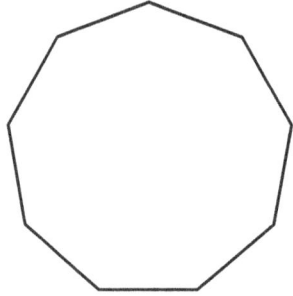

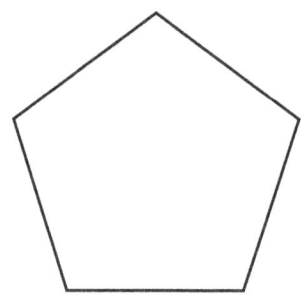

_____

_____

_____

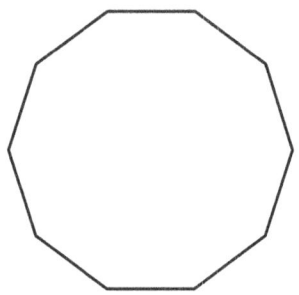

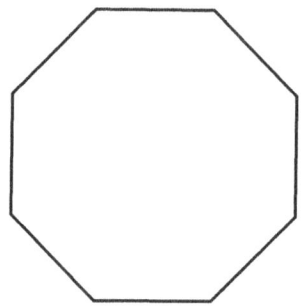

_____

_____

_____

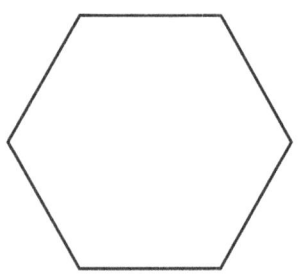

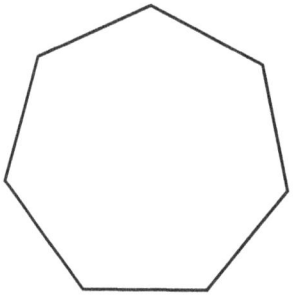

_____

_____

_____

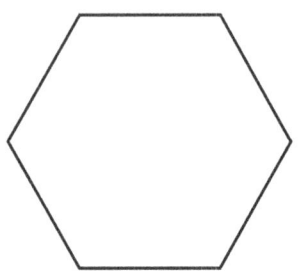

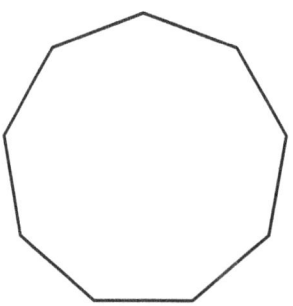

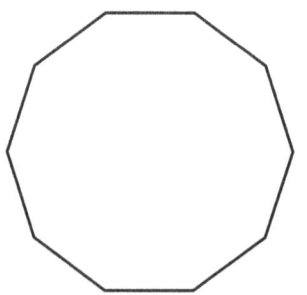

_____

_____

_____

Name _____ Date _____

Write the name of each polygon.

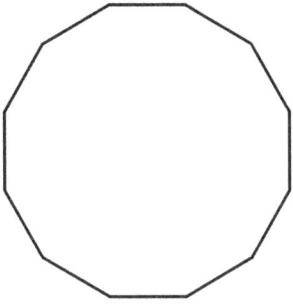

_____

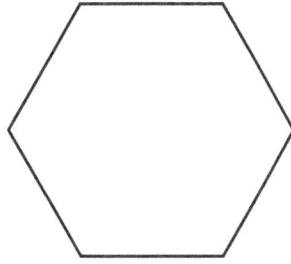

_____

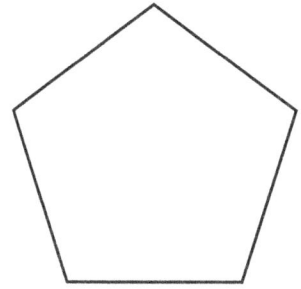

_____

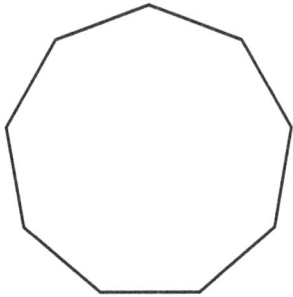

_____

_____

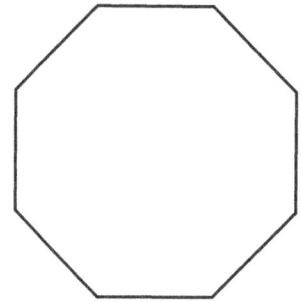

_____

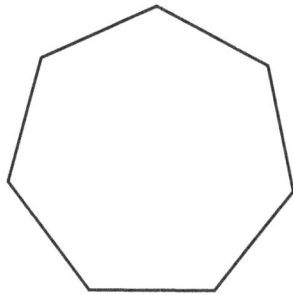

_____

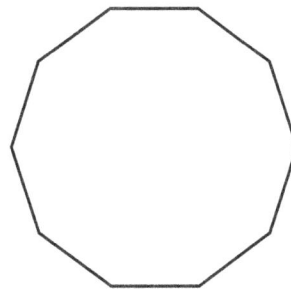

_____

_____

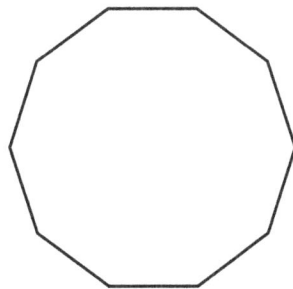

_____

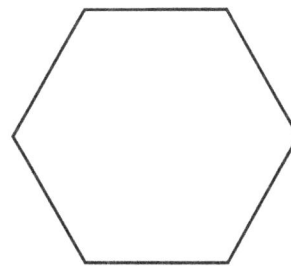

_____

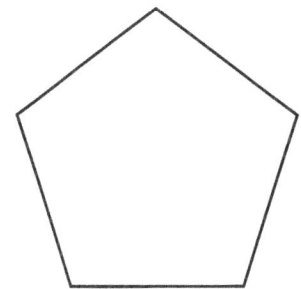

_____

Name _____ Date _____

Write the name of each polygon.

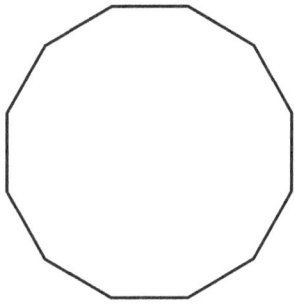

_____

_____

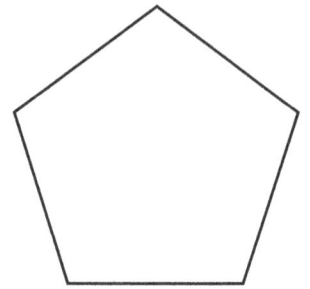

_____

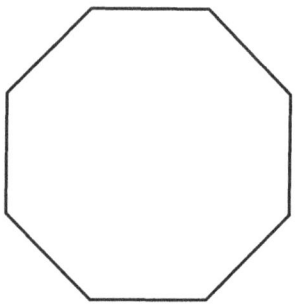

_____

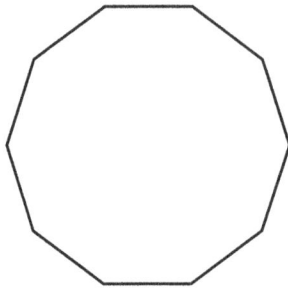

_____

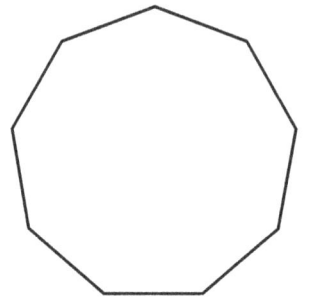

_____

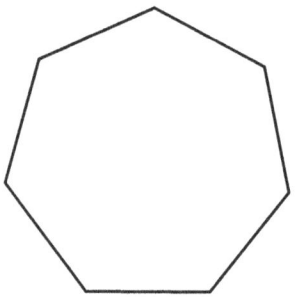

_____

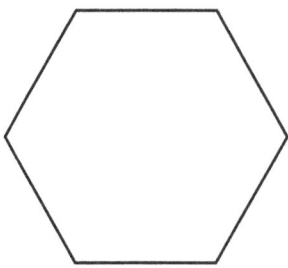

_____

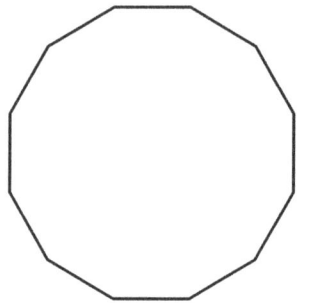

_____

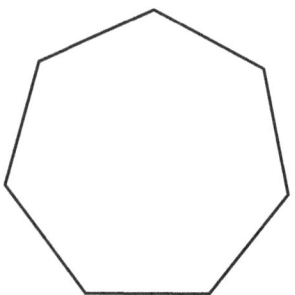

_____

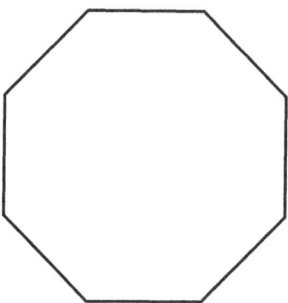

_____

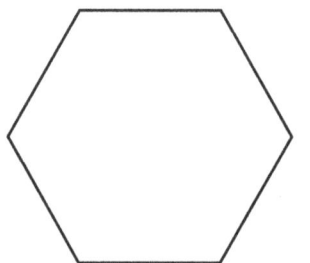

_____

Name _____ Date _____

Write the name of each polygon.

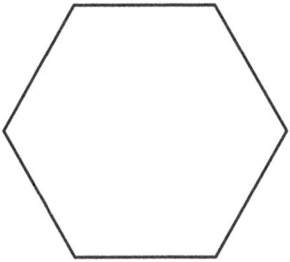

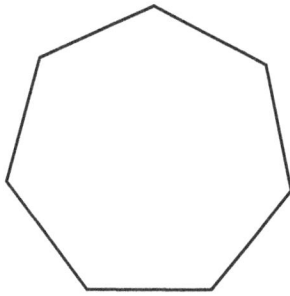

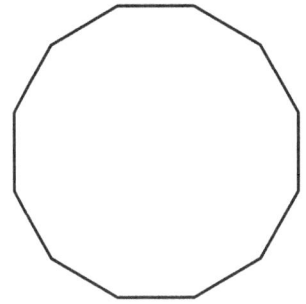

_____   _____   _____

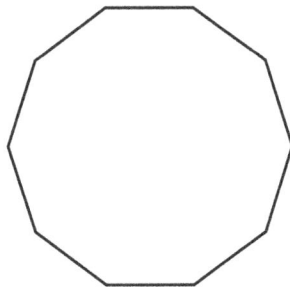

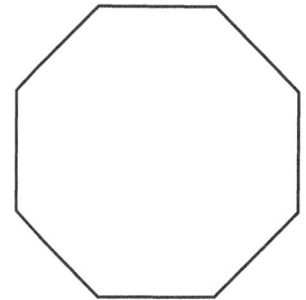

_____   _____   _____

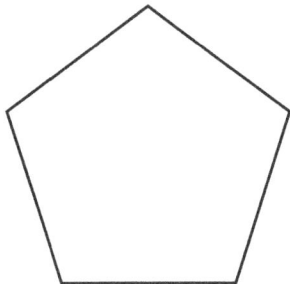

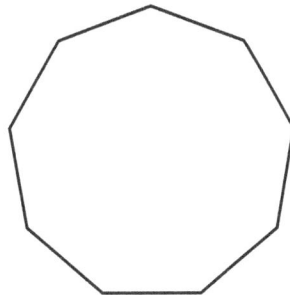

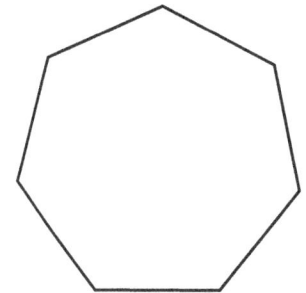

_____   _____   _____

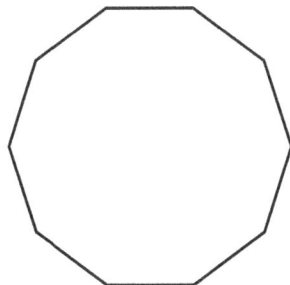

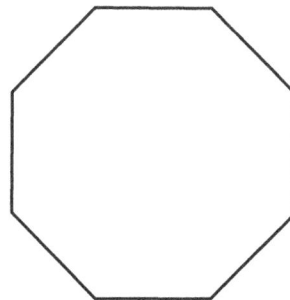

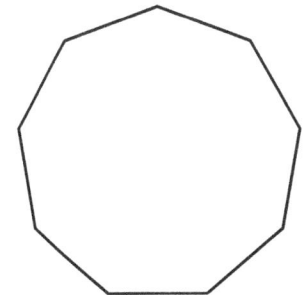

_____   _____   _____

Page 35

Name _____ Date _____

Write the name of each 3-dimensional solid.

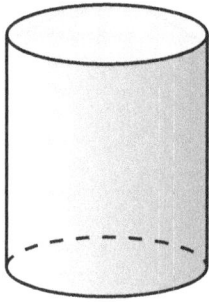

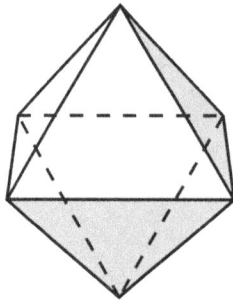

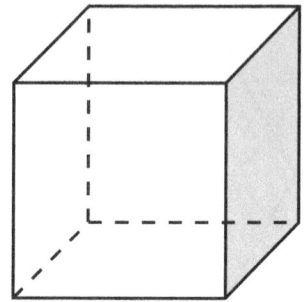

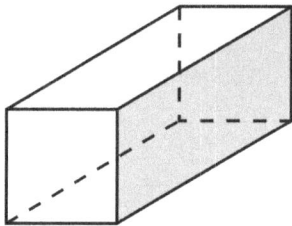

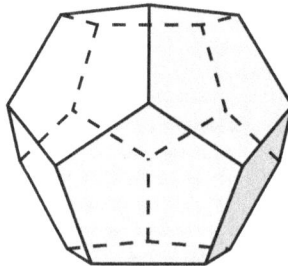

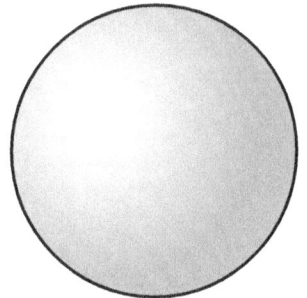

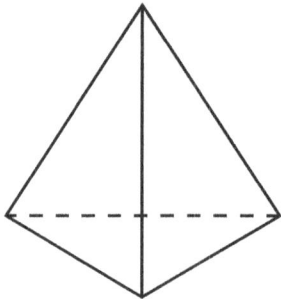

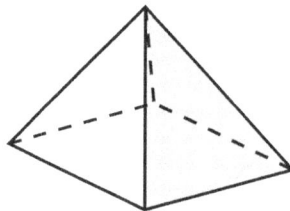

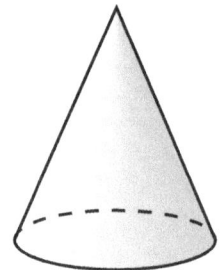

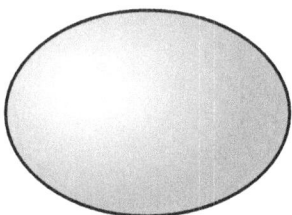

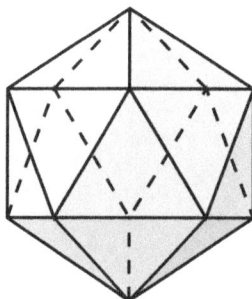

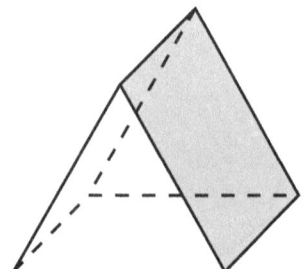

_____   _____   _____

_____   _____   _____

_____   _____   _____

_____   _____   _____

Name _____ Date _____

Write the name of each 3-dimensional solid.

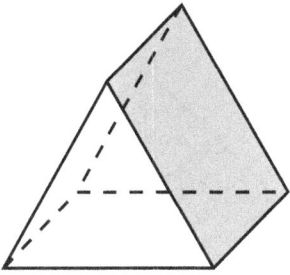

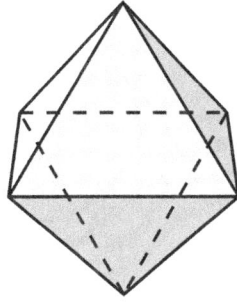

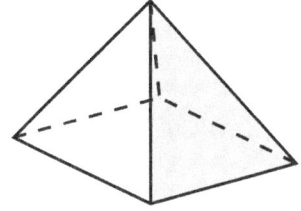

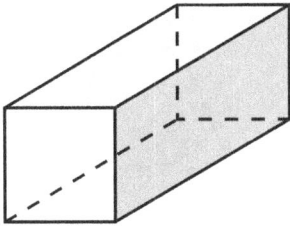

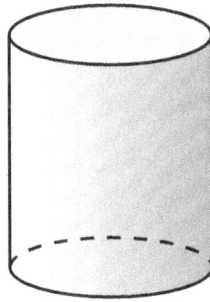

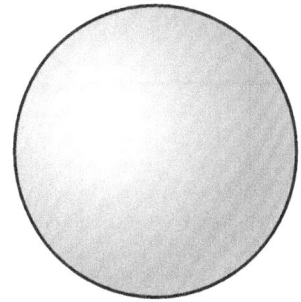

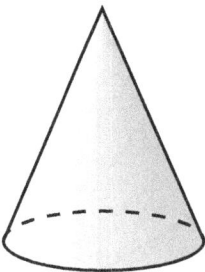

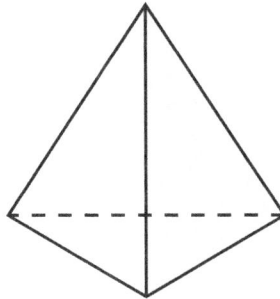

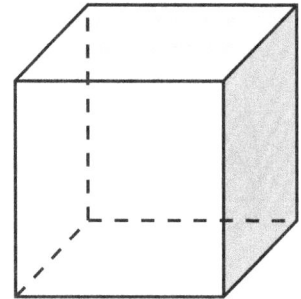

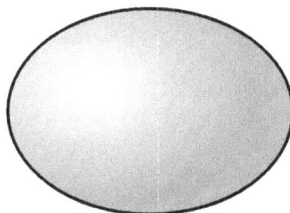

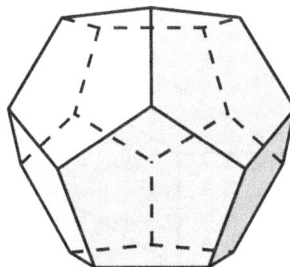

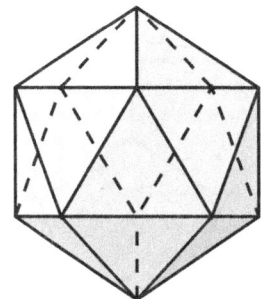

_____   _____   _____

_____   _____   _____

_____   _____   _____

_____   _____   _____

Name _____ Date _____

Write the name of each 3-dimensional solid.

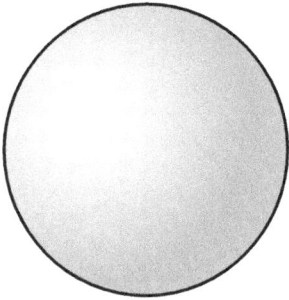

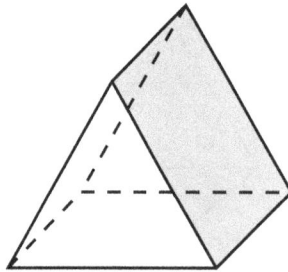

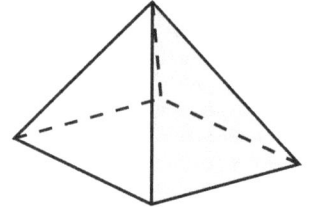

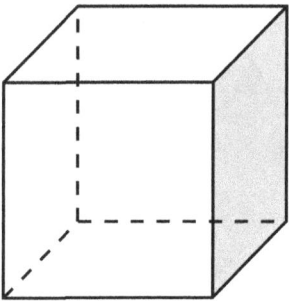

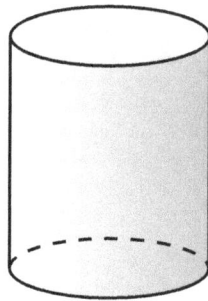

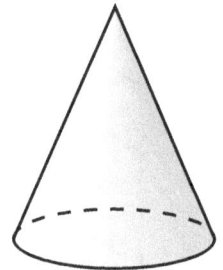

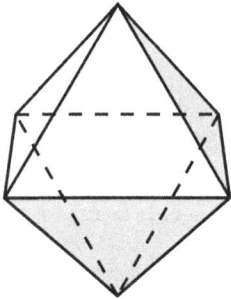

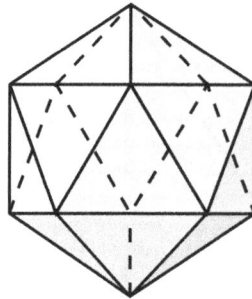

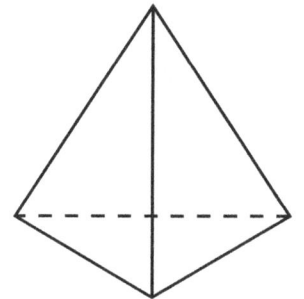

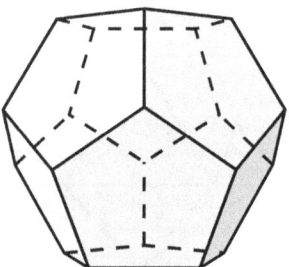

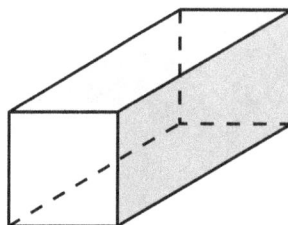

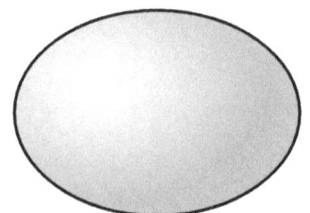

_____   _____   _____

_____   _____   _____

_____   _____   _____

_____   _____   _____

Name _____ Date _____

Write the name of each 3-dimensional solid.

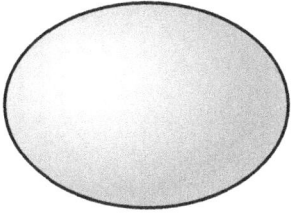

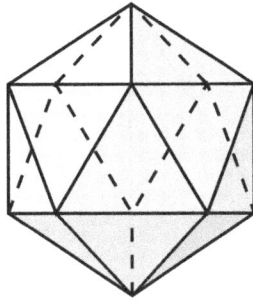

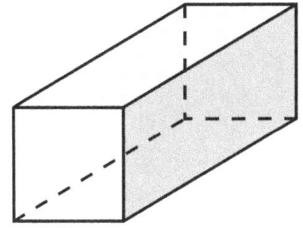

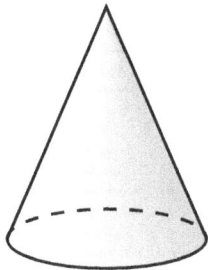

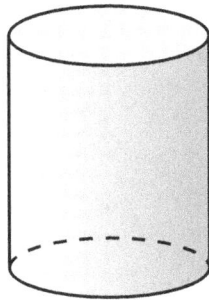

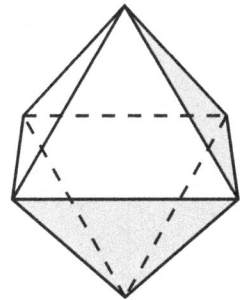

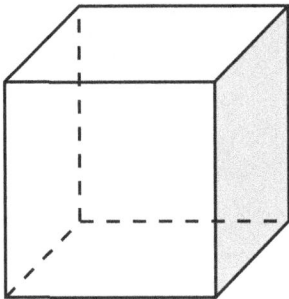

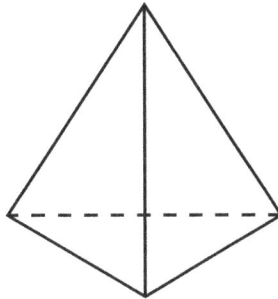

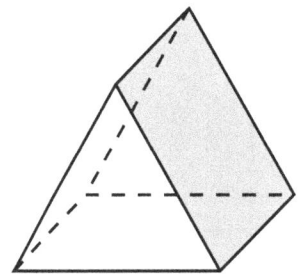

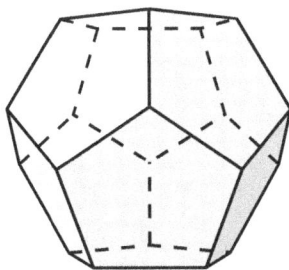

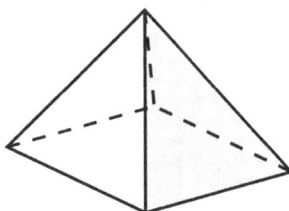

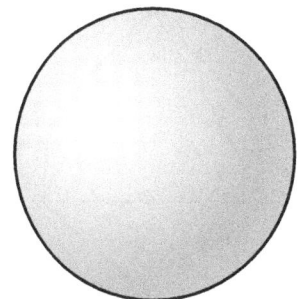

_____   _____   _____

_____   _____   _____

_____   _____   _____

_____   _____   _____

Name _____ Date _____

Write the name of each 3-dimensional solid.

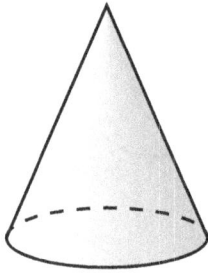

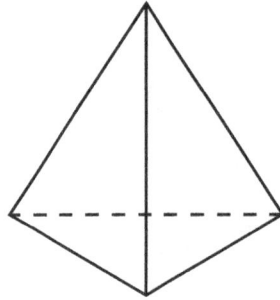

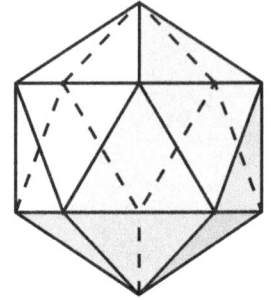

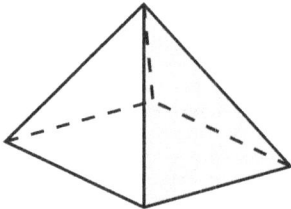

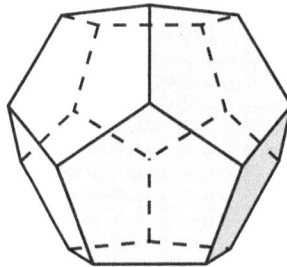

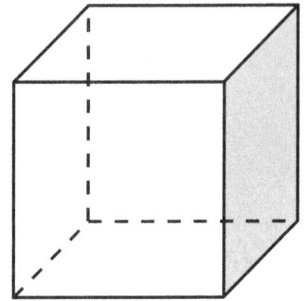

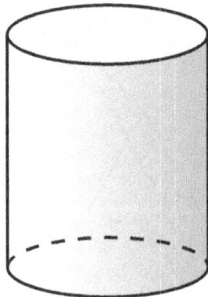

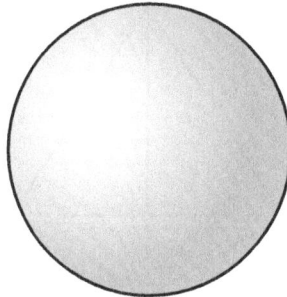

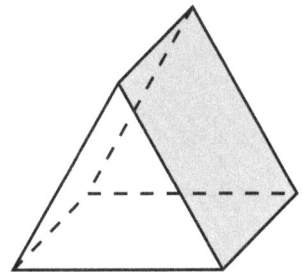

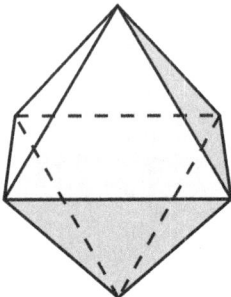

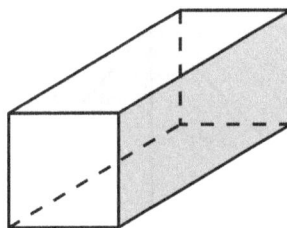

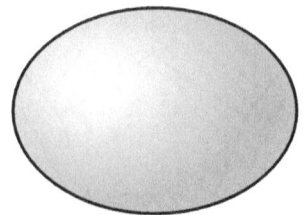

_____   _____   _____

_____   _____   _____

_____   _____   _____

_____   _____   _____

Name _____ Date _____

Write the name of each 3-dimensional solid.

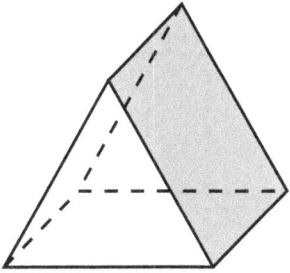

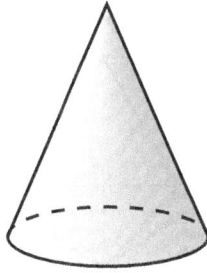

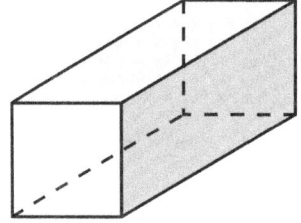

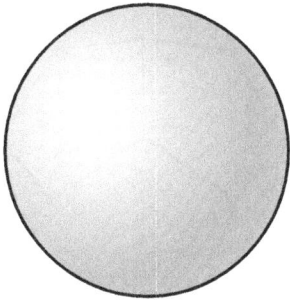

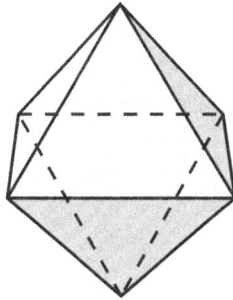

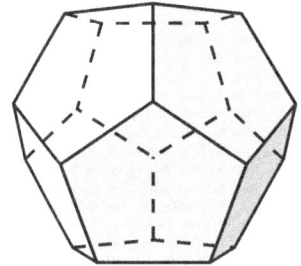

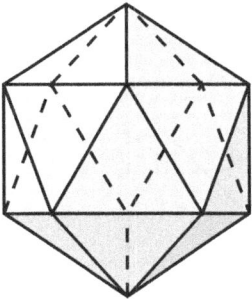

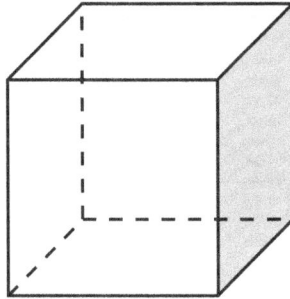

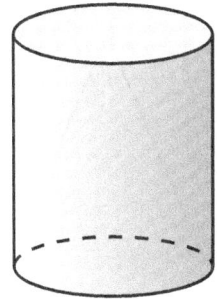

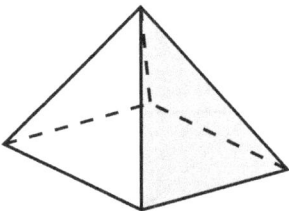

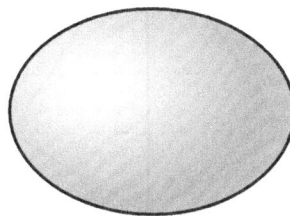

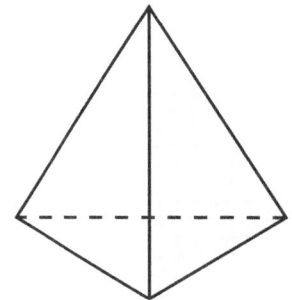

_____   _____   _____

_____   _____   _____

_____   _____   _____

_____   _____   _____

Name _____ Date _____

Write the name of each 3-dimensional solid.

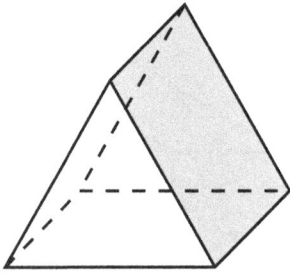

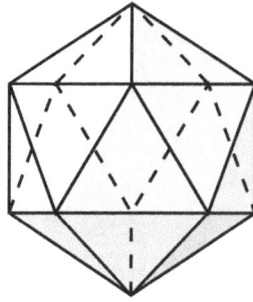

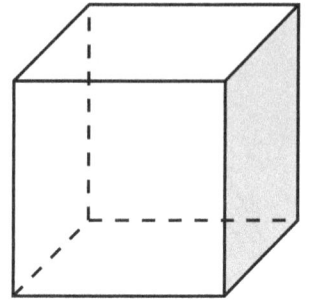

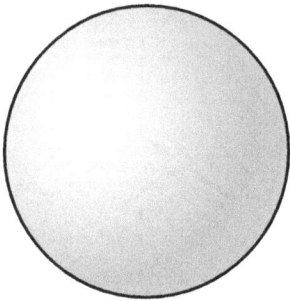

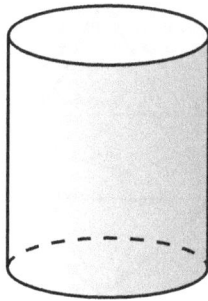

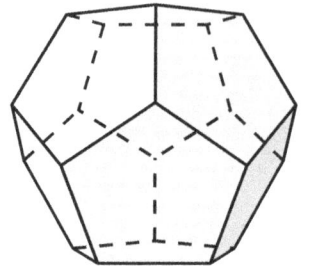

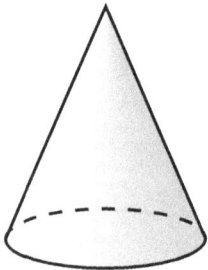

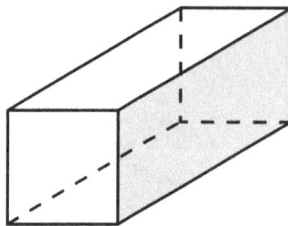

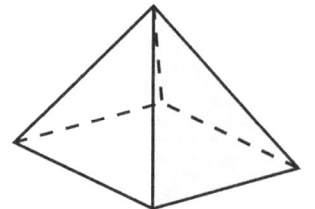

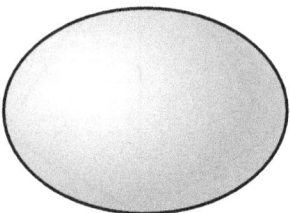

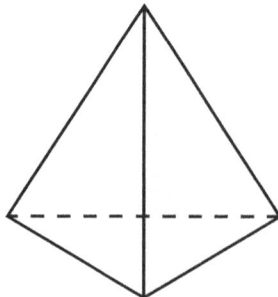

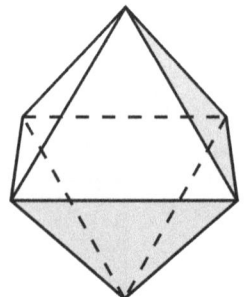

_____   _____   _____

_____   _____   _____

_____   _____   _____

_____   _____   _____

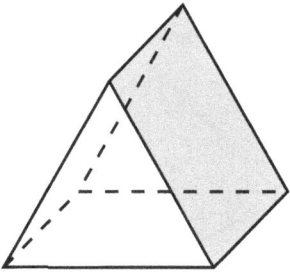

This is a

_____

It has _____ faces.

It has _____ edges.

It has _____ vertices.

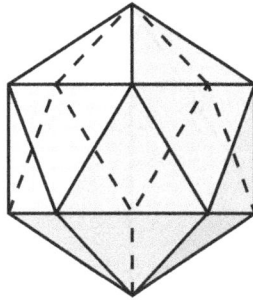

This is a

_____

It has _____ faces.

It has _____ edges.

It has _____ vertices.

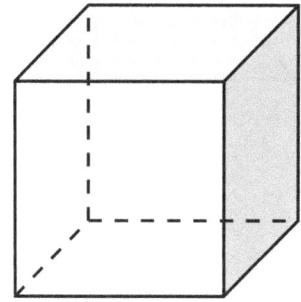

This is a

_____

It has _____ faces.

It has _____ edges.

It has _____ vertices.

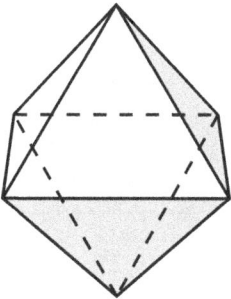

This is a

_____

It has _____ faces.

It has _____ edges.

It has _____ vertices.

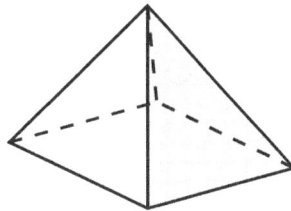

This is a

_____

It has _____ faces.

It has _____ edges.

It has _____ vertices.

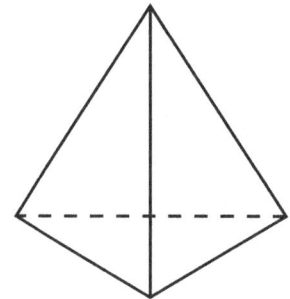

This is a

_____

It has _____ faces.

It has _____ edges.

It has _____ vertices.

Name _____ Date _____

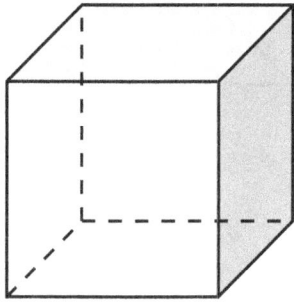

This is a

_____

It has _____ faces.

It has _____ edges.

It has _____ vertices.

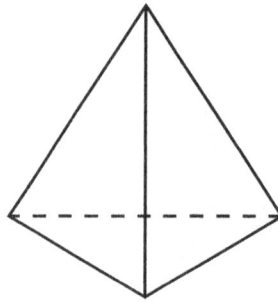

This is a

_____

It has _____ faces.

It has _____ edges.

It has _____ vertices.

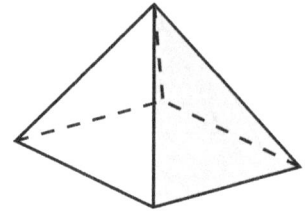

This is a

_____

It has _____ faces.

It has _____ edges.

It has _____ vertices.

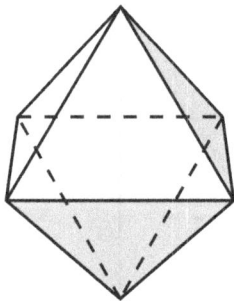

This is a

_____

It has _____ faces.

It has _____ edges.

It has _____ vertices.

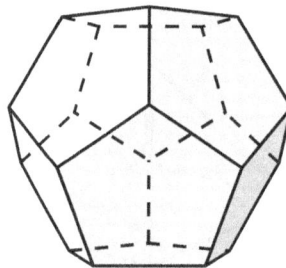

This is a

_____

It has _____ faces.

It has _____ edges.

It has _____ vertices.

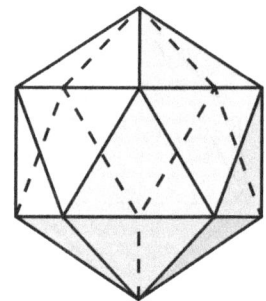

This is a

_____

It has _____ faces.

It has _____ edges.

It has _____ vertices.

Name _____   Date _____

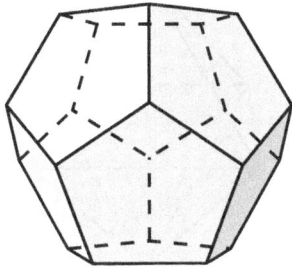

This is a

_____

It has _____ faces.

It has _____ edges.

It has _____ vertices.

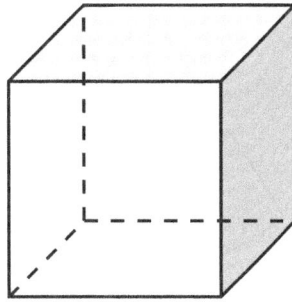

This is a

_____

It has _____ faces.

It has _____ edges.

It has _____ vertices.

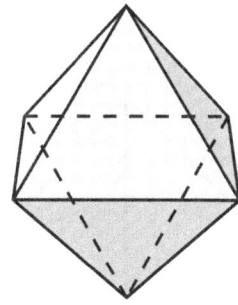

This is a

_____

It has _____ faces.

It has _____ edges.

It has _____ vertices.

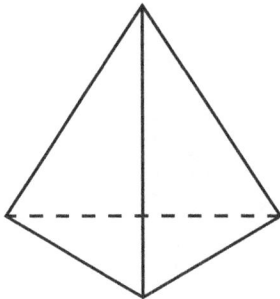

This is a

_____

It has _____ faces.

It has _____ edges.

It has _____ vertices.

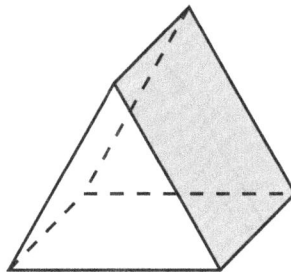

This is a

_____

It has _____ faces.

It has _____ edges.

It has _____ vertices.

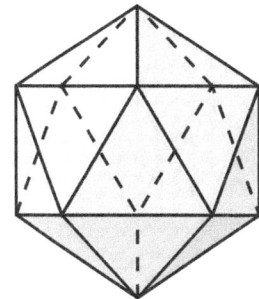

This is a

_____

It has _____ faces.

It has _____ edges.

It has _____ vertices.

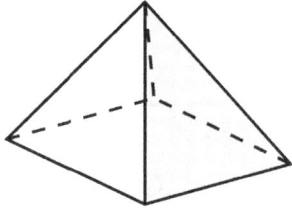

This is a

_____

It has _____ faces.

It has _____ edges.

It has _____ vertices.

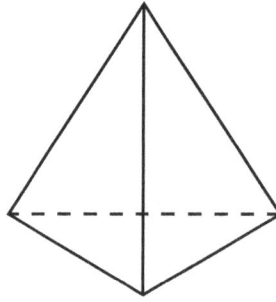

This is a

_____

It has _____ faces.

It has _____ edges.

It has _____ vertices.

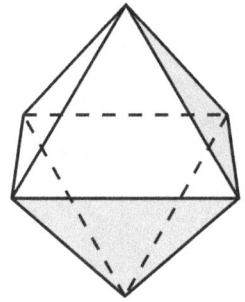

This is a

_____

It has _____ faces.

It has _____ edges.

It has _____ vertices.

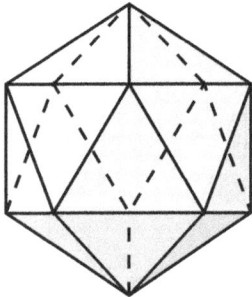

This is a

_____

It has _____ faces.

It has _____ edges.

It has _____ vertices.

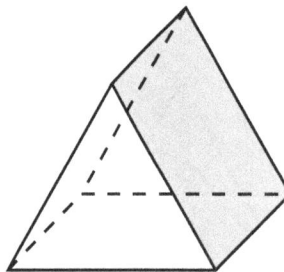

This is a

_____

It has _____ faces.

It has _____ edges.

It has _____ vertices.

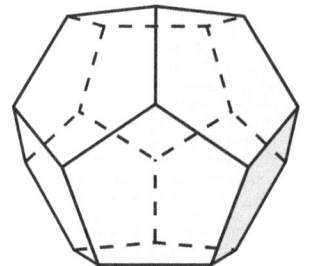

This is a

_____

It has _____ faces.

It has _____ edges.

It has _____ vertices.

Name _____ Date _____

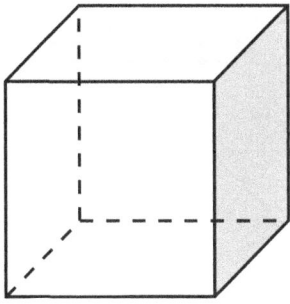

This is a

_____

It has _____ faces.

It has _____ edges.

It has _____ vertices.

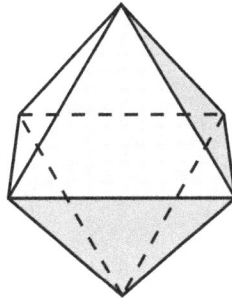

This is a

_____

It has _____ faces.

It has _____ edges.

It has _____ vertices.

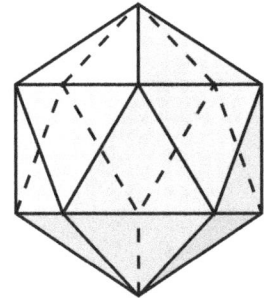

This is a

_____

It has _____ faces.

It has _____ edges.

It has _____ vertices.

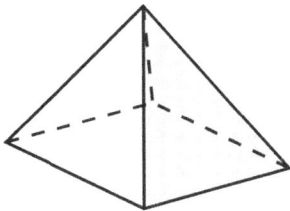

This is a

_____

It has _____ faces.

It has _____ edges.

It has _____ vertices.

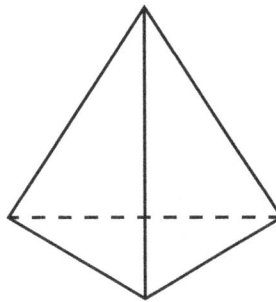

This is a

_____

It has _____ faces.

It has _____ edges.

It has _____ vertices.

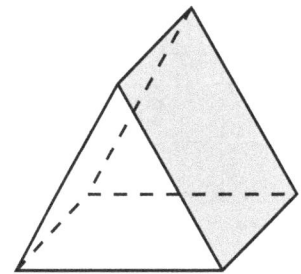

This is a

_____

It has _____ faces.

It has _____ edges.

It has _____ vertices.

Name _____ Date _____

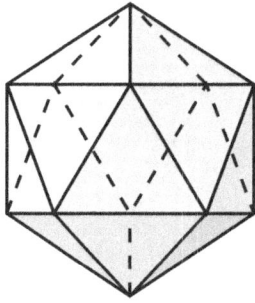

This is a

_____

It has _____ faces.

It has _____ edges.

It has _____ vertices.

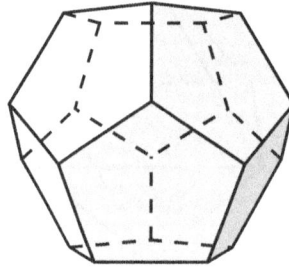

This is a

_____

It has _____ faces.

It has _____ edges.

It has _____ vertices.

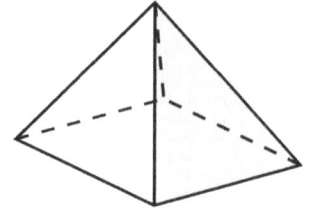

This is a

_____

It has _____ faces.

It has _____ edges.

It has _____ vertices.

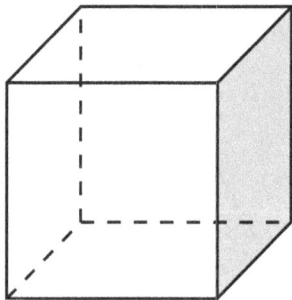

This is a

_____

It has _____ faces.

It has _____ edges.

It has _____ vertices.

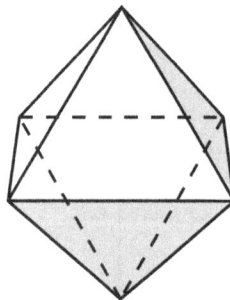

This is a

_____

It has _____ faces.

It has _____ edges.

It has _____ vertices.

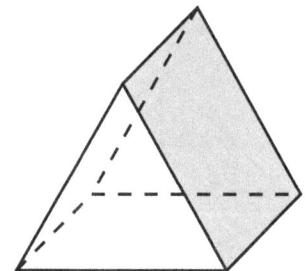

This is a

_____

It has _____ faces.

It has _____ edges.

It has _____ vertices.

Name _____ Date _____

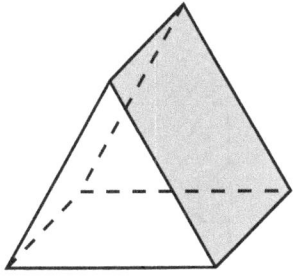

This is a

_____

It has _____ faces.

It has _____ edges.

It has _____ vertices.

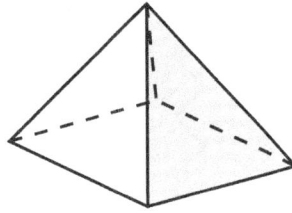

This is a

_____

It has _____ faces.

It has _____ edges.

It has _____ vertices.

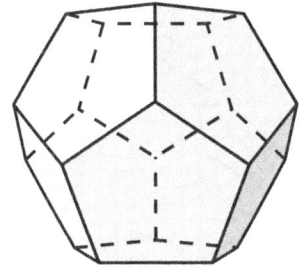

This is a

_____

It has _____ faces.

It has _____ edges.

It has _____ vertices.

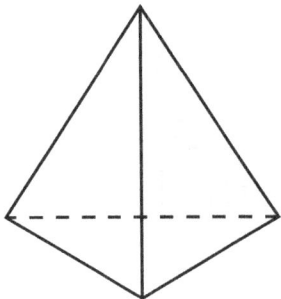

This is a

_____

It has _____ faces.

It has _____ edges.

It has _____ vertices.

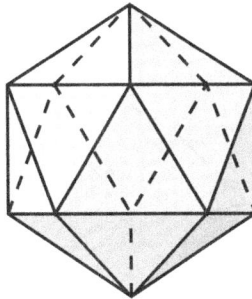

This is a

_____

It has _____ faces.

It has _____ edges.

It has _____ vertices.

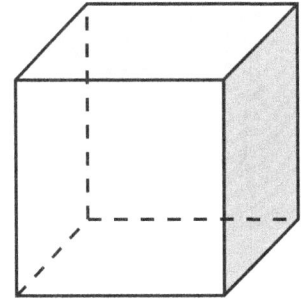

This is a

_____

It has _____ faces.

It has _____ edges.

It has _____ vertices.

Name _____ Date _____

What type of symmetry does each shape have?
Label each shape Reflective, Rotational, Both or None.

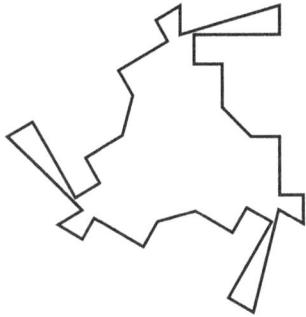

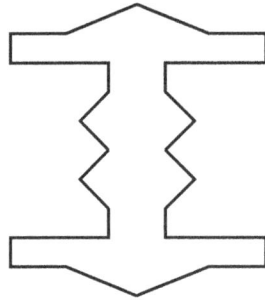

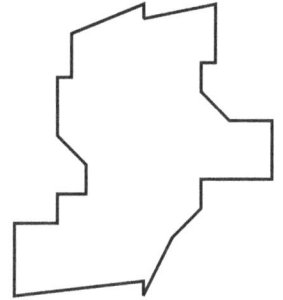

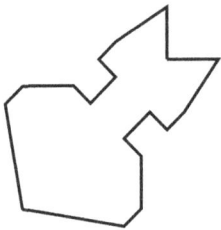

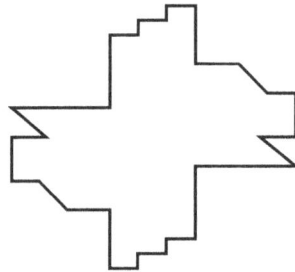

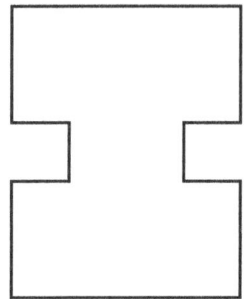

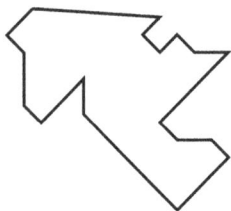

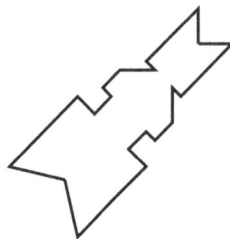

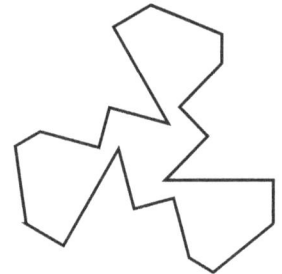

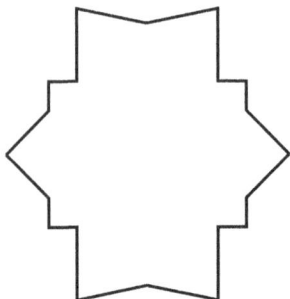

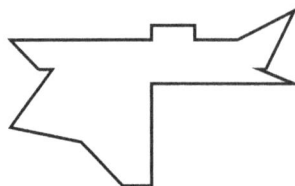

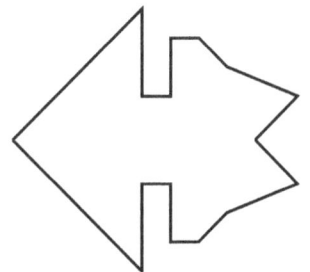

_____   _____   _____

_____   _____   _____

_____   _____   _____

_____   _____   _____

What type of symmetry does each shape have?
Label each shape Reflective, Rotational, Both or None.

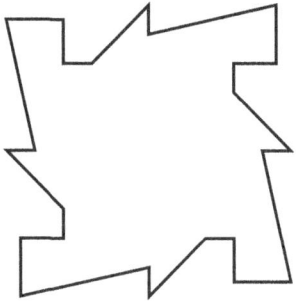

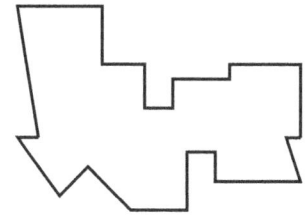

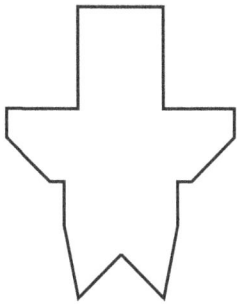

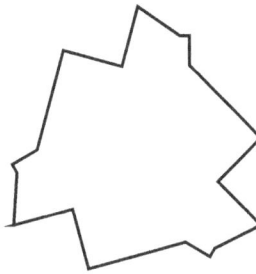

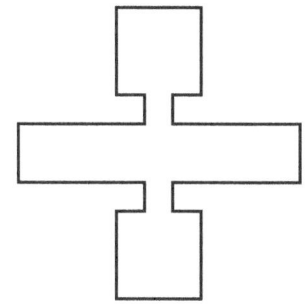

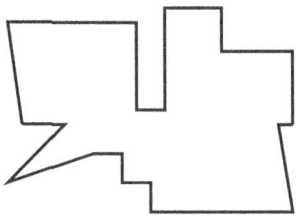

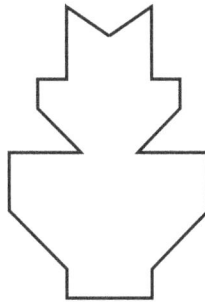

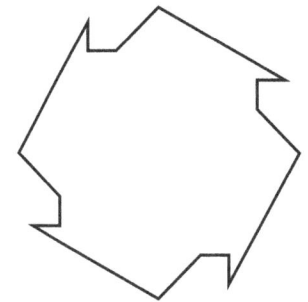

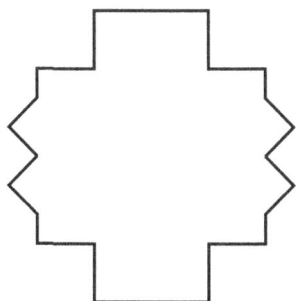

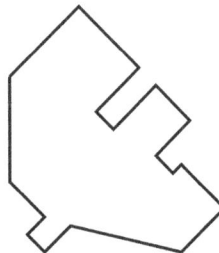

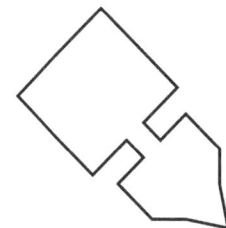

_____   _____   _____

_____   _____   _____

_____   _____   _____

_____   _____   _____

Name _____ Date _____

What type of symmetry does each shape have?
Label each shape Reflective, Rotational, Both or None.

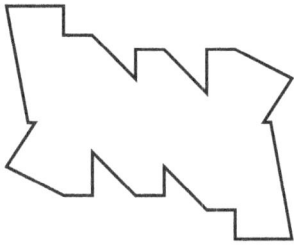

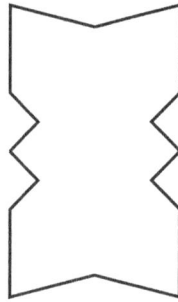

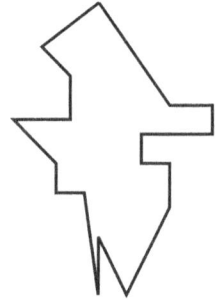

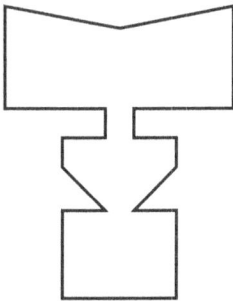

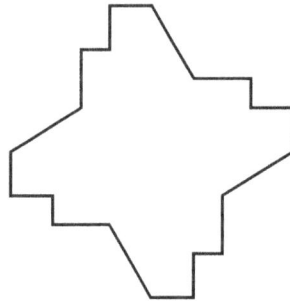

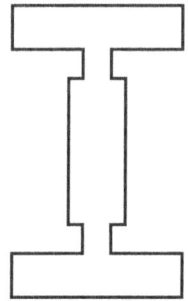

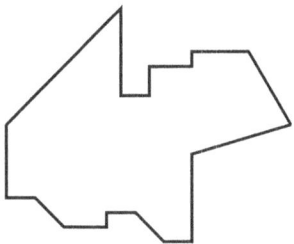

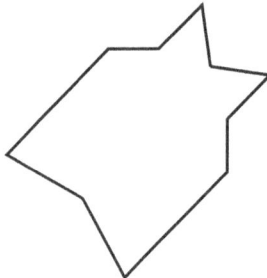

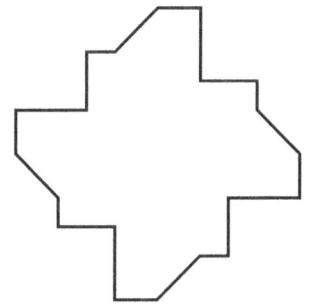

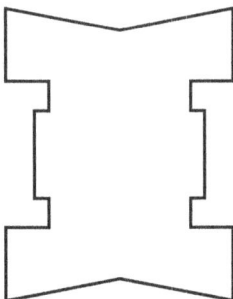

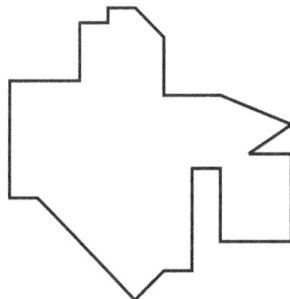

Name _____ Date _____

What type of symmetry does each shape have?
Label each shape Reflective, Rotational, Both or None.

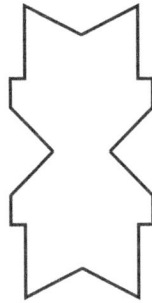

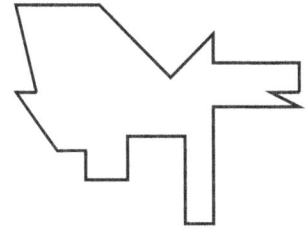

_____   _____   _____

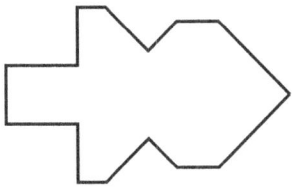

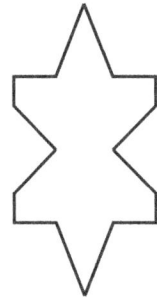

_____   _____   _____

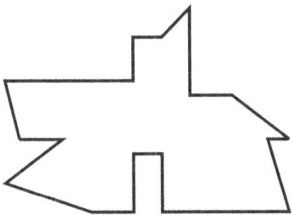

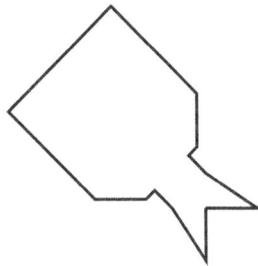

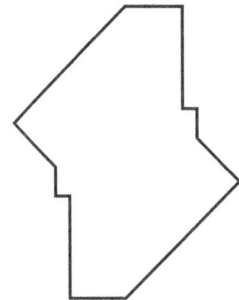

_____   _____   _____

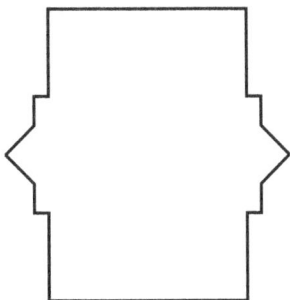

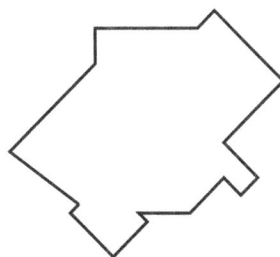

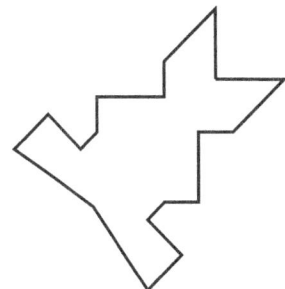

_____   _____   _____

Name _____ Date _____

What type of symmetry does each shape have?
Label each shape Reflective, Rotational, Both or None.

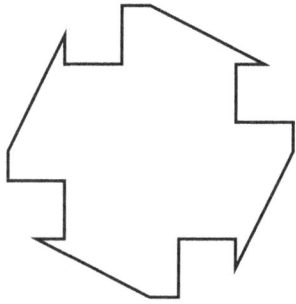   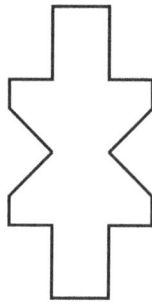   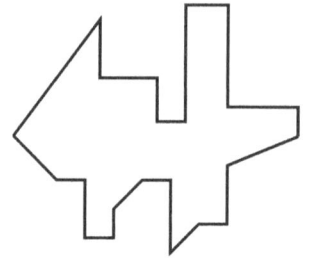

_____   _____   _____

   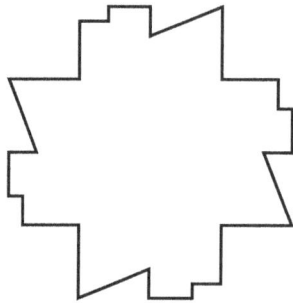   

_____   _____   _____

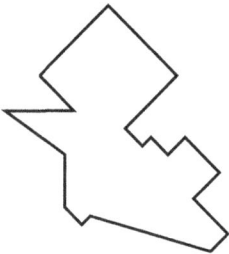      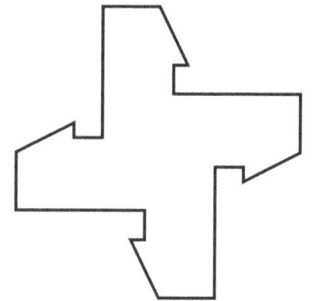

_____   _____   _____

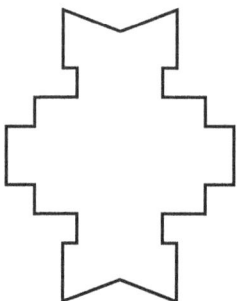   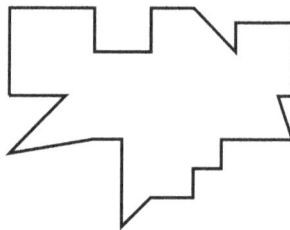   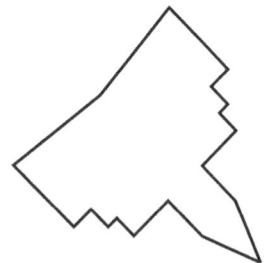

_____   _____   _____

Name _____ Date _____

What type of symmetry does each shape have?
Label each shape Reflective, Rotational, Both or None.

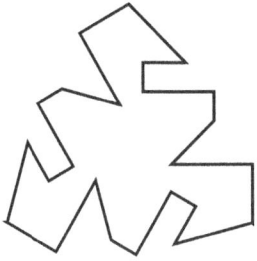

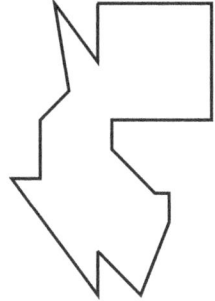

_____ _____ _____

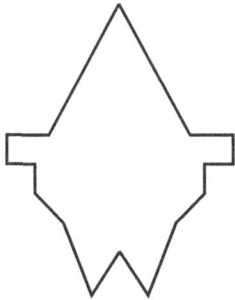

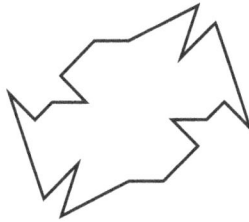

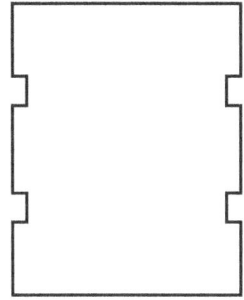

_____ _____ _____

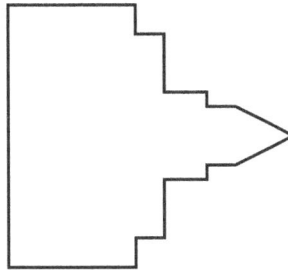

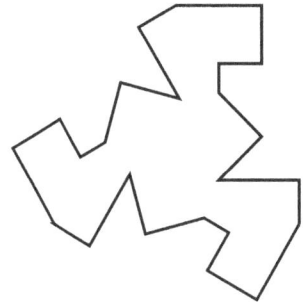

_____ _____ _____

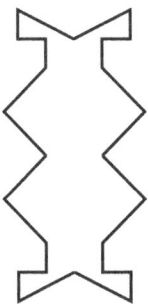

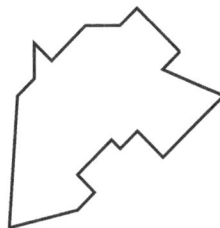

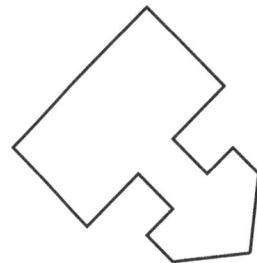

_____ _____ _____

Name _____ Date _____

What type of symmetry does each shape have?
Label each shape Reflective, Rotational, Both or None.

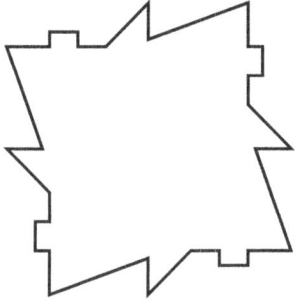

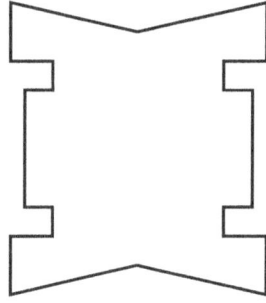

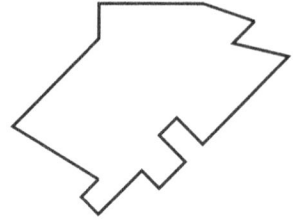

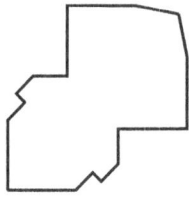

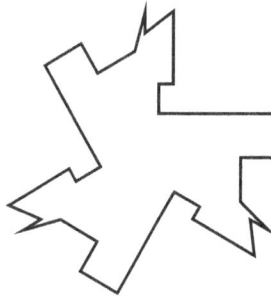

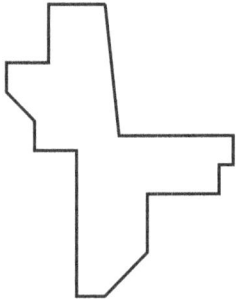

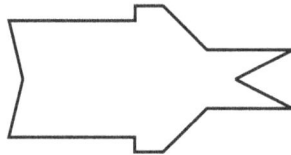

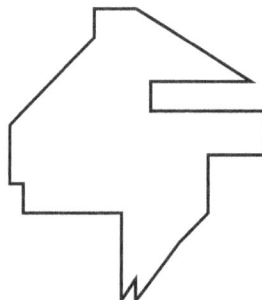

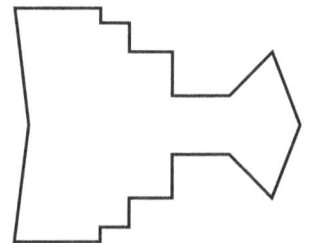

_____   _____   _____

_____   _____   _____

_____   _____   _____

_____   _____   _____

Name _____ Date _____

Draw the line of symmetry for each shape.
Some shapes may have more than one line of symmetry.

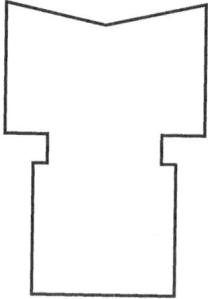

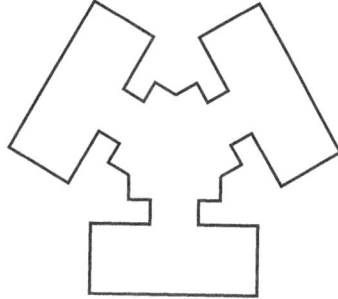

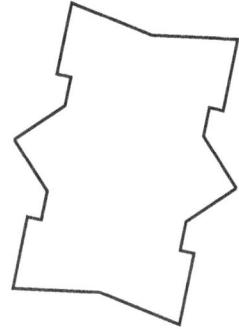

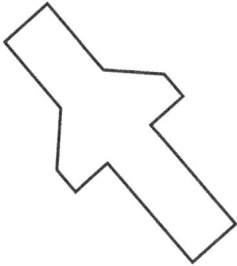

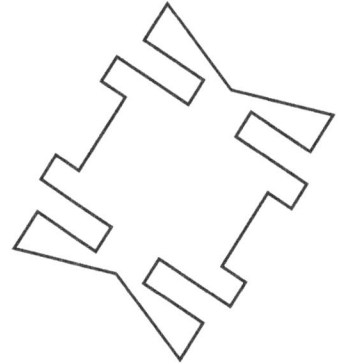

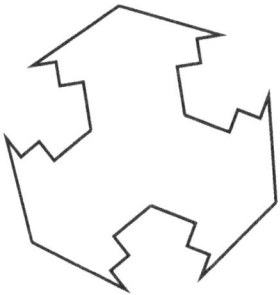

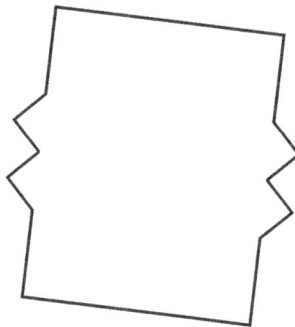

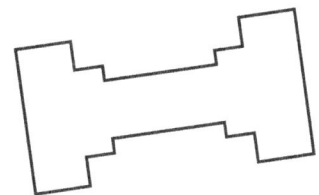

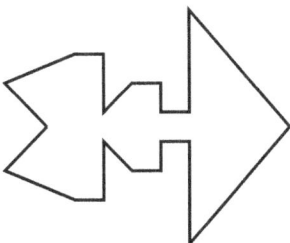

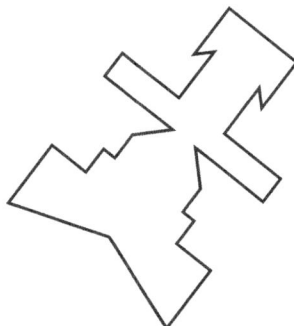

Name _____ Date _____

Draw the line of symmetry for each shape.
Some shapes may have more than one line of symmetry.

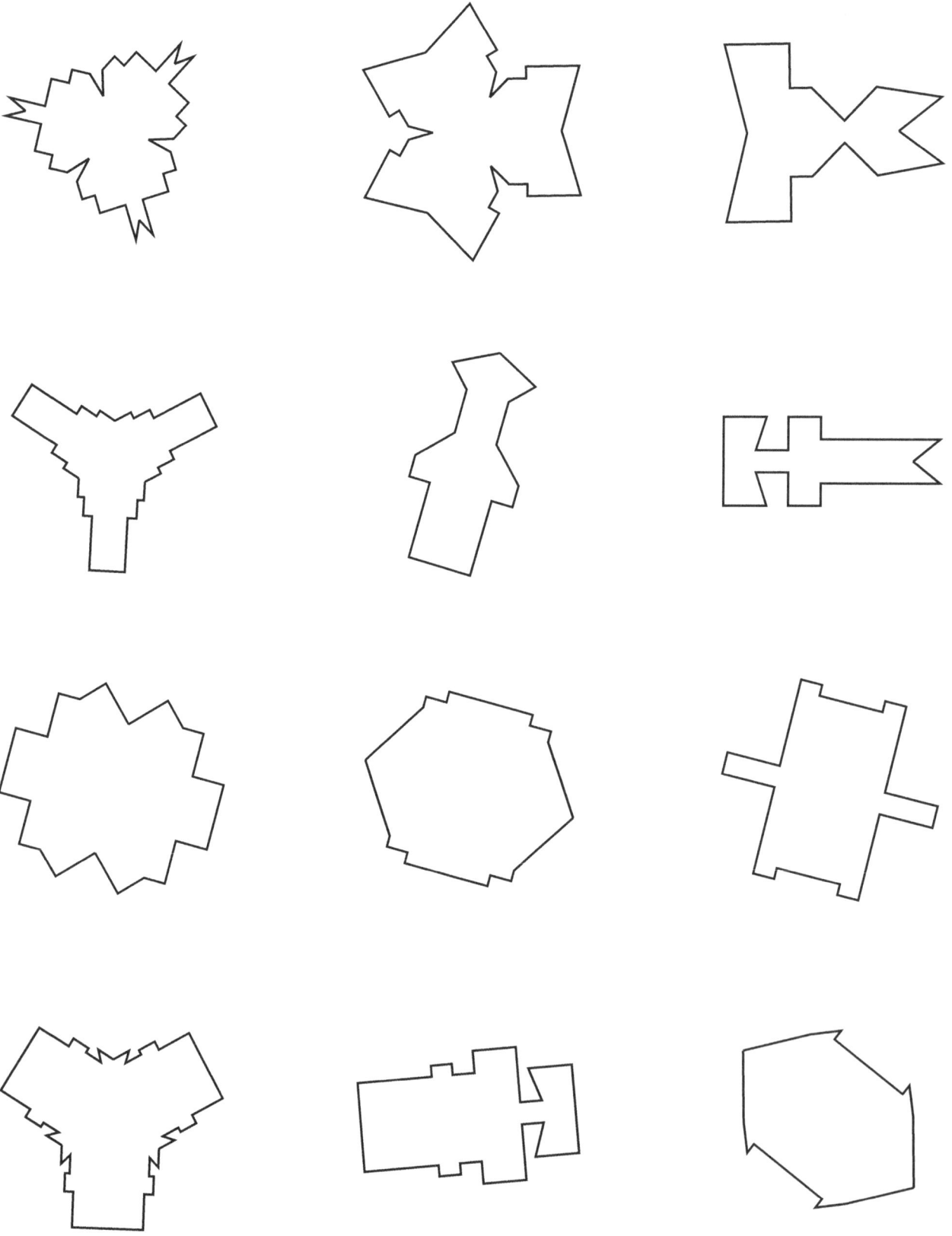

Name _____ Date _____

Draw the line of symmetry for each shape.
Some shapes may have more than one line of symmetry.

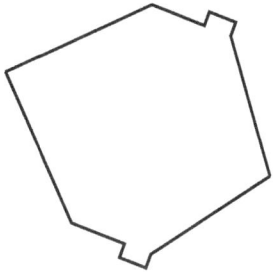

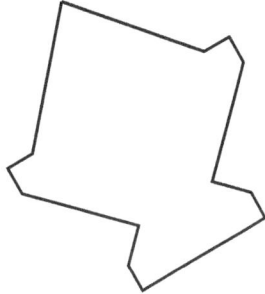

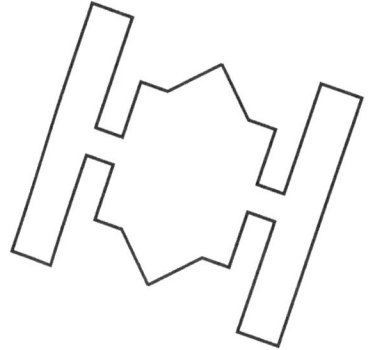

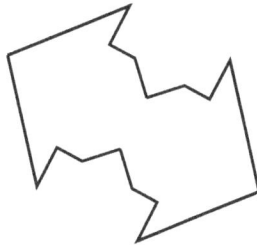

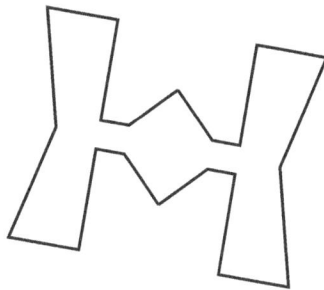

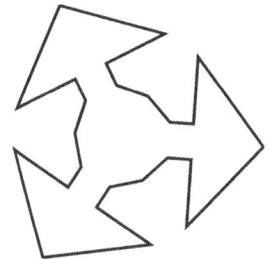

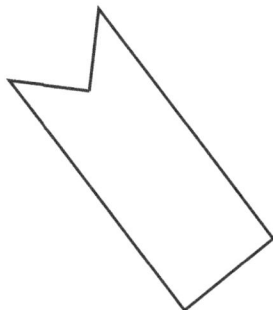

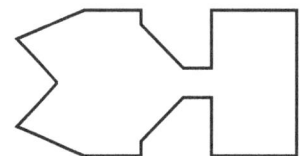

Name _____ Date _____

Draw the line of symmetry for each shape.
Some shapes may have more than one line of symmetry.

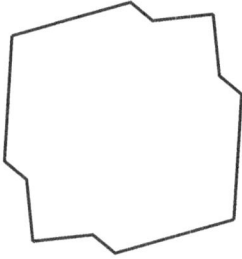

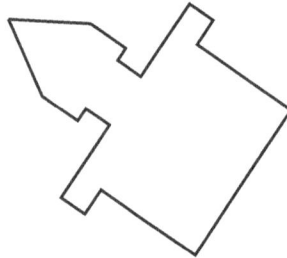

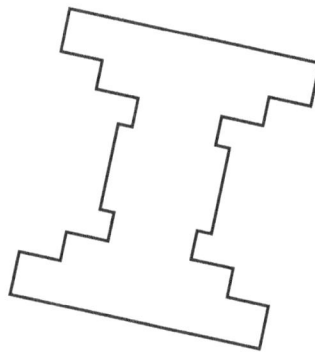

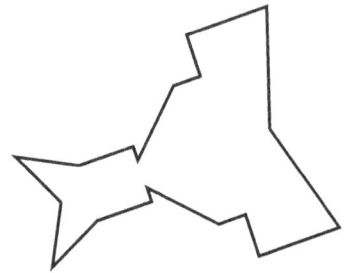

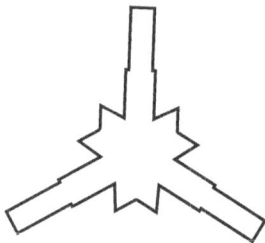

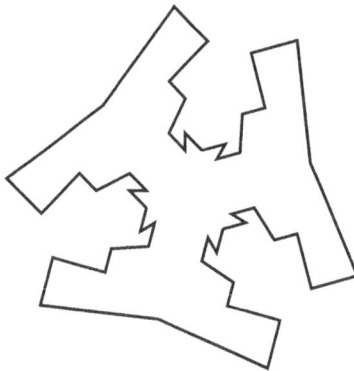

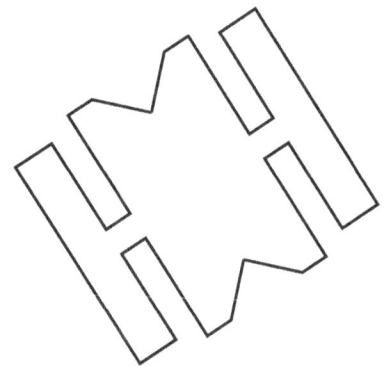

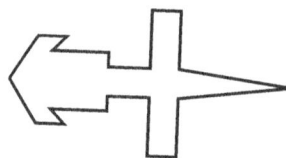

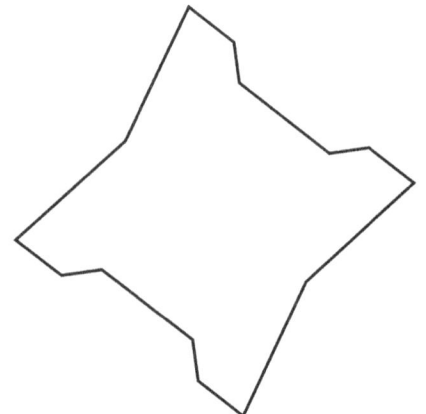

Name _____ Date _____

Draw the line of symmetry for each shape.
Some shapes may have more than one line of symmetry.

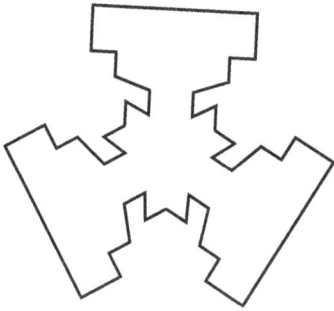

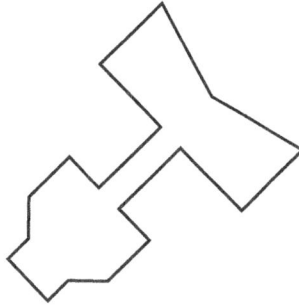

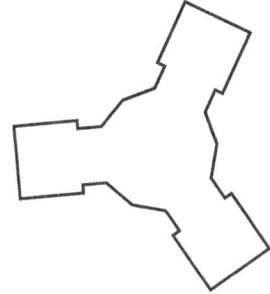

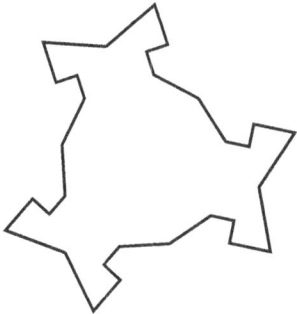

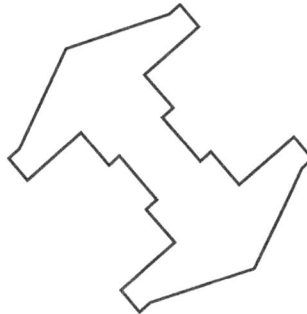

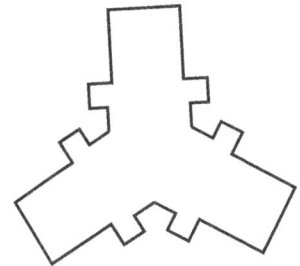

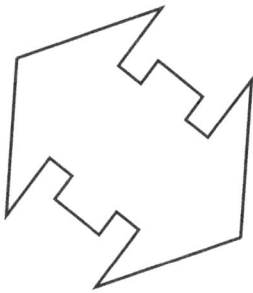

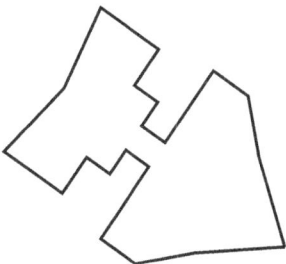

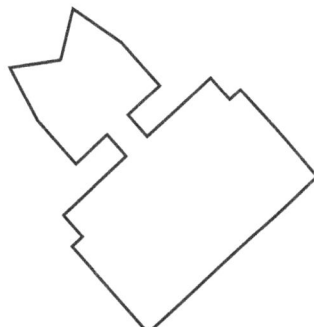

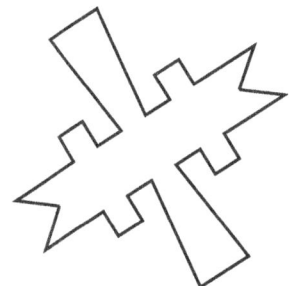

Name _____ Date _____

Draw the line of symmetry for each shape.
Some shapes may have more than one line of symmetry.

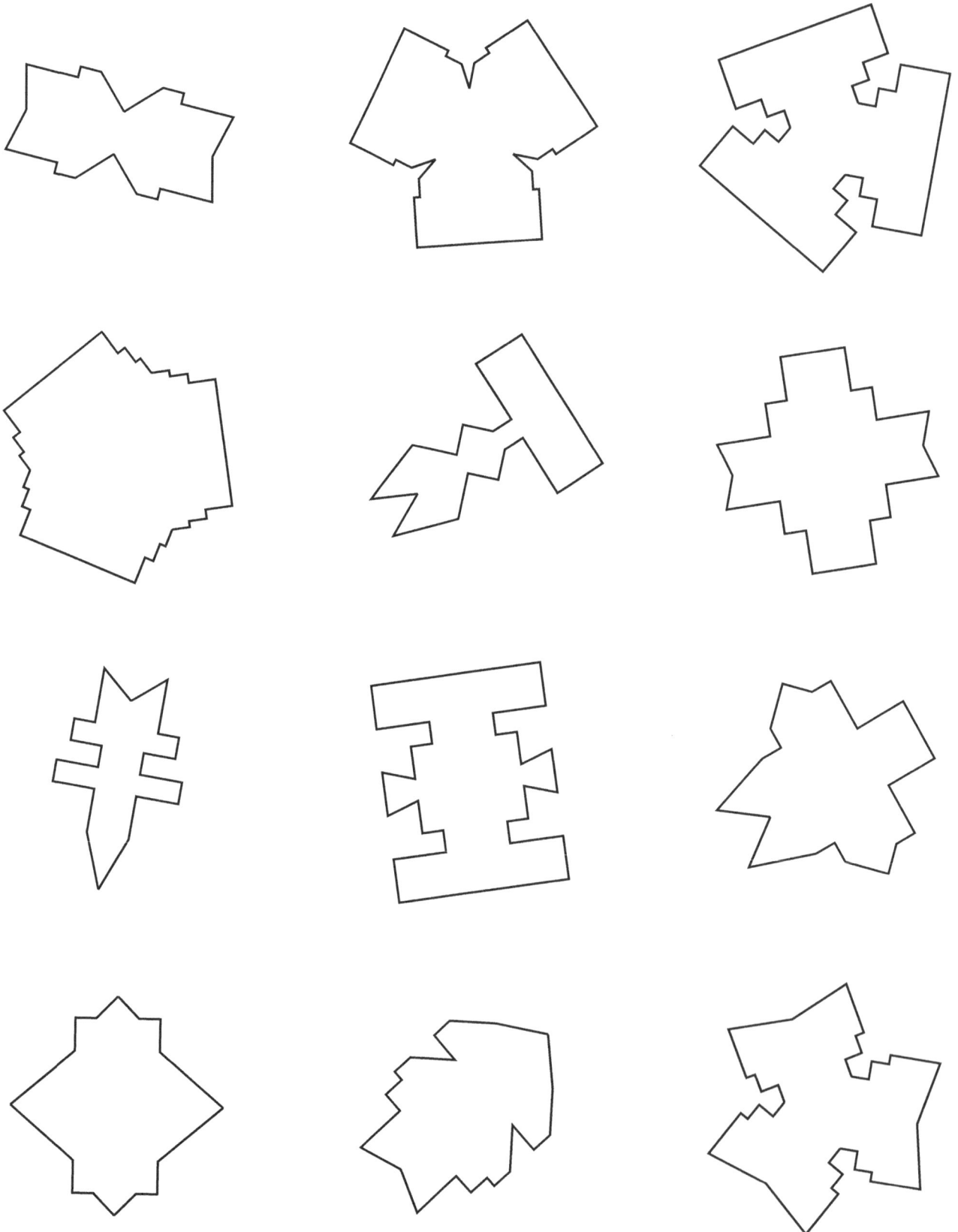

Name _____ Date _____

Draw the line of symmetry for each shape.
Some shapes may have more than one line of symmetry.

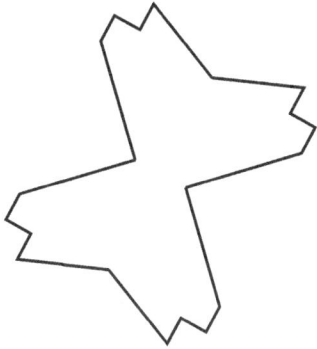

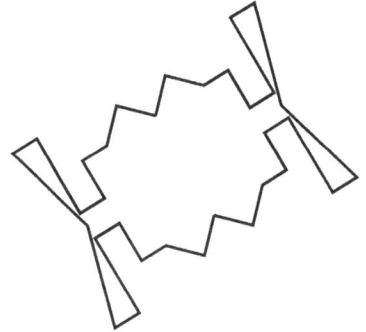

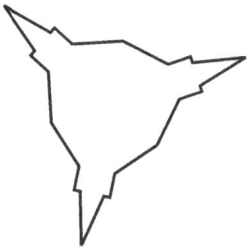

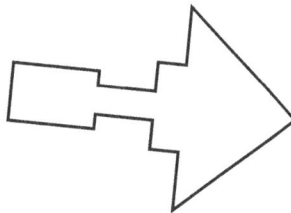

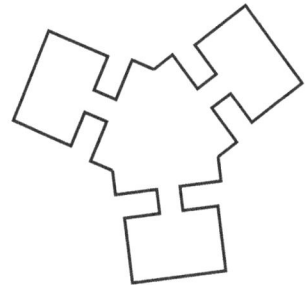

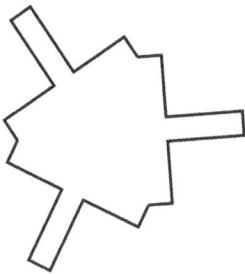

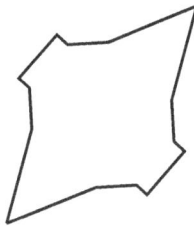

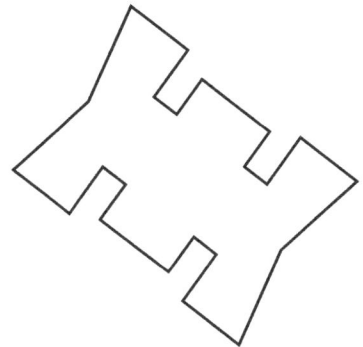

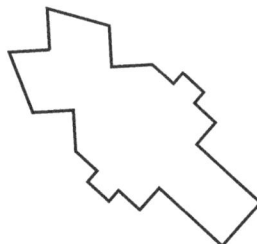

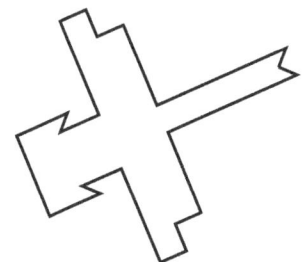

Name _____ Date _____

Draw the reflection of each shape across its line of symmetry.

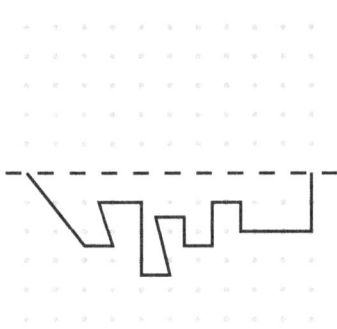

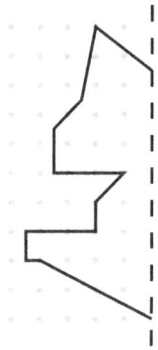

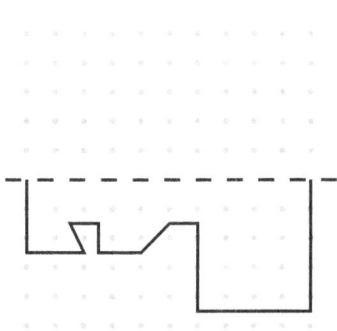

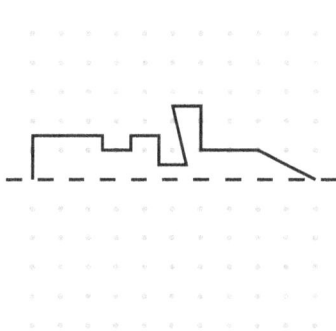

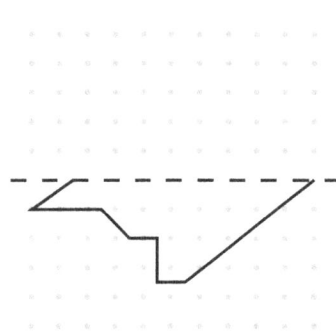

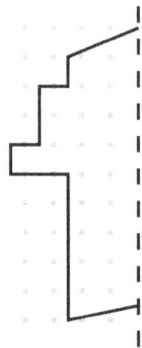

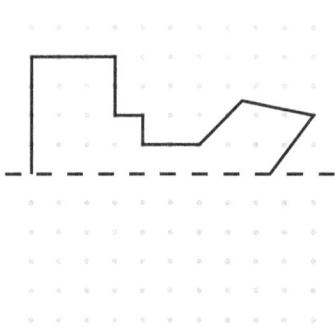

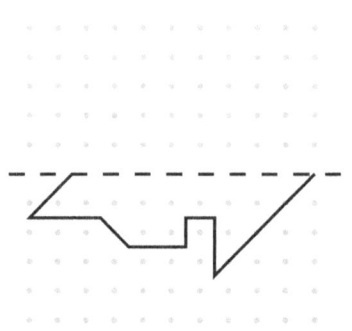

Name _____ Date _____

Draw the reflection of each shape across its line of symmetry.

Name _____ Date _____

Draw the reflection of each shape across its line of symmetry.

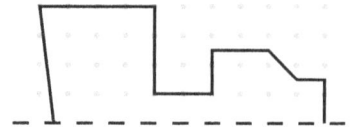

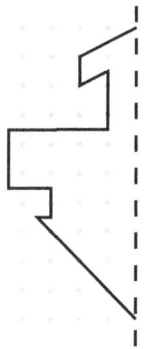

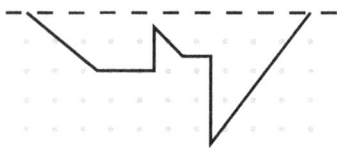

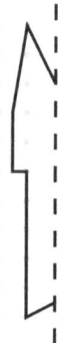

Name _____ Date _____

Draw the reflection of each shape across its line of symmetry.

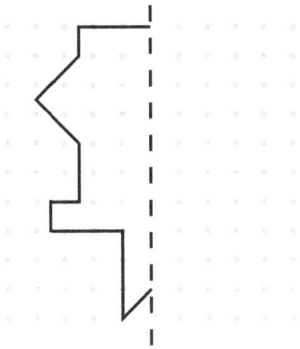

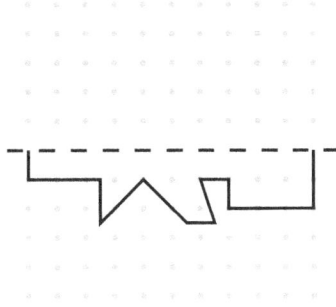

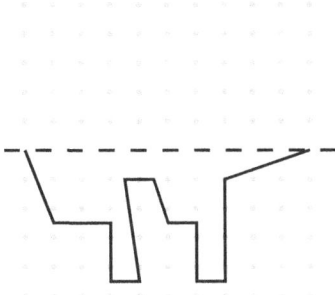

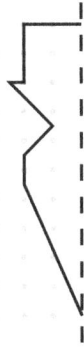

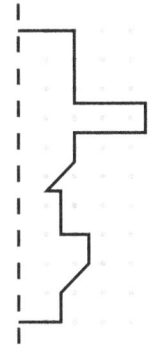

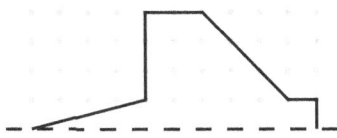

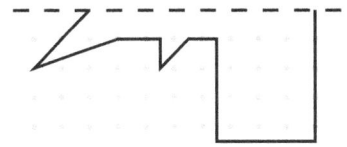

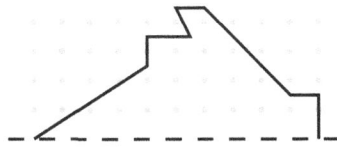

Draw the reflection of each shape across its line of symmetry.

Name _____ Date _____

Draw the reflection of each shape across its line of symmetry.

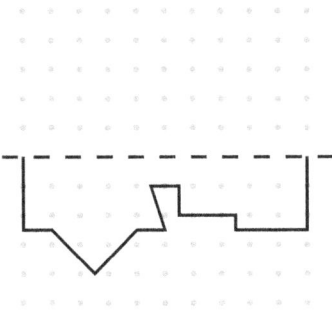

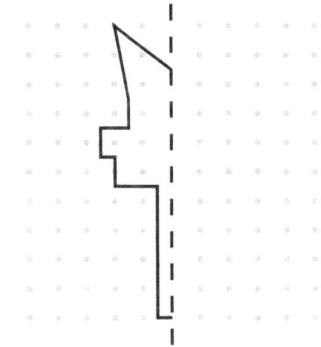

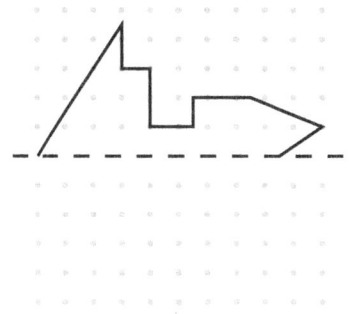

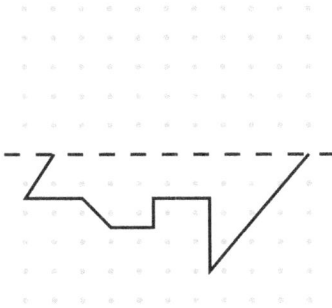

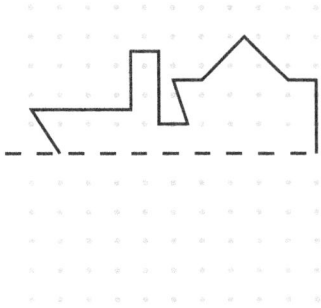

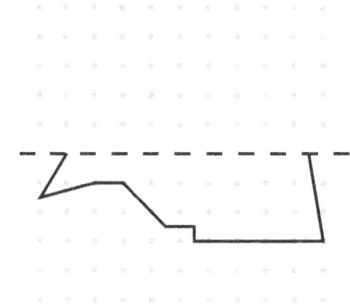

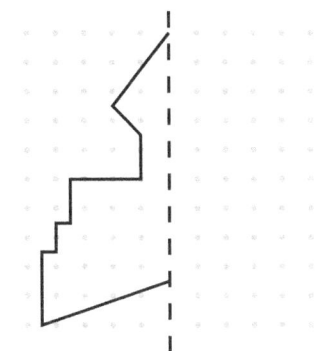

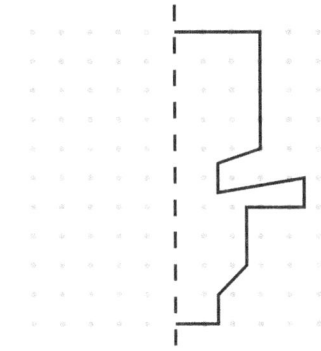

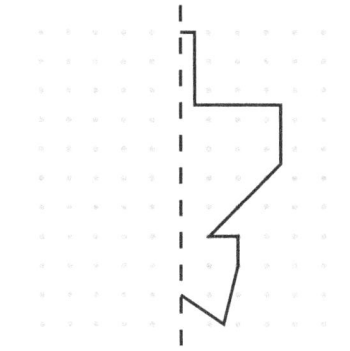

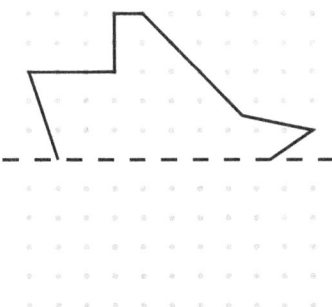

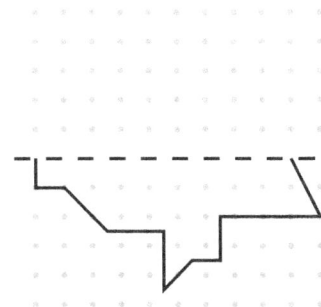

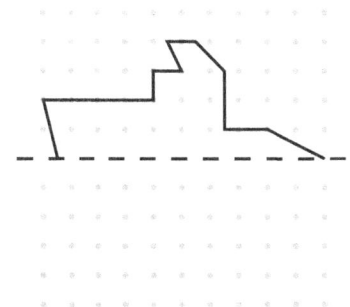

Name _____ Date _____

Draw the reflection of each shape across its line of symmetry.

Name _____ Date _____

Fill in the measures of the unknown angles.

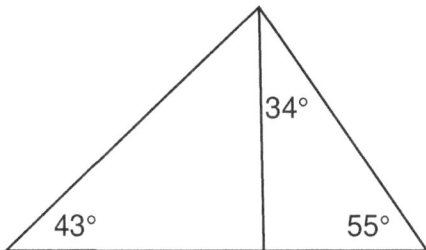

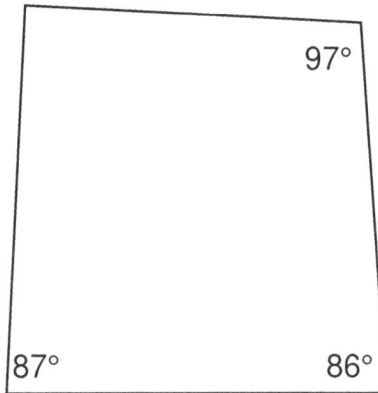

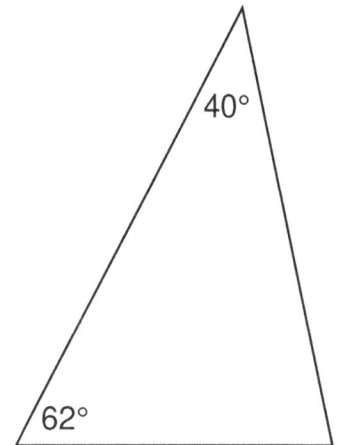

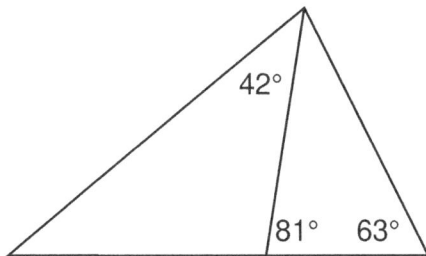

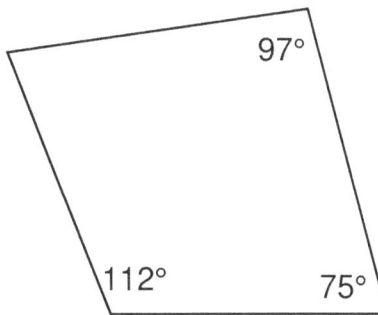

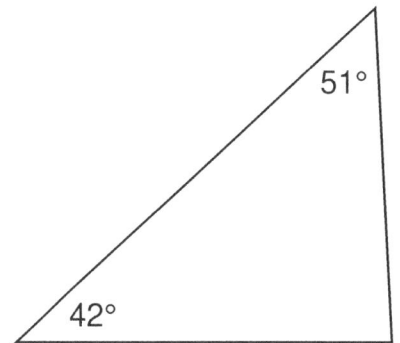

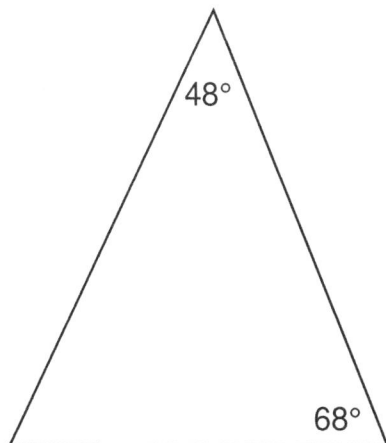

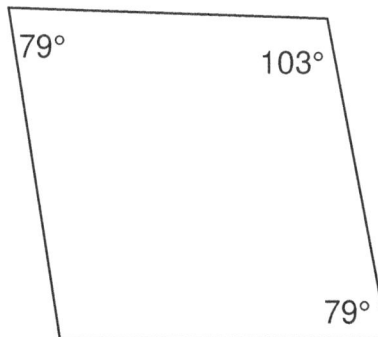

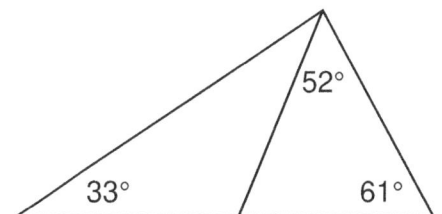

97°

40°

34°

43°   55°

87°   86°

62°

42°

97°

51°

81° 63°

112°   75°

42°

48°

79°   103°

52°

68°

79°

33°   61°

Name _____ Date _____

Fill in the measures of the unknown angles.

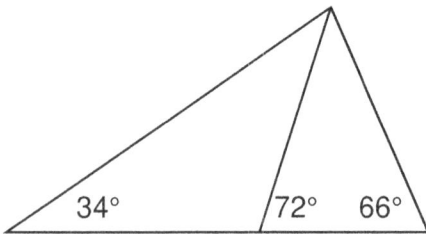

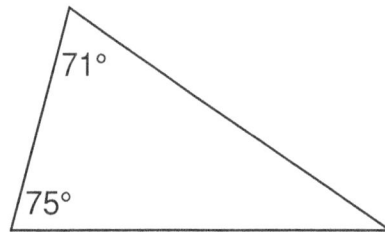

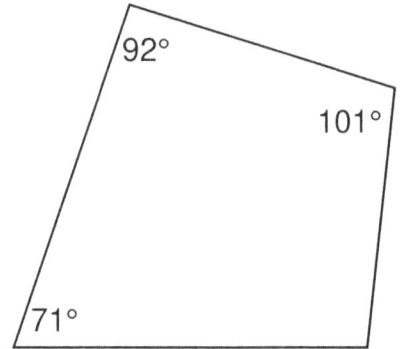

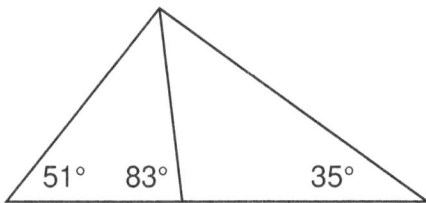

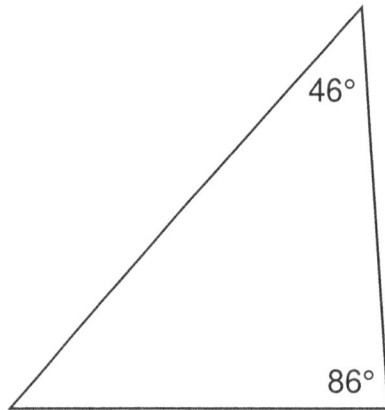

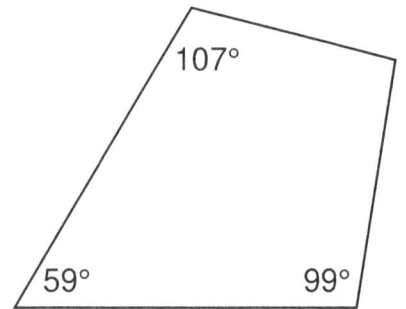

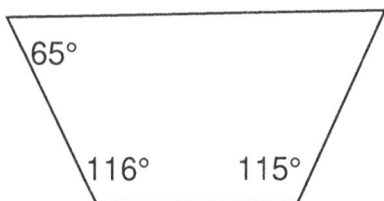

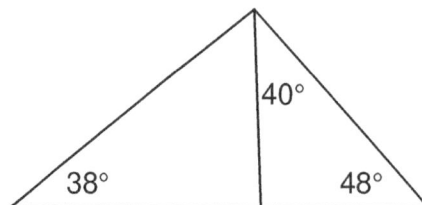

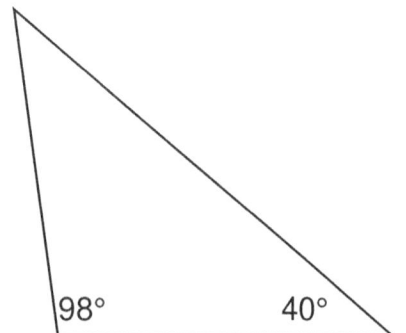

34°   72°   66°

71°   75°

92°   101°   71°

51°   83°   35°

46°   86°

107°   59°   99°

65°   116°   115°

40°   38°   48°

98°   40°

Page 72

Name _____ Date _____

Fill in the measures of the unknown angles.

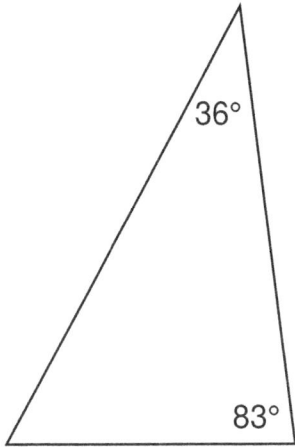

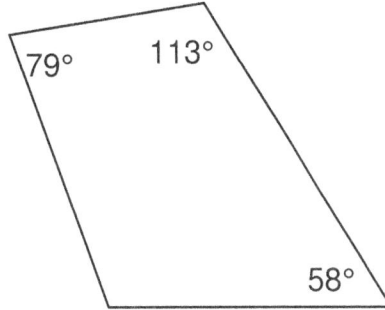

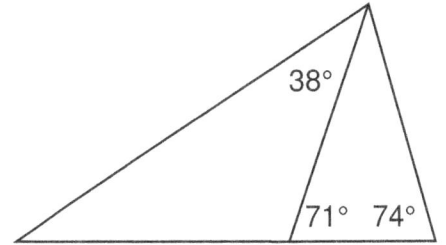

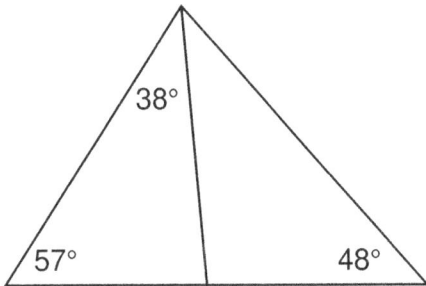

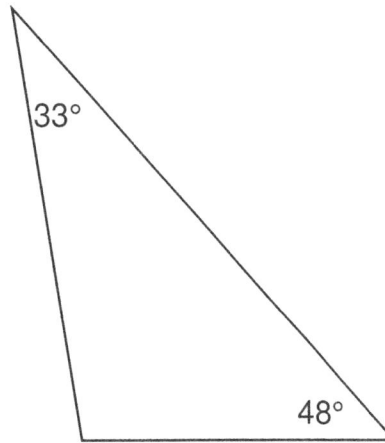

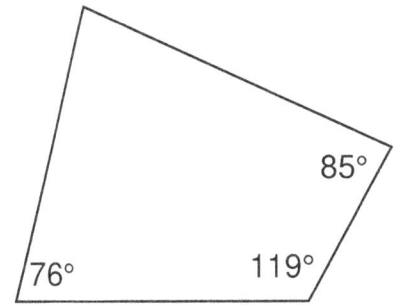

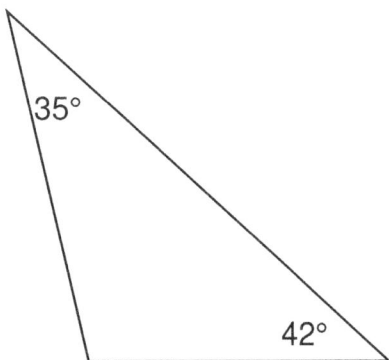

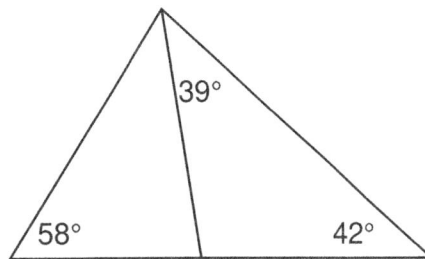

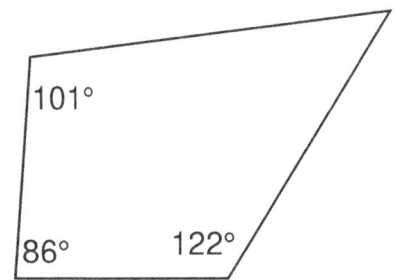

36°

83°

79° 113°

58°

38°

71° 74°

38°

57° 48°

33°

48°

85°

76° 119°

35°

42°

39°

58° 42°

101°

86° 122°

Name _____ Date _____

Fill in the measures of the unknown angles.

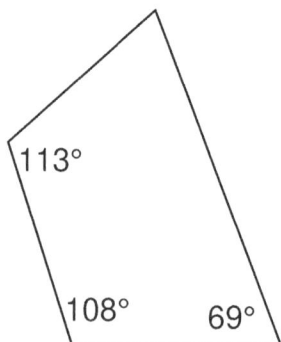

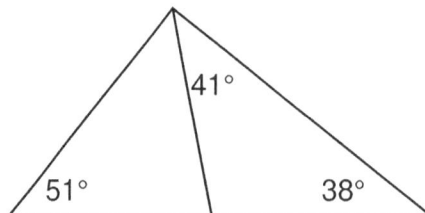

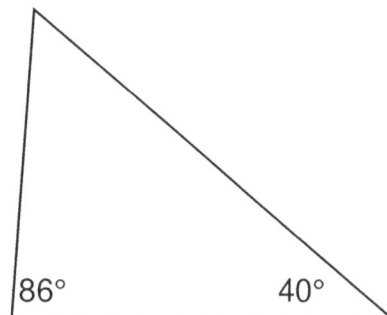

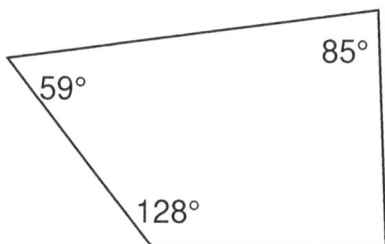

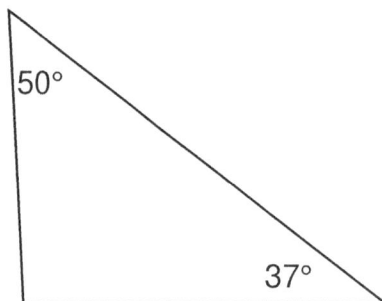

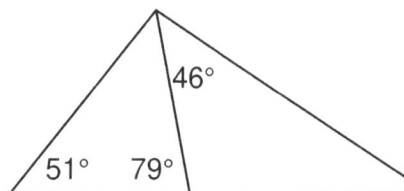

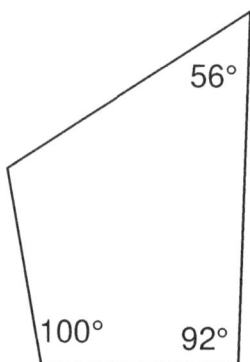

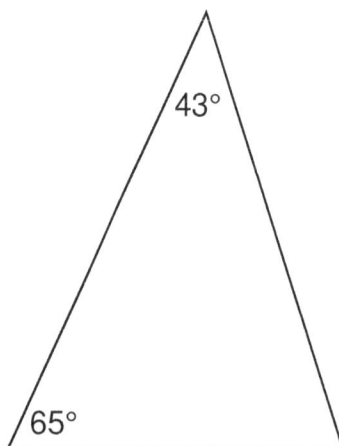

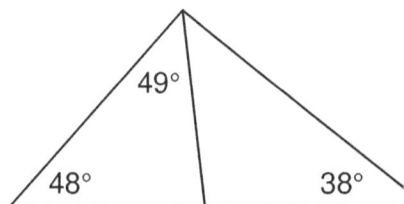

113°
108°   69°

41°
51°   38°

86°   40°

85°
59°
128°

50°
37°

46°
51° 79°

56°
100°   92°

43°
65°

49°
48°   38°

Name _____ Date _____

Fill in the measures of the unknown angles.

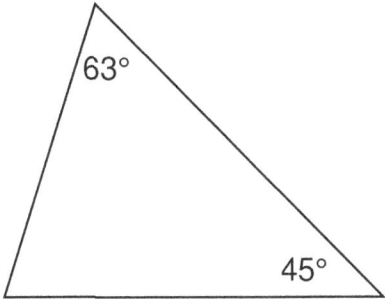

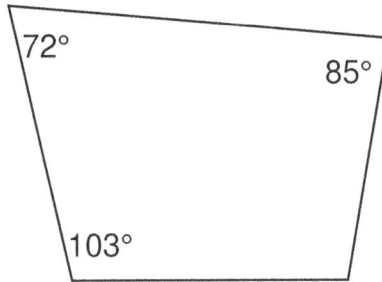

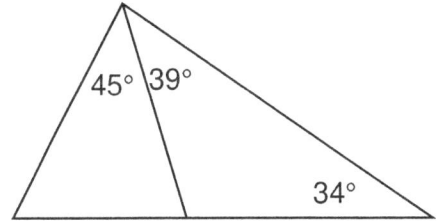

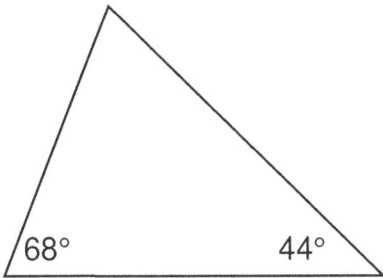

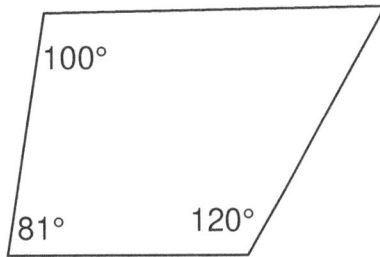

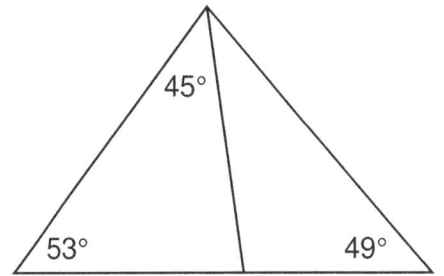

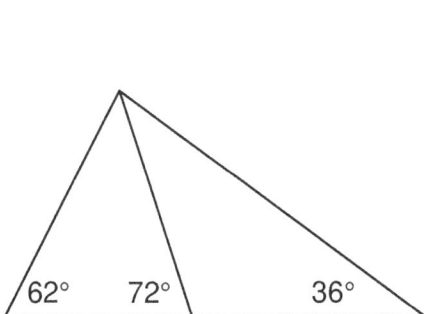

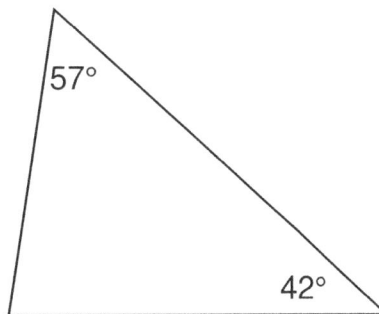

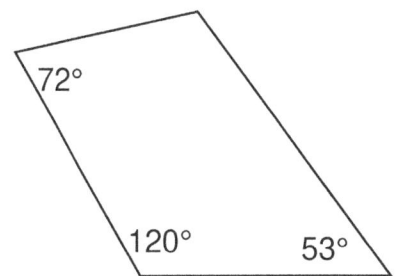

63°
45°

72°
85°
103°

45° 39°
34°

68°
44°

100°
81°
120°

45°
53°
49°

62° 72°
36°

57°
42°

72°
120°
53°

Name _____ Date _____

Fill in the measures of the unknown angles.

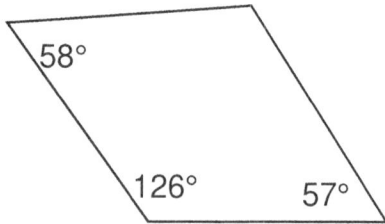

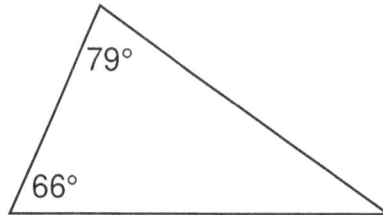

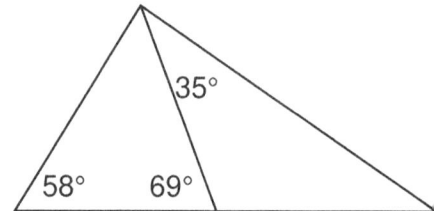

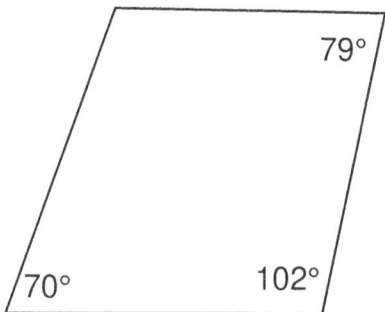

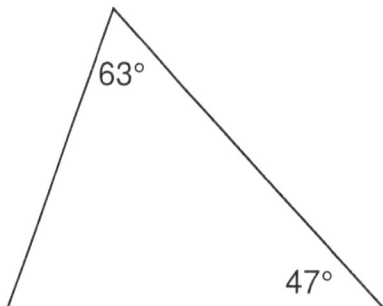

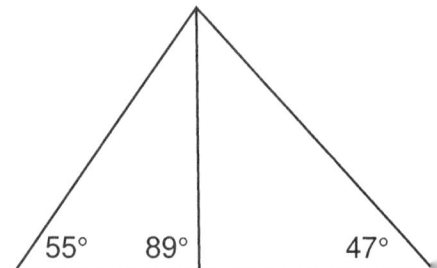

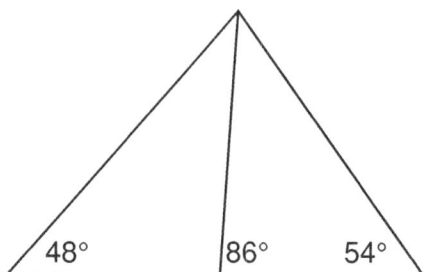

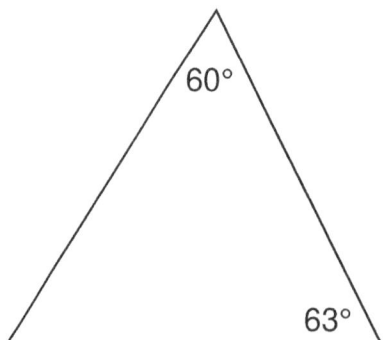

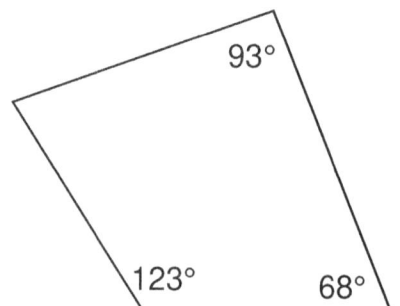

58°
126°   57°

79°
66°

35°
58°   69°

79°
70°   102°

63°
47°

55°   89°   47°

48°   86°   54°

60°
63°

93°
123°   68°

Name _____ Date _____

Fill in the measures of the unknown angles.

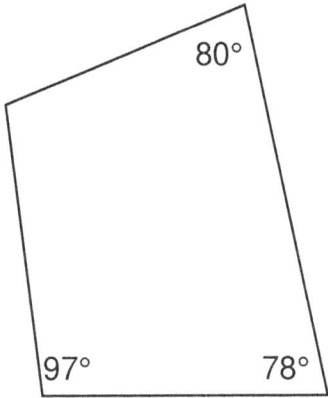

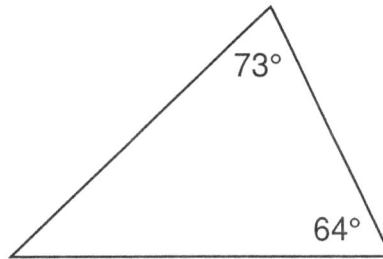

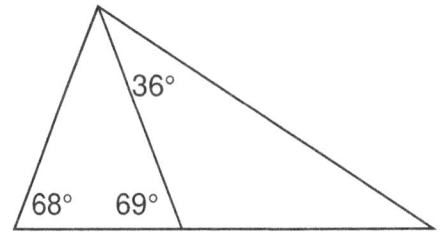

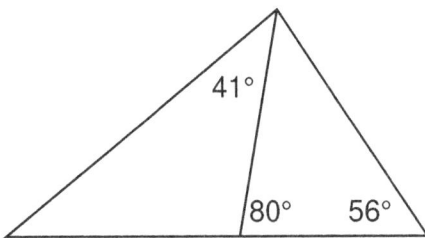

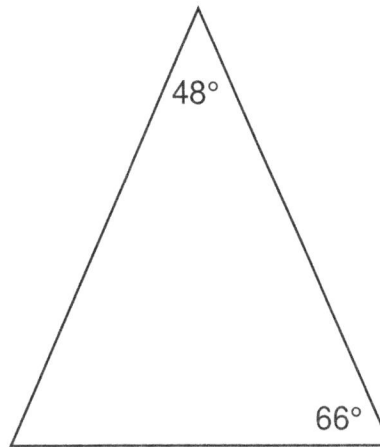

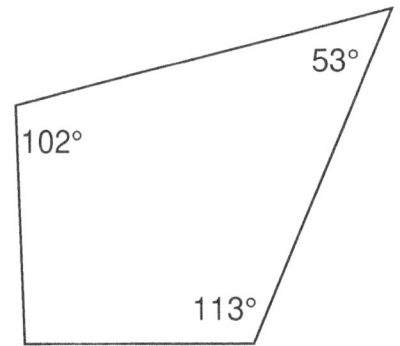

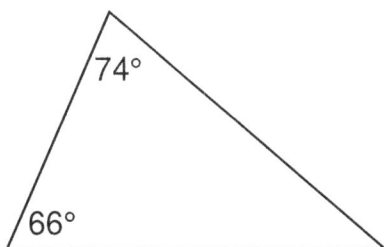

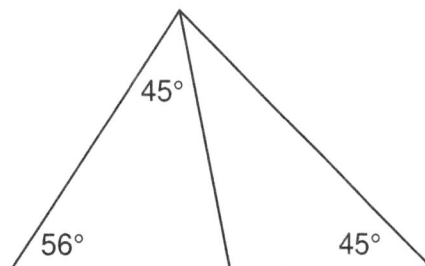

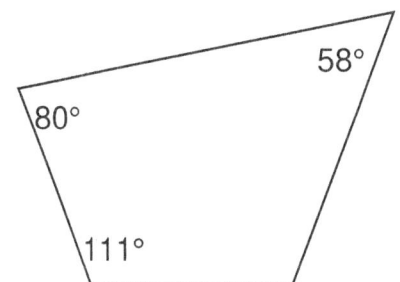

80°

97° 78°

73°

64°

36°

68° 69°

41°

80° 56°

48°

66°

53°

102°

113°

74°

66°

45°

56° 45°

58°

80°

111°

Name _____ Date _____

Fill in the measures of the unknown angles.
Horizontal lines that appear to be parallel are.

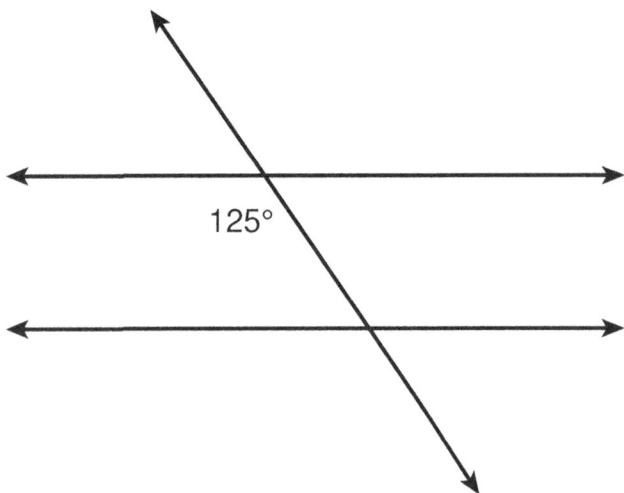

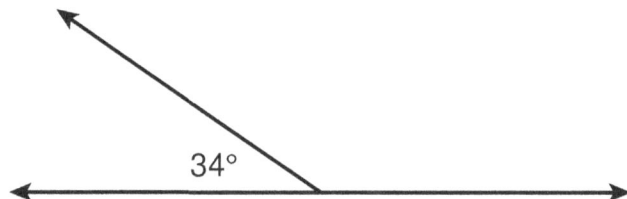

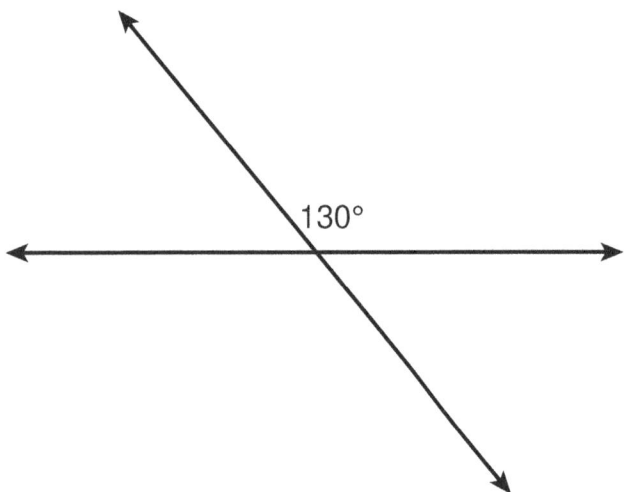

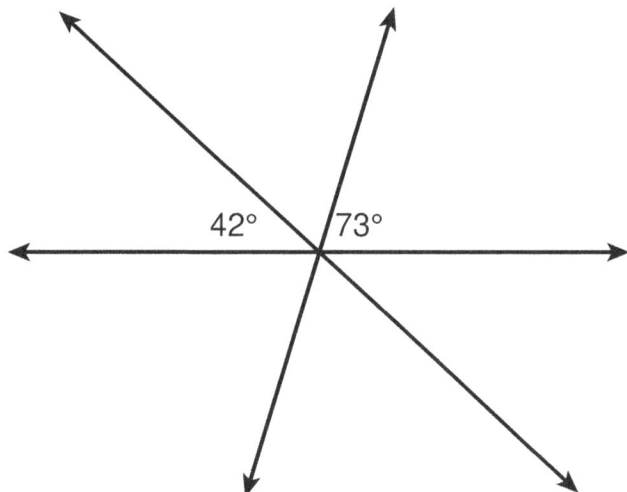

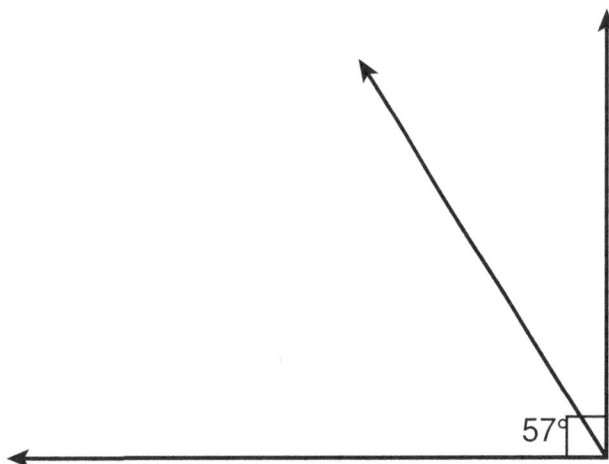

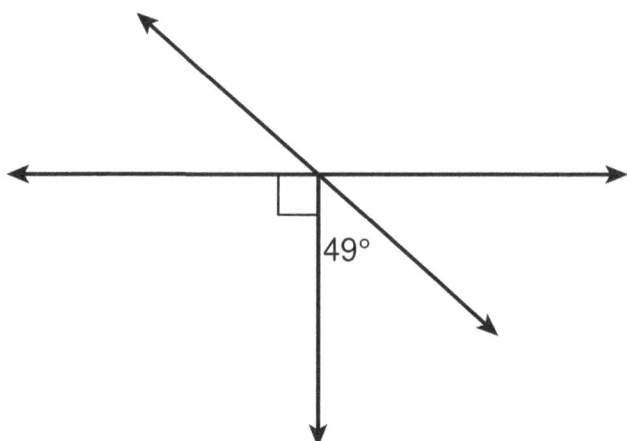

125°

34°

130°

42° 73°

57°

49°

Name _____ Date _____

Fill in the measures of the unknown angles.
Horizontal lines that appear to be parallel are.

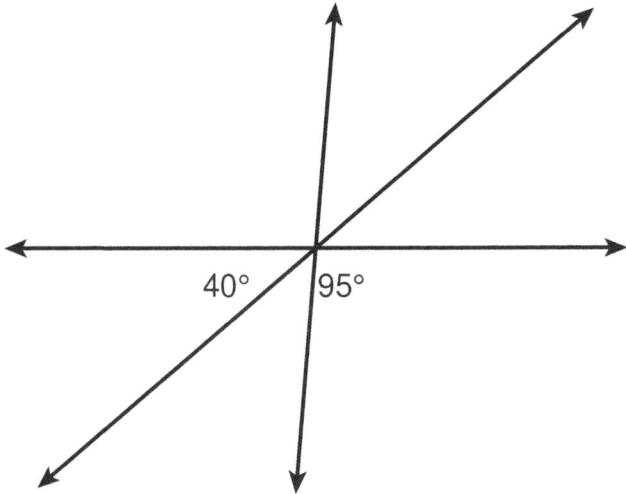

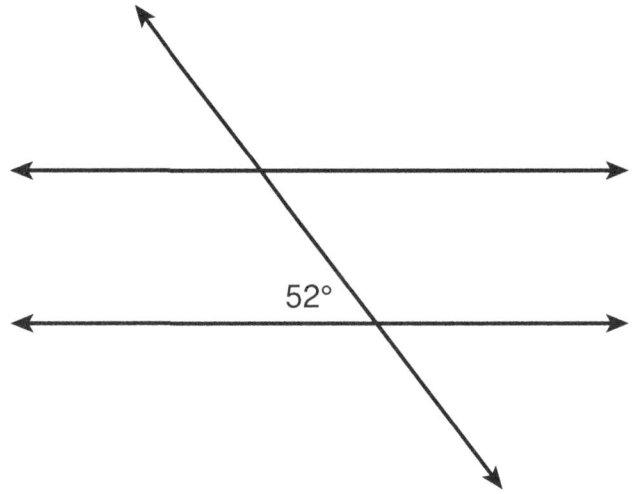

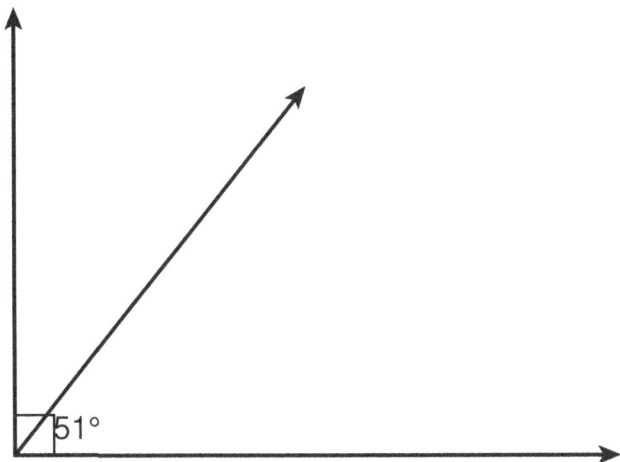

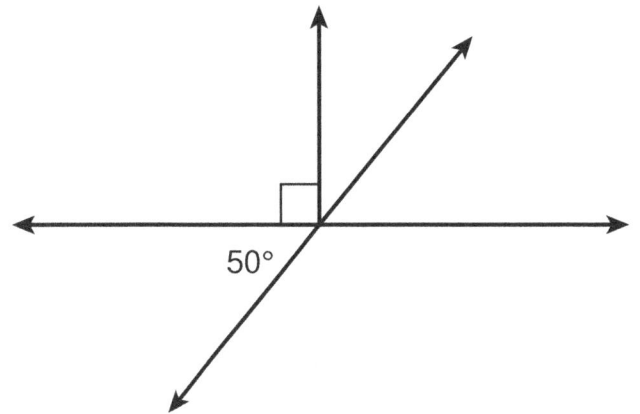

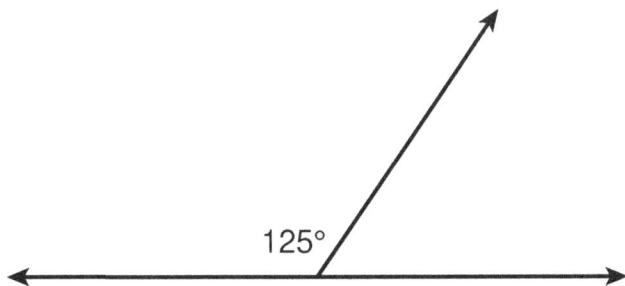

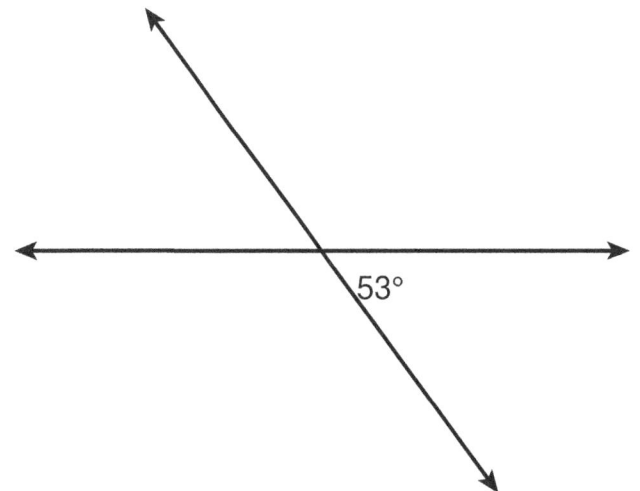

Name _____ Date _____

Fill in the measures of the unknown angles.
Horizontal lines that appear to be parallel are.

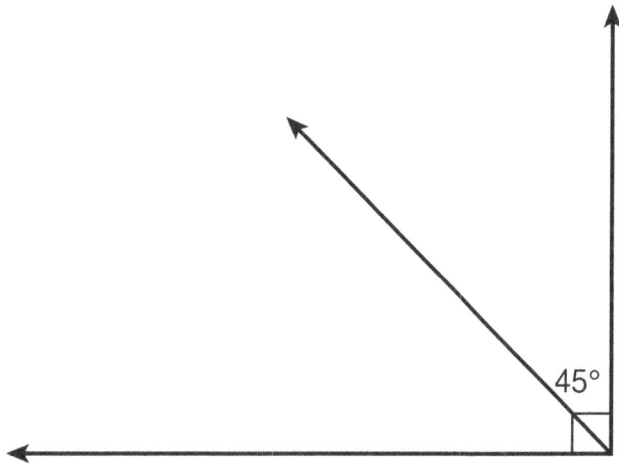

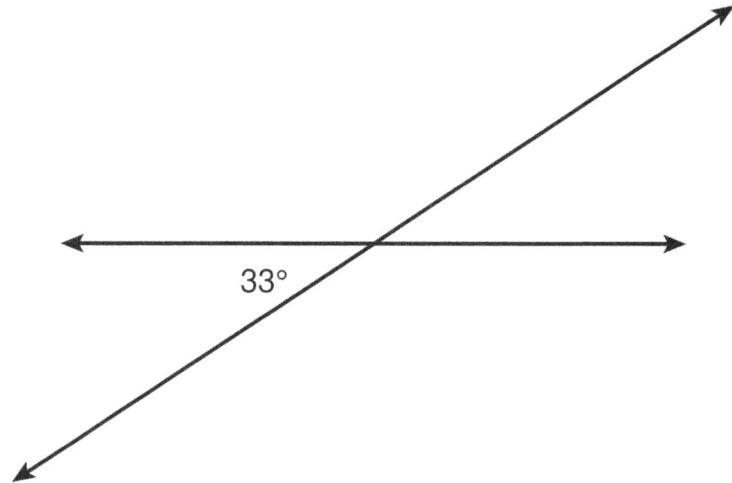

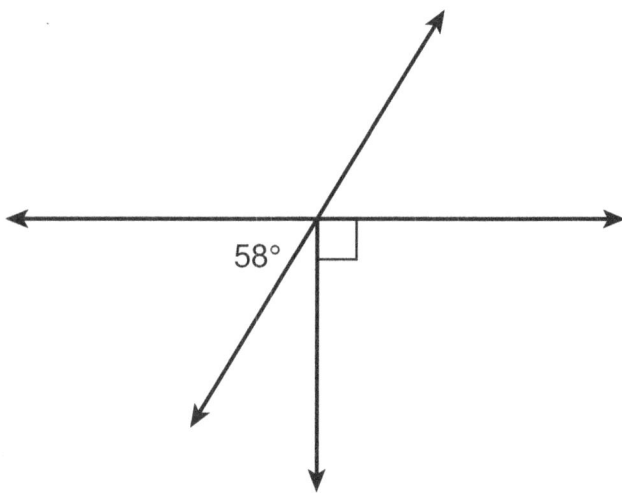

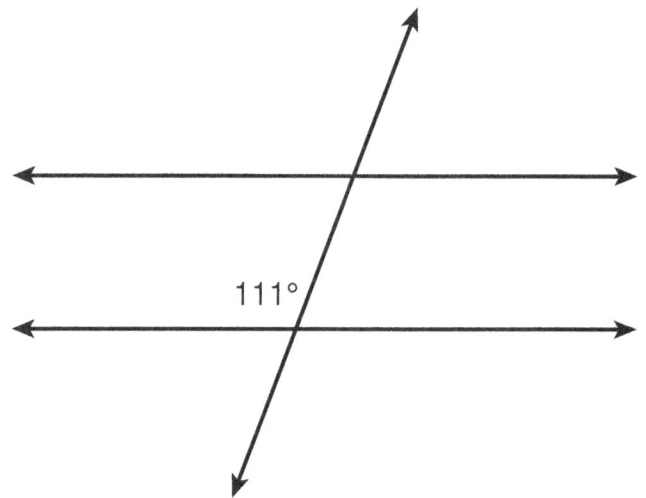

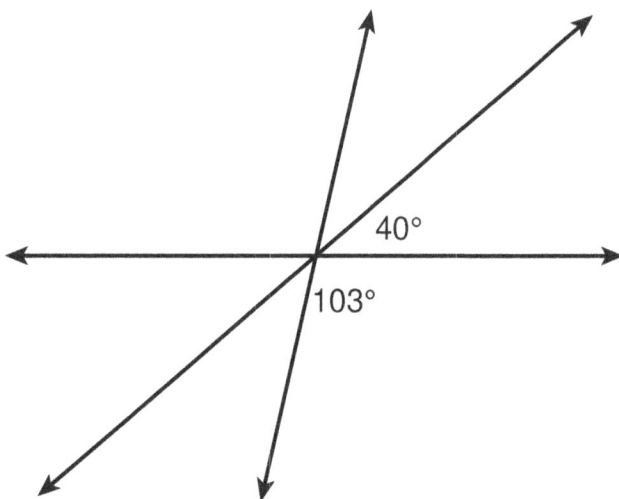

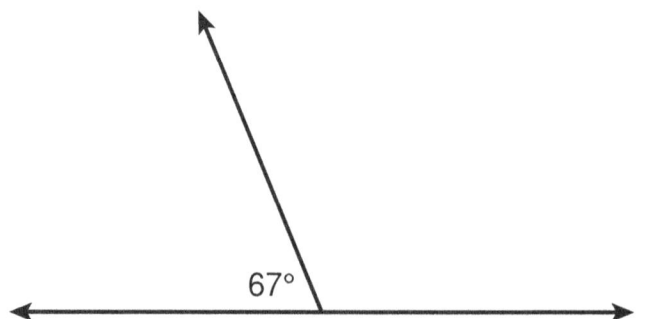

Name _____ Date _____

Fill in the measures of the unknown angles.
Horizontal lines that appear to be parallel are.

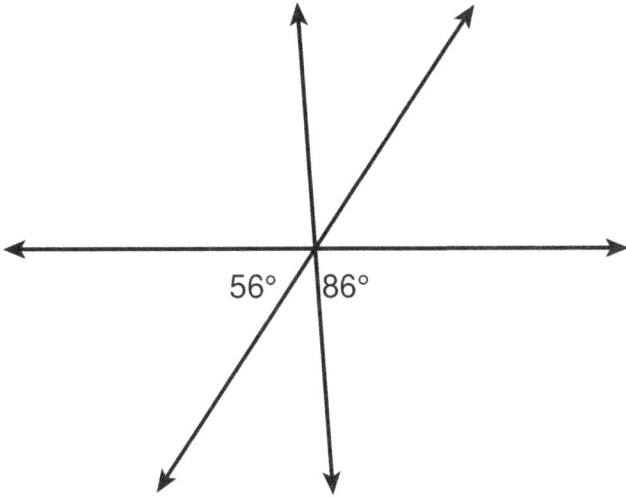

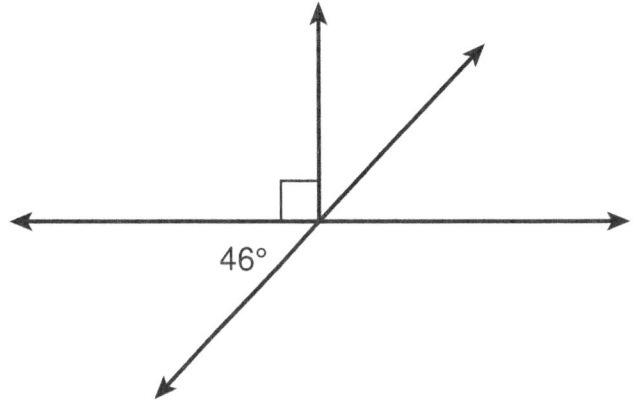

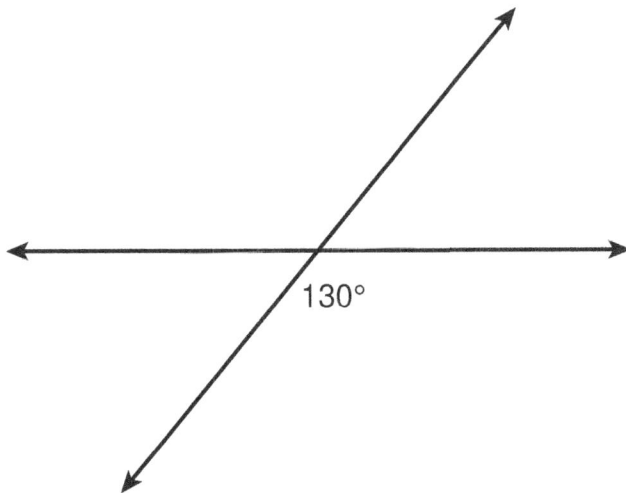

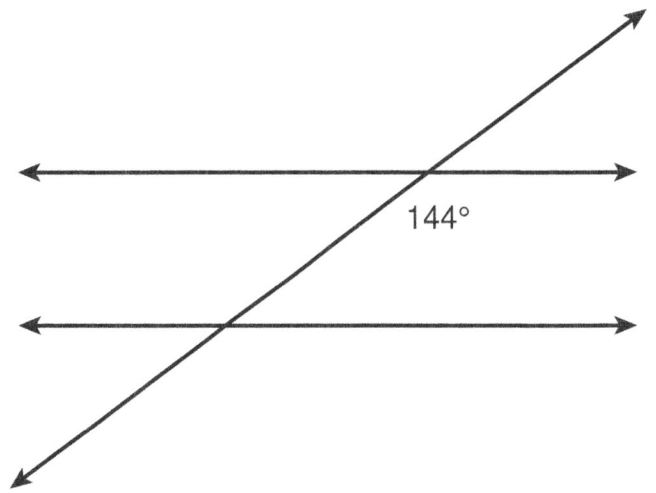

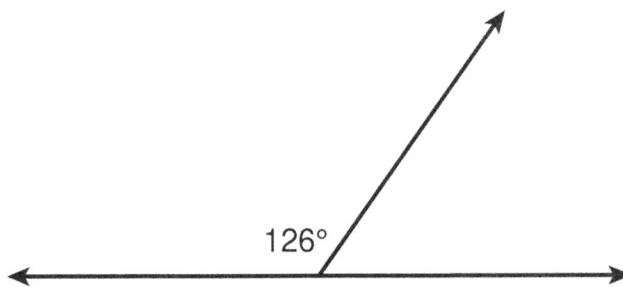

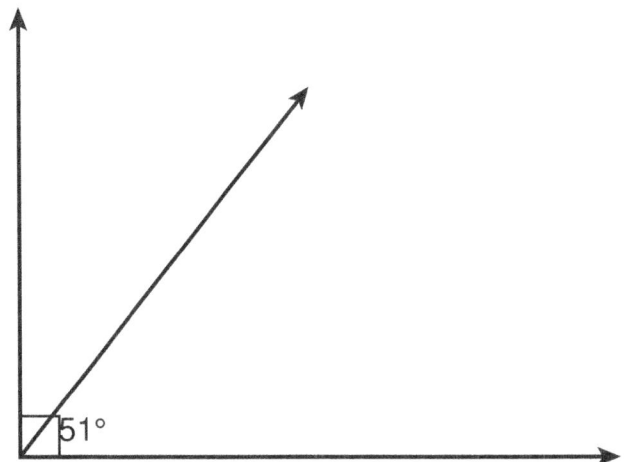

56° 86°

46°

130°

144°

126°

51°

Name _____ Date _____

Fill in the measures of the unknown angles.
Horizontal lines that appear to be parallel are.

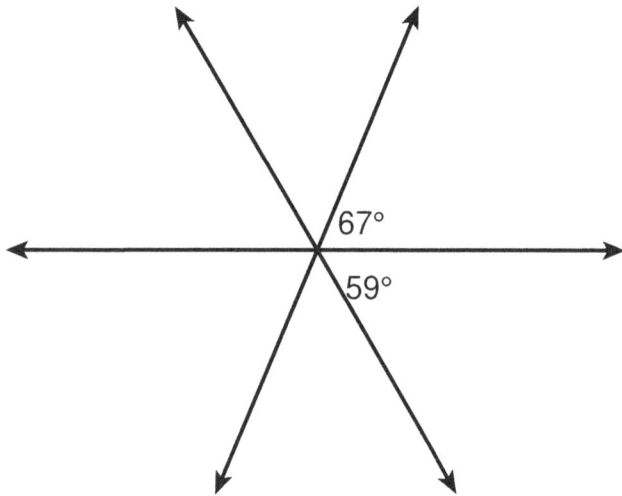

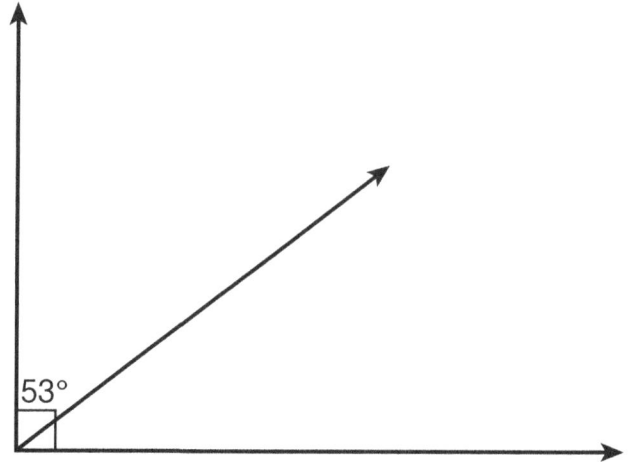

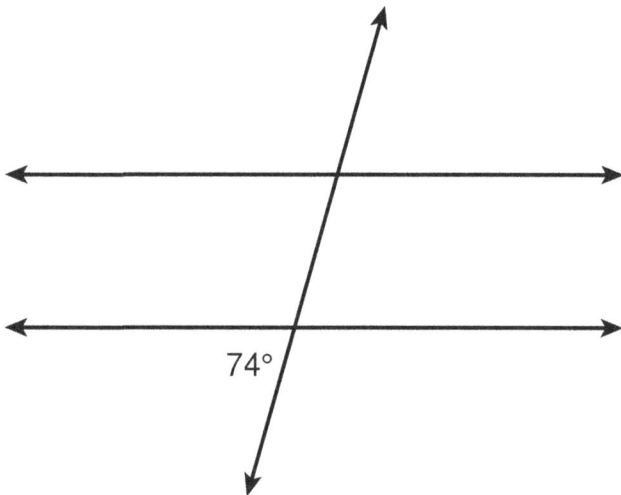

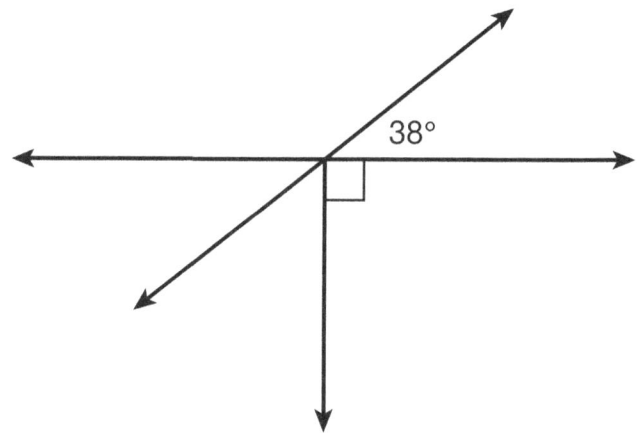

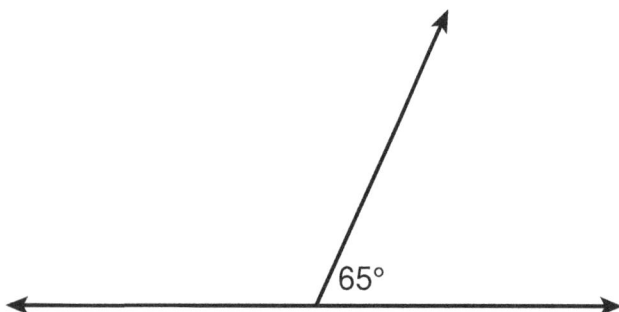

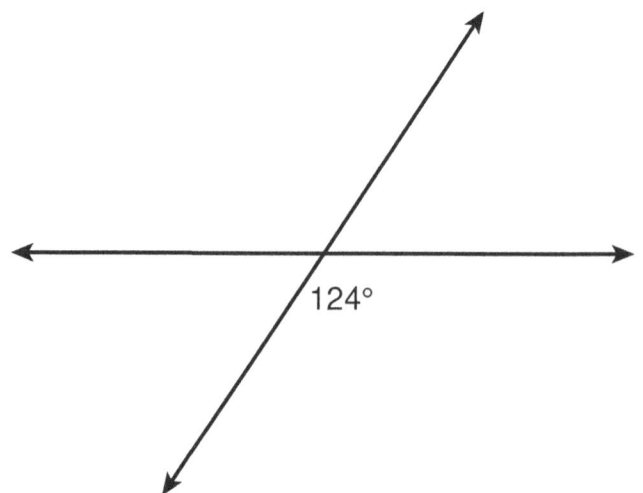

67°
59°

53°

74°

38°

65°

124°

Name _____ Date _____

Fill in the measures of the unknown angles.
Horizontal lines that appear to be parallel are.

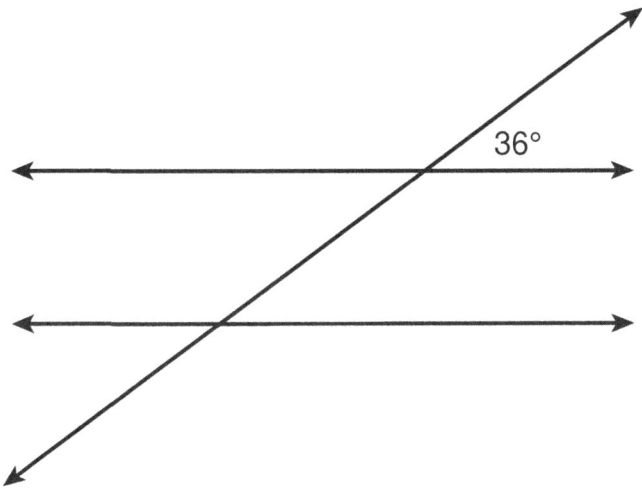

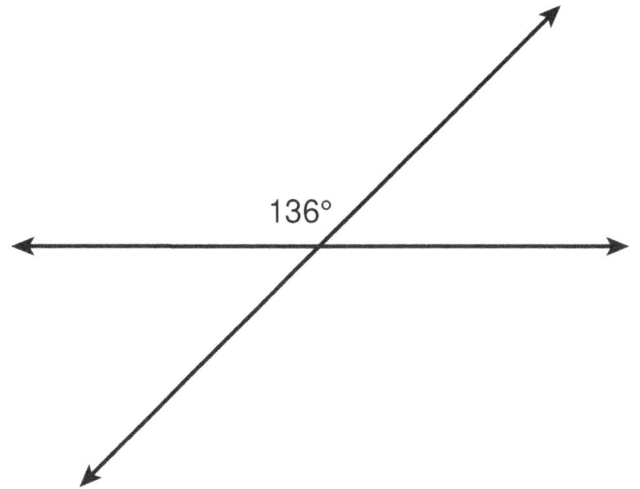

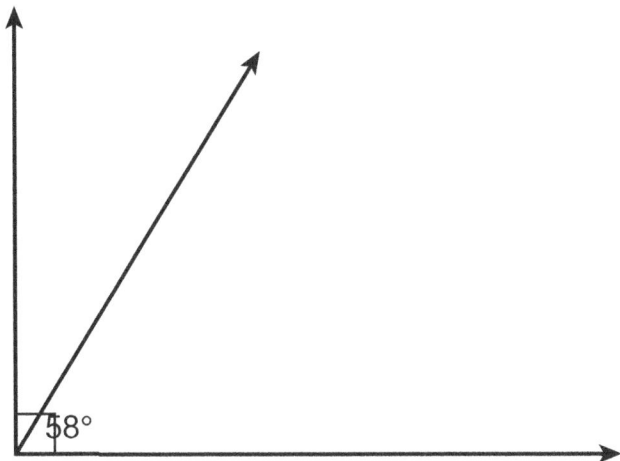

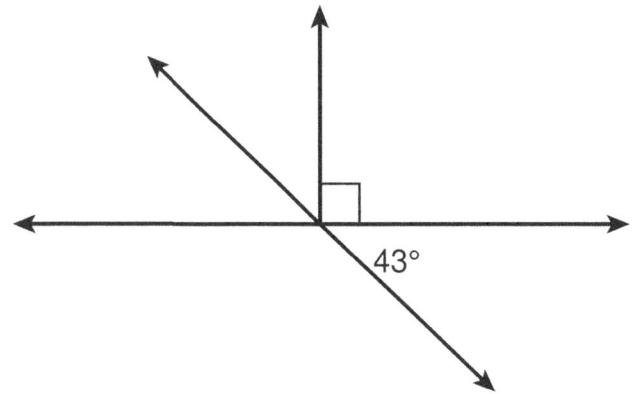

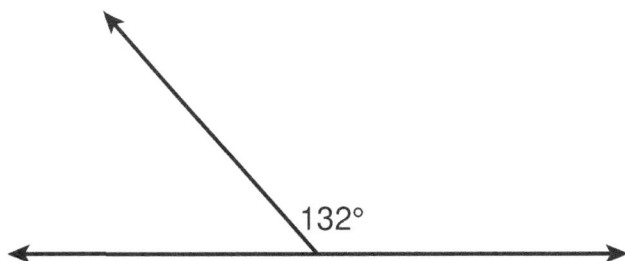

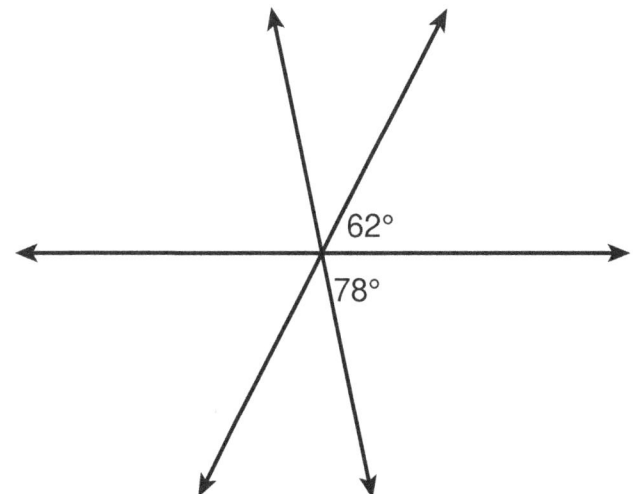

36°

136°

58°

43°

132°

62°

78°

Name _____ Date _____

Fill in the measures of the unknown angles.
Horizontal lines that appear to be parallel are.

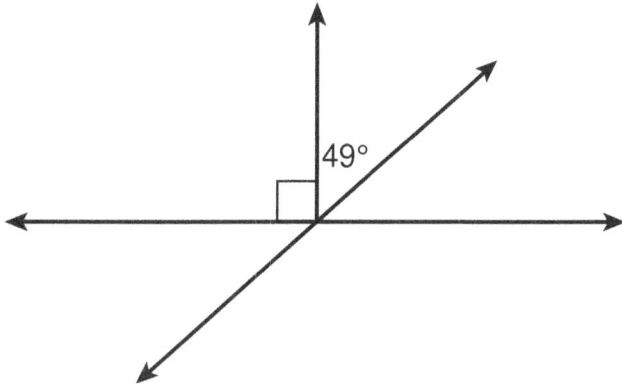

49°

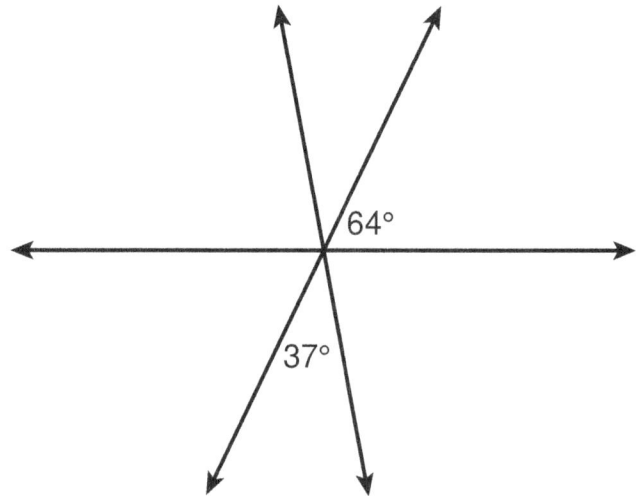

64°

37°

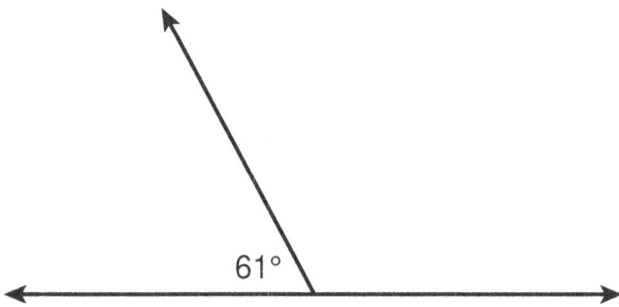

61°

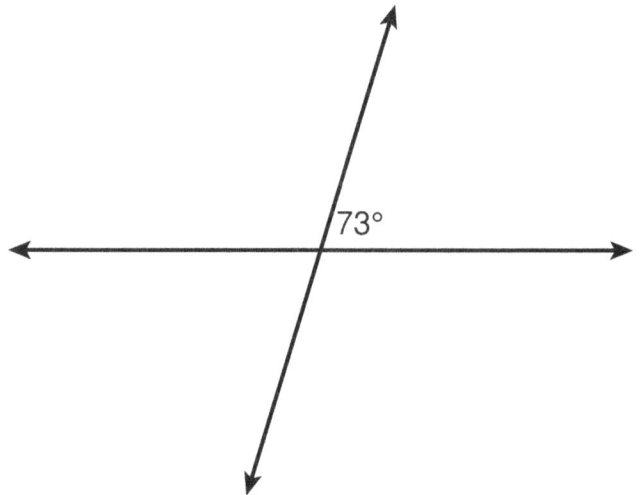

73°

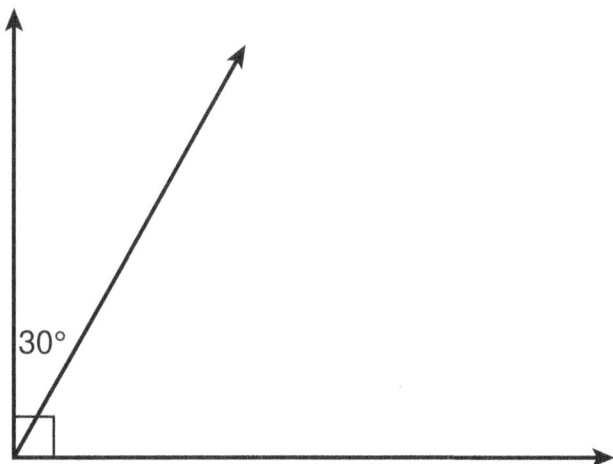

30°

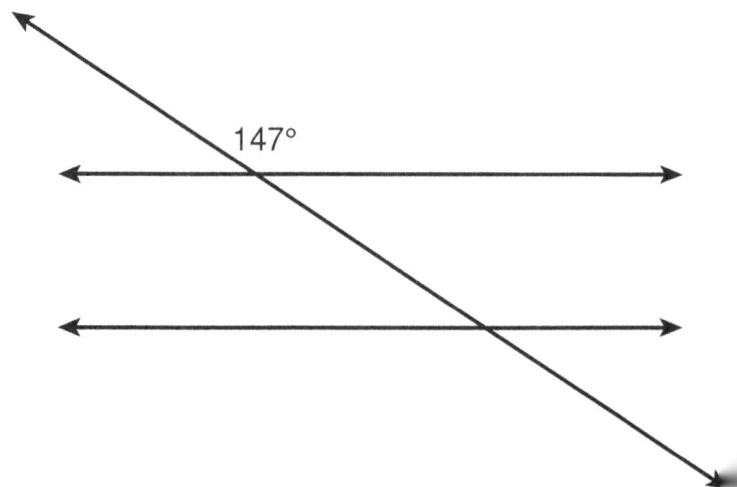

147°

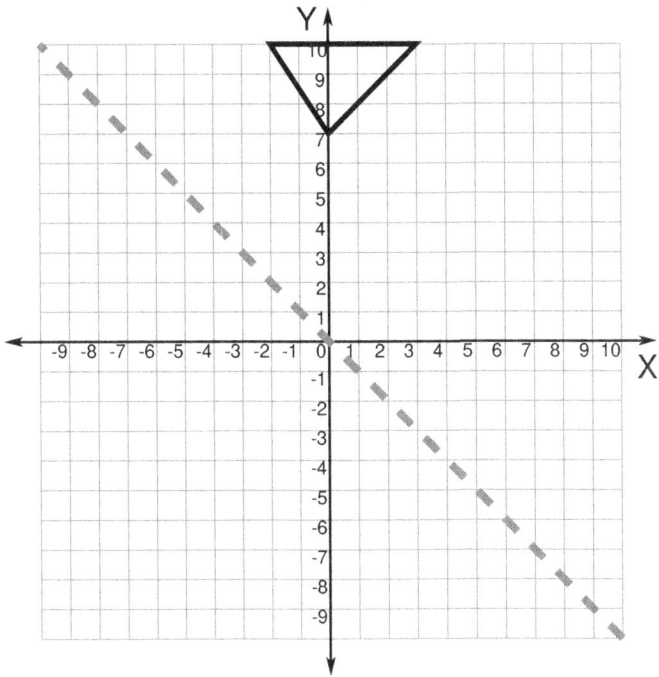

Reflect across y = -x.

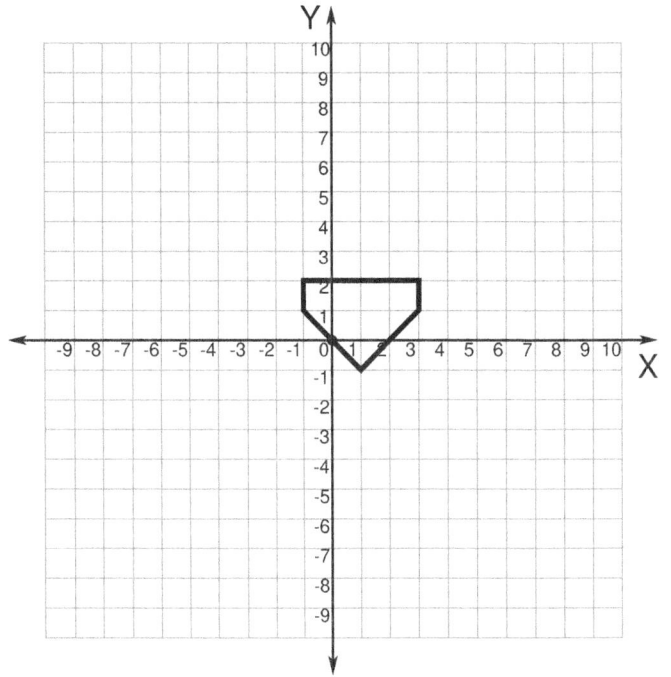

Dilate with a scale factor of 2, centered at the origin.

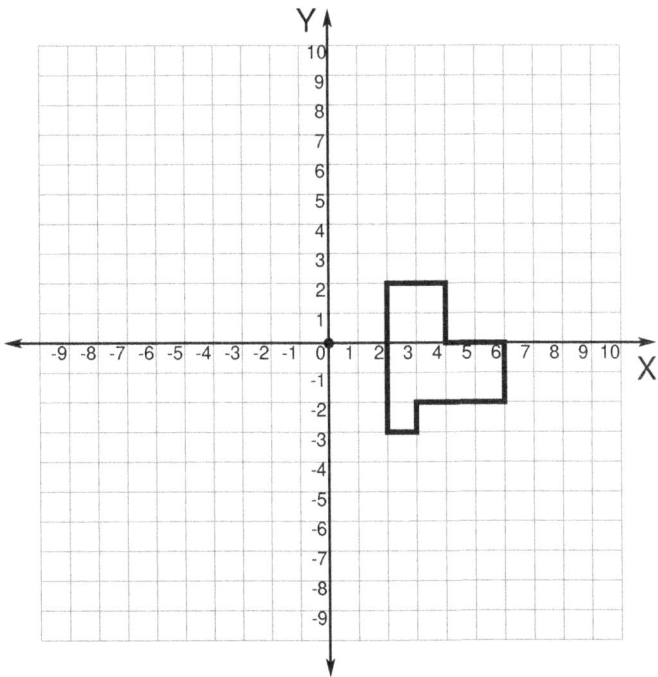

Reflect across (0, 0)

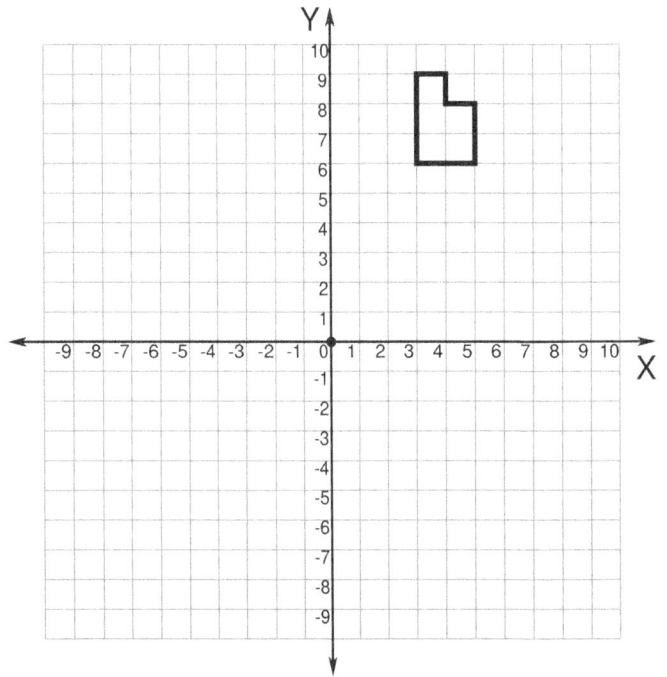

Rotate 75º about the origin.

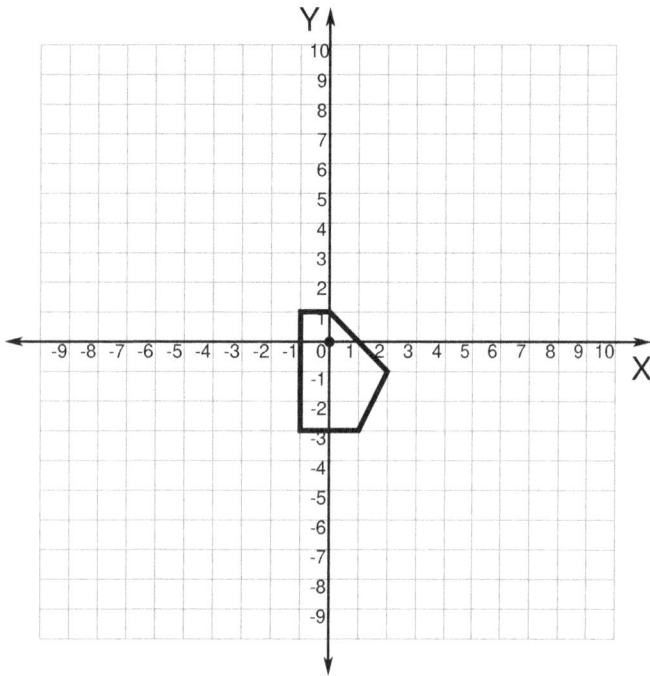

Rotate 180° about the origin.

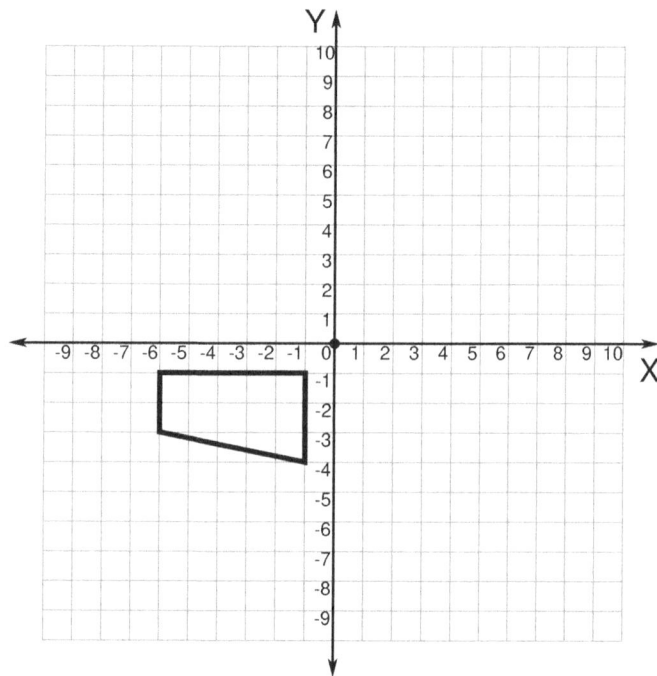

Dilate with a scale factor of 1.5, centered at the origin.

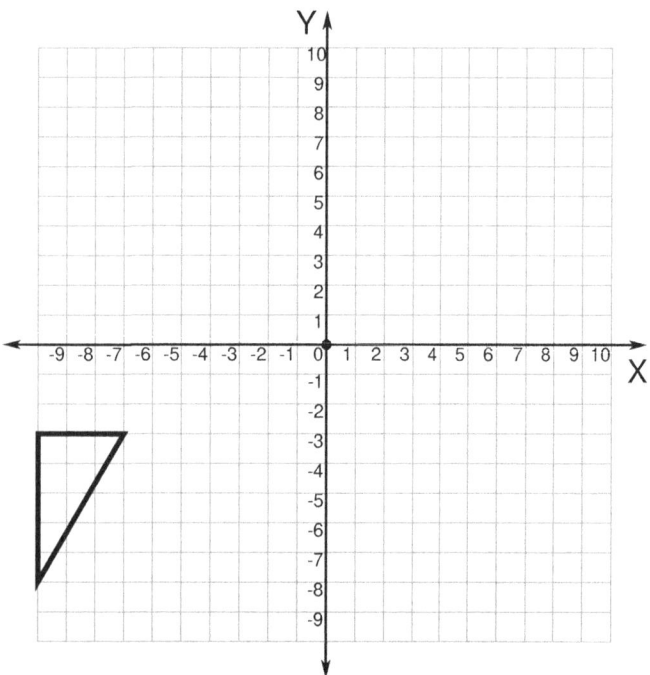

Reflect across (0, 0)

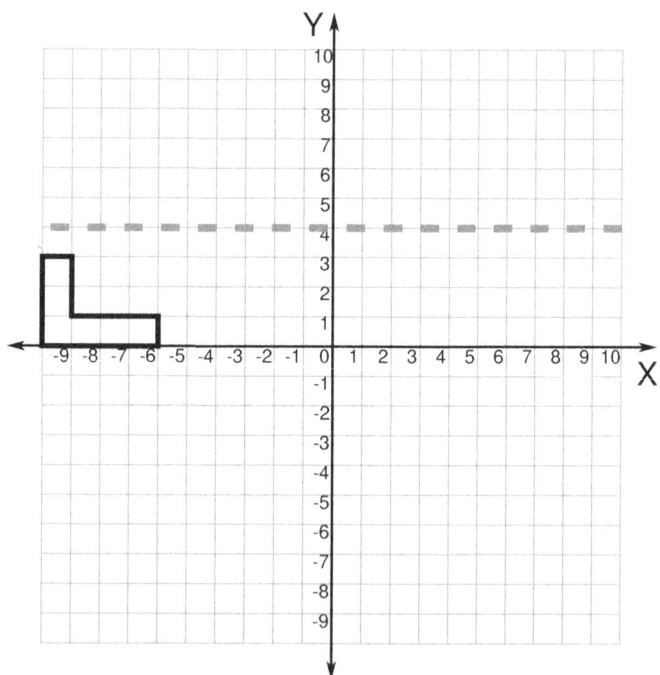

Reflect across y = 4.

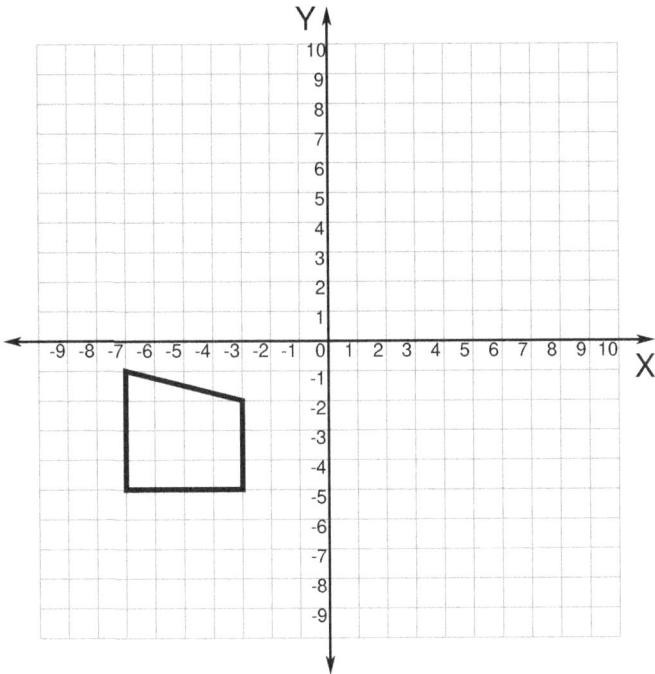

Translate 4 right and 7 up.

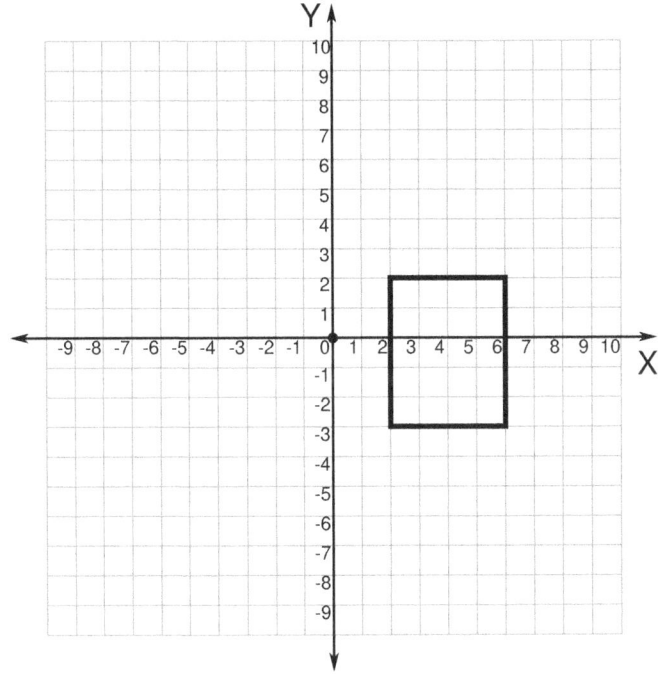

Rotate 60° about the origin.

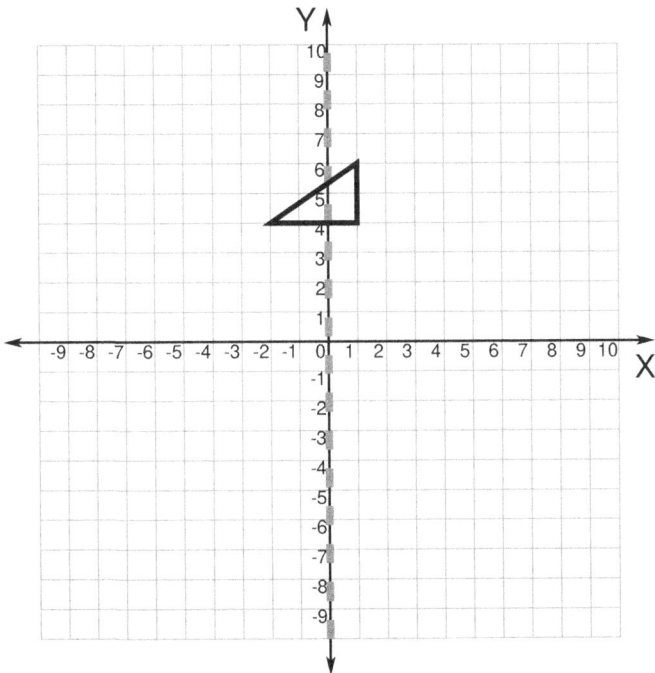

Reflect across the Y axis.

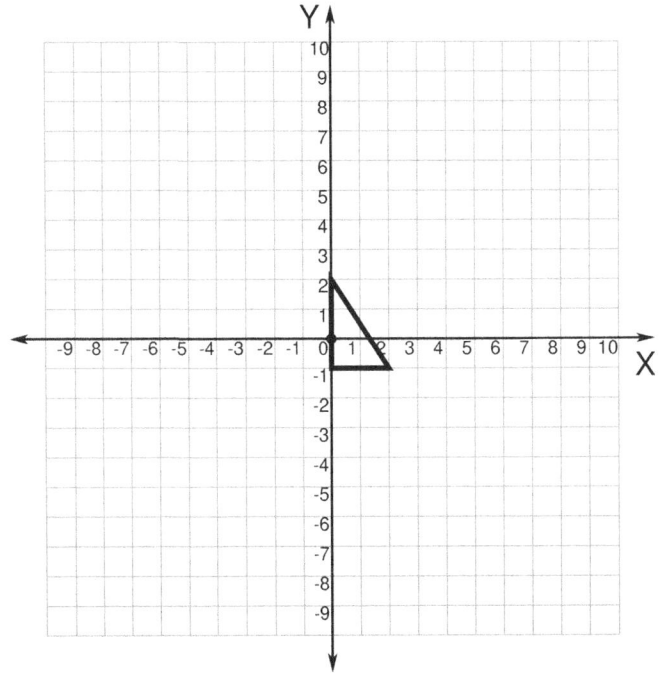

Dilate with a scale factor of 2.5, centered at the origin.

Name _____ Date _____

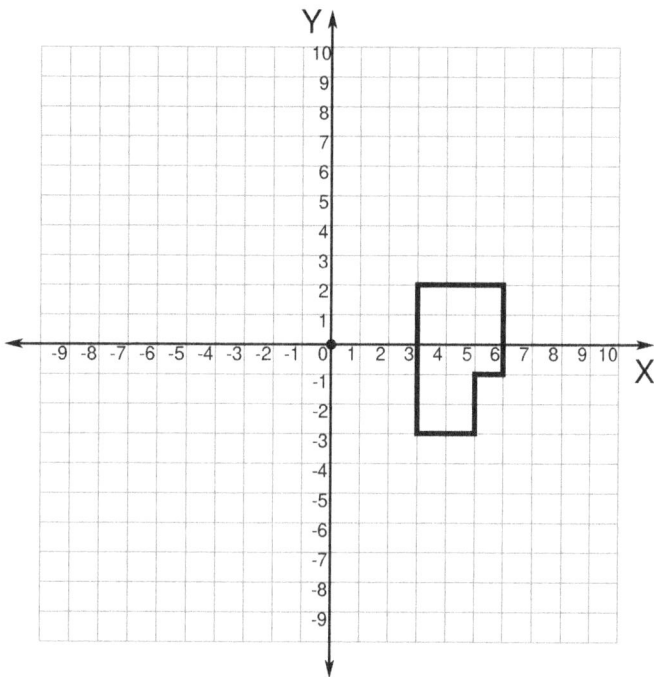

Reflect across (0, 0)

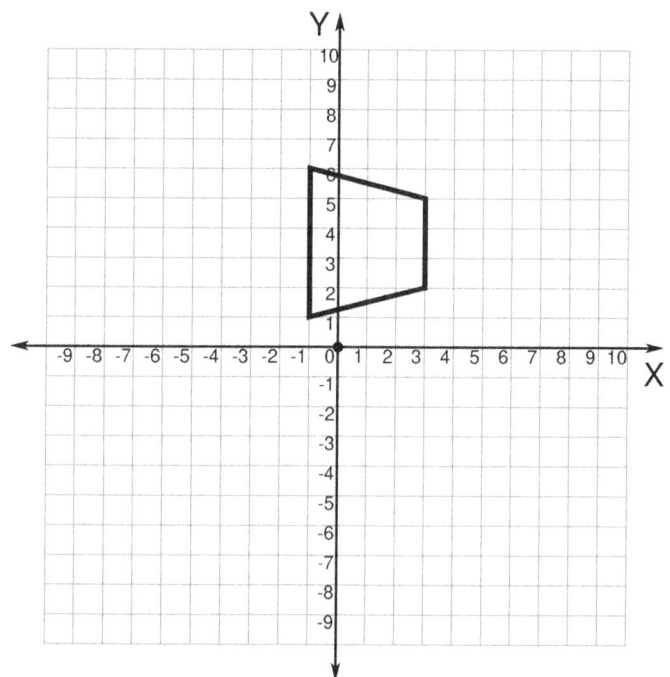

Dilate with a scale factor of 1.5, centered at the origin.

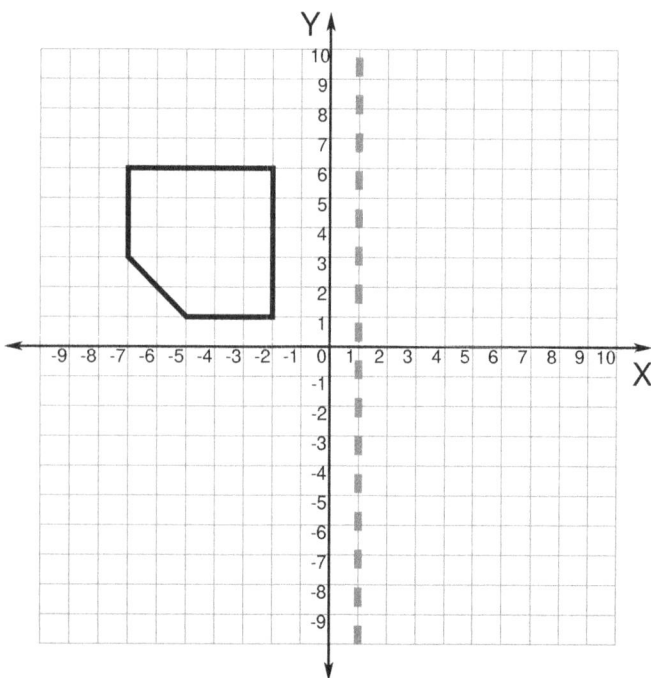

Reflect across x = 1.

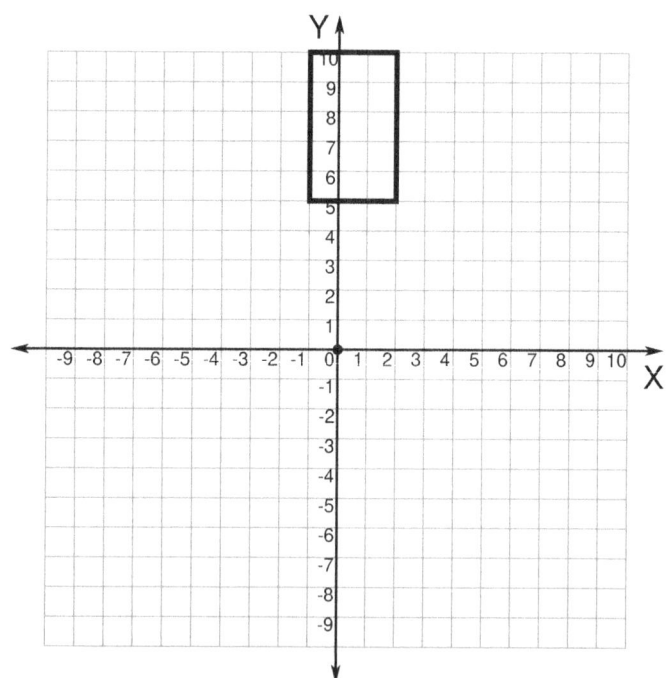

Rotate 60º about the origin.

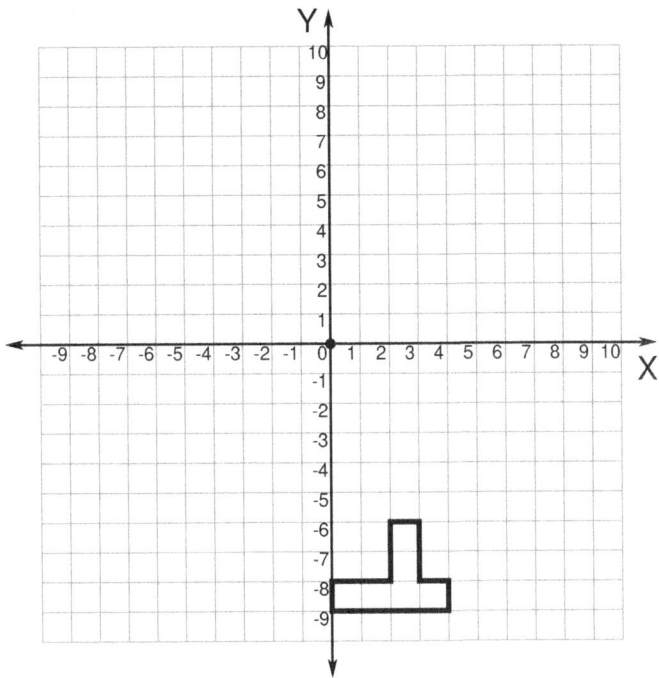

Reflect across (0, 0)

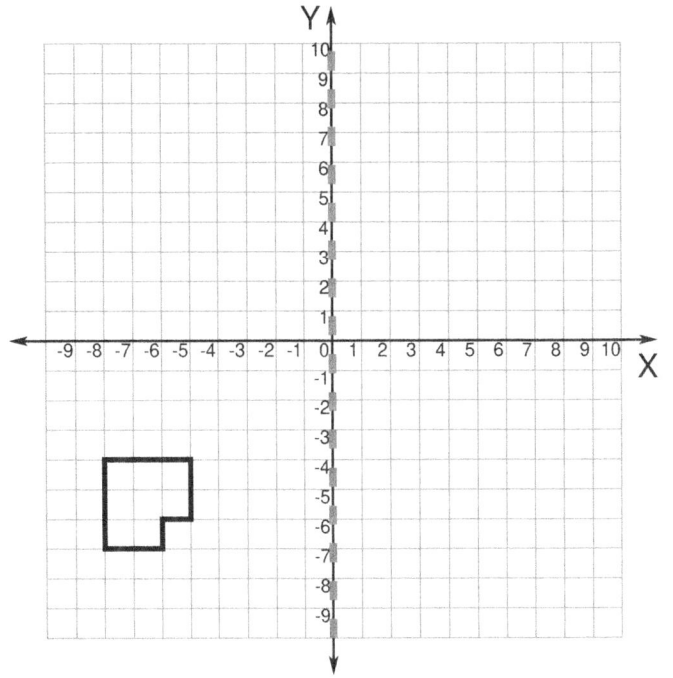

Reflect across the Y axis.

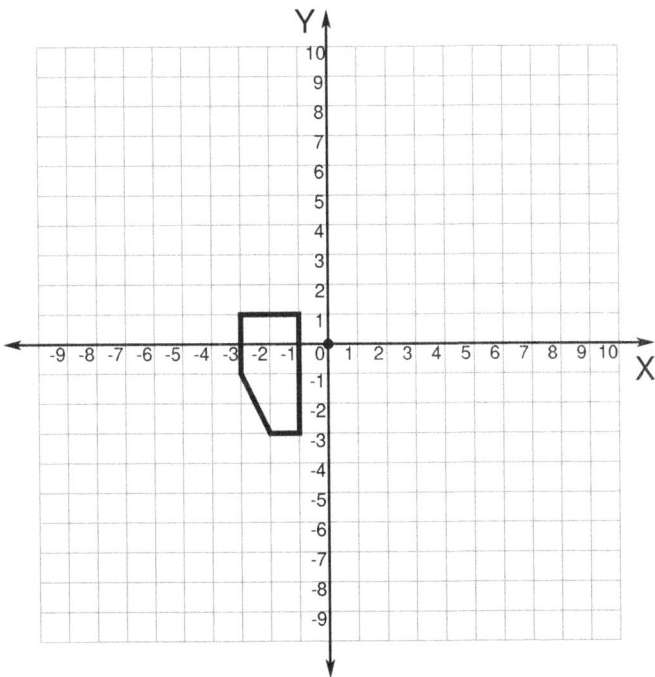

Dilate with a scale factor of 2.5, centered at the origin.

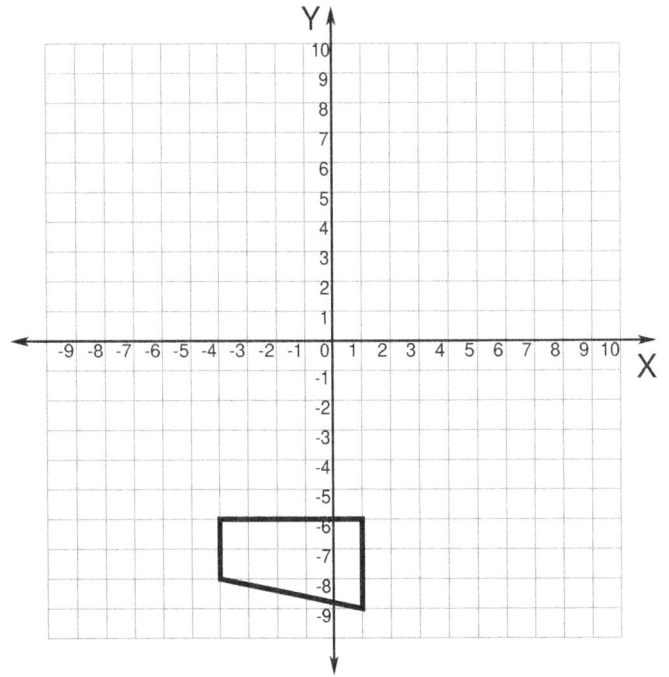

Translate 3 right and 4 up.

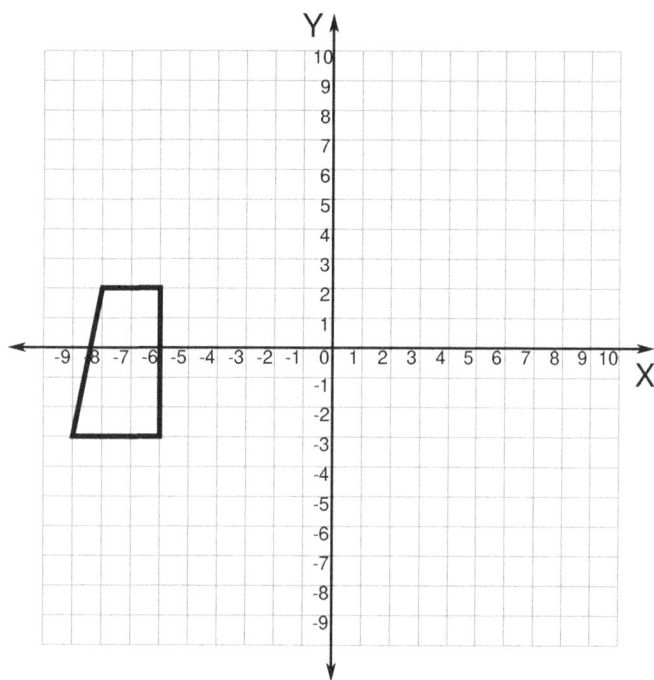

Translate 9 right and 4 down.

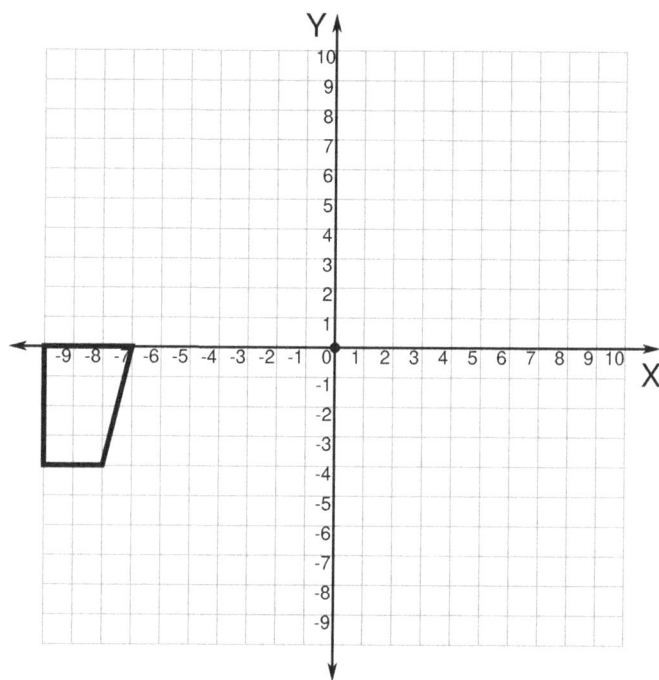

Rotate 180° about the origin.

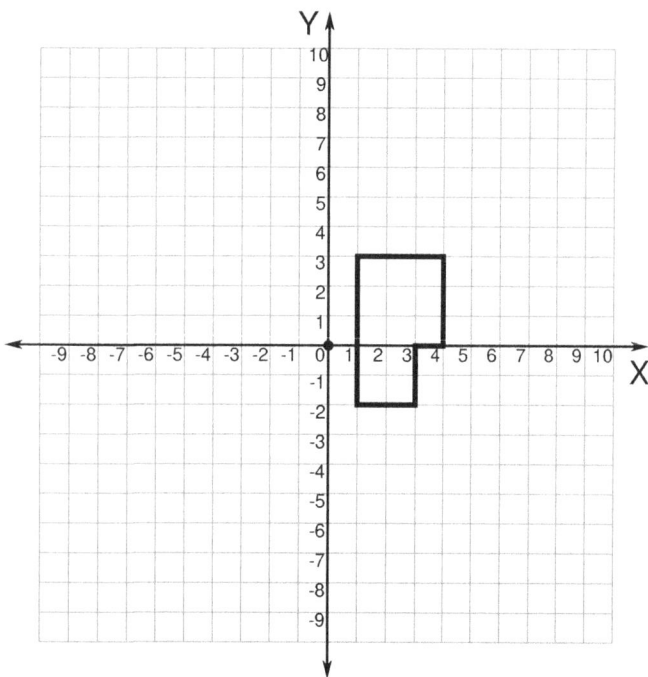

Dilate with a scale factor of 2.5, centered at the origin.

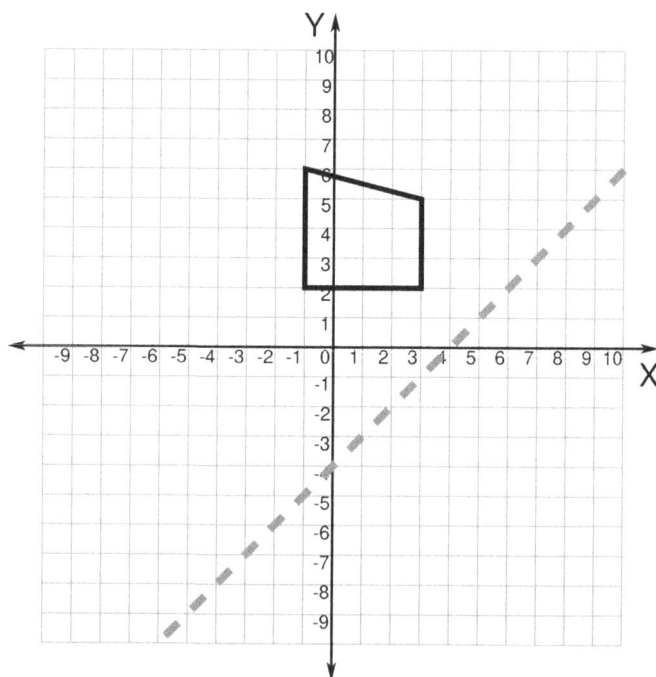

Reflect across y = x - 4.

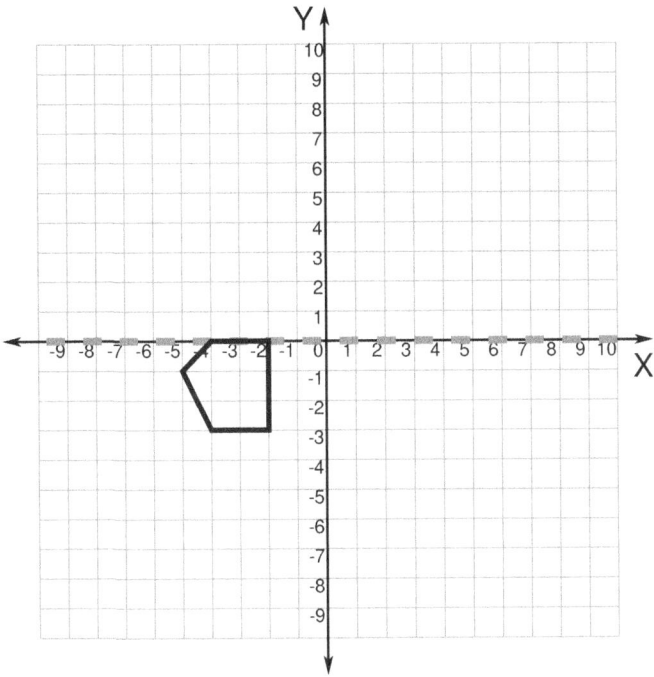

Reflect across the X axis.

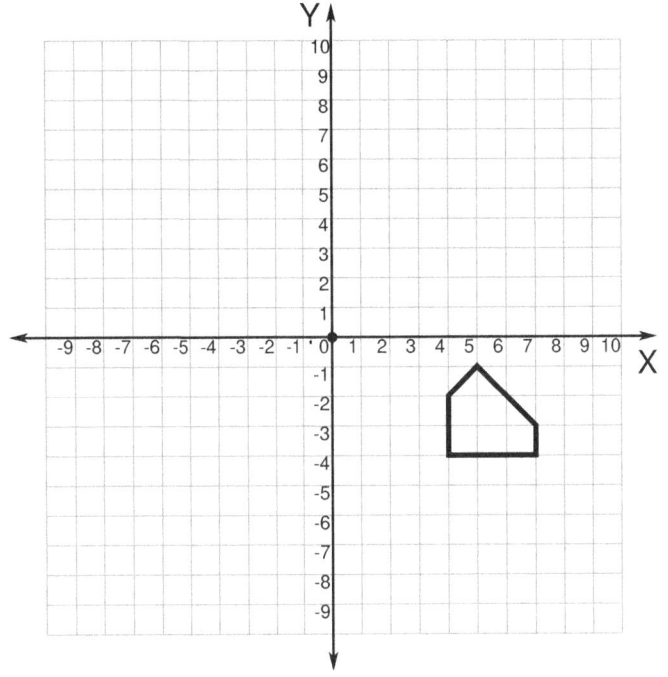

Reflect across (0, 0)

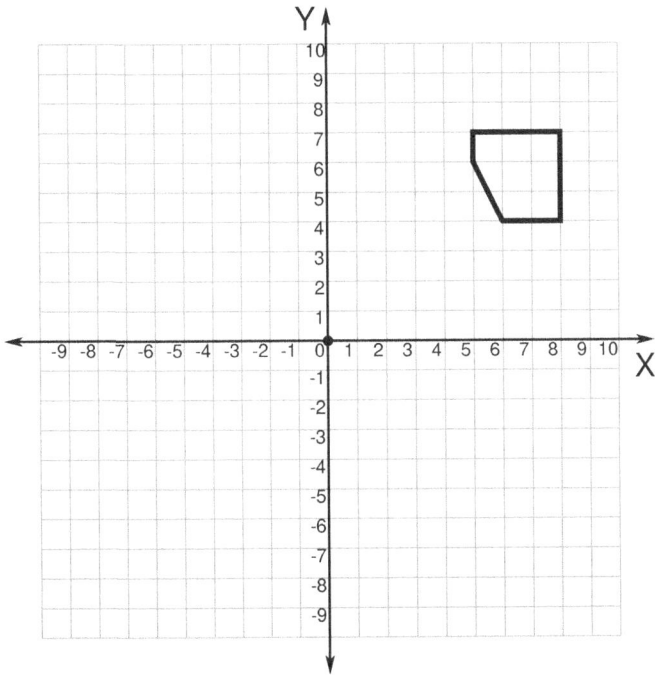

Rotate 180° about the origin.

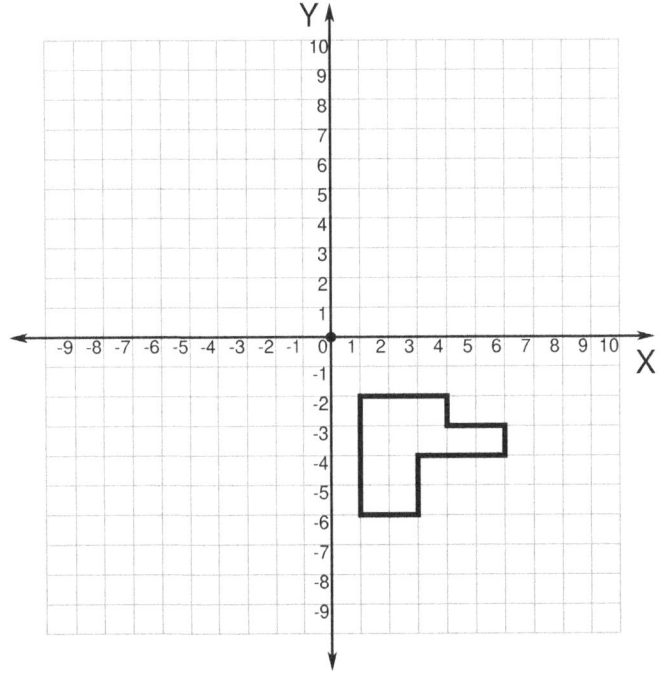

Dilate with a scale factor of 1.5, centered at the origin.

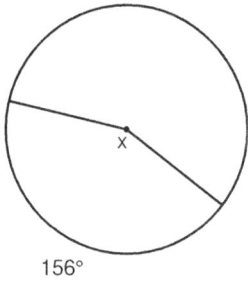

What is the measure of angle x?

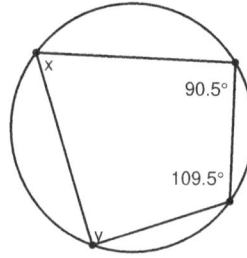

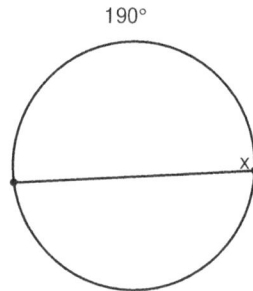

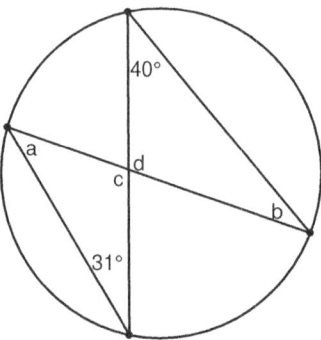

156°

What are the measures of angle x and angle y?

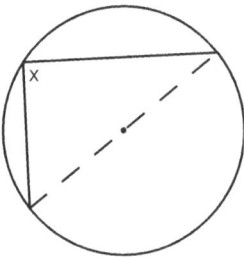

90.5°

109.5°

What is the measure of angle x?

What is the measure of angle x?

190°

What are the measures of angle a, angle b, angle c and angle d?

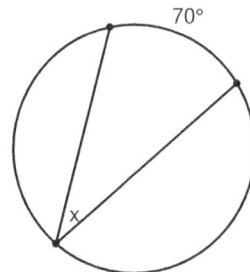

40°

31°

a

d

c

b

What is the measure of angle x?

70°

x

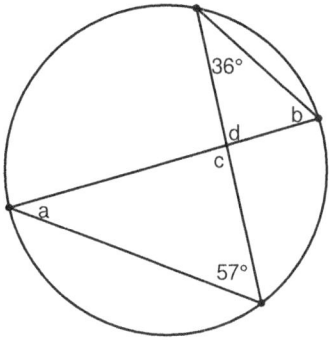

What are the measures of angle a, angle b, angle c and angle d?

36°
b
d
c
a
57°

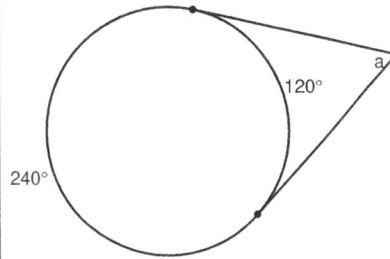

What is the measure of angle a?

120°
a
240°

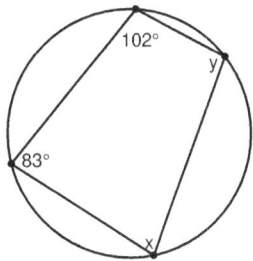

What are the measures of angle x and angle y?

102°
y
83°
x

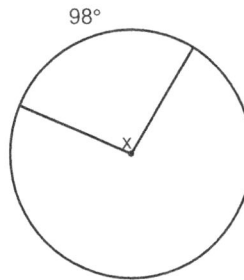

What is the measure of angle x?

98°
x

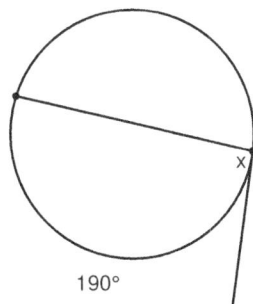

What is the measure of angle x?

x
190°

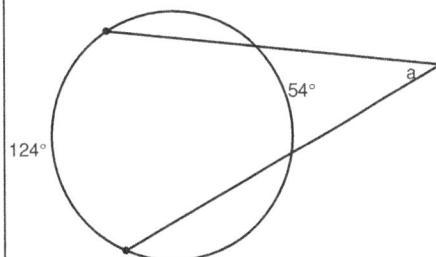

What is the measure of angle a?

54°
a
124°

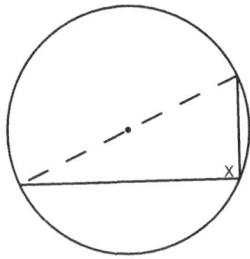

What is the measure of angle x?

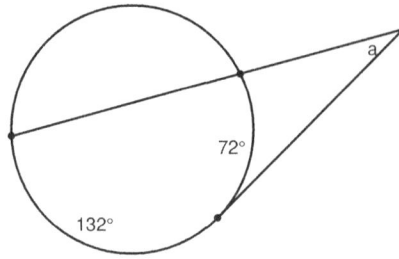

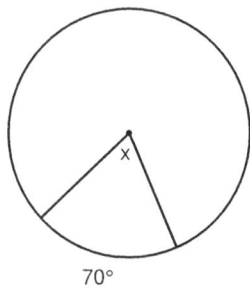

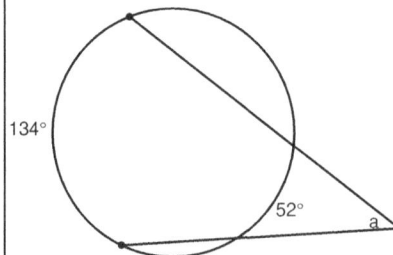

What is the measure of angle a?

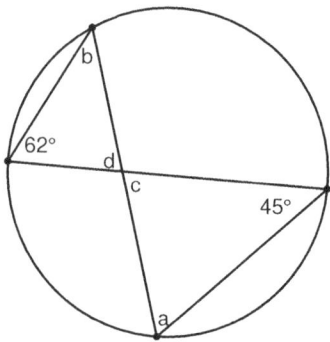

What are the measures of angle a, angle b, angle c and angle d?

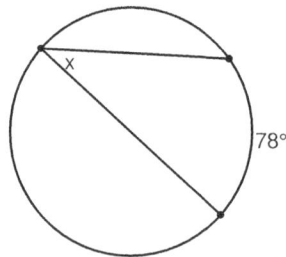

What is the measure of angle x?

What is the measure of angle x?

What is the measure of angle a?

What is the
measure of
angle a?

What is the measure of
angle x?

What is the measure of
angle x?

What are the measures
of angle x and angle y?

What is the measure of
angle x?

What is the
measure of
angle a?

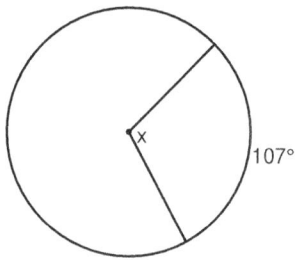

What is the measure of angle x?

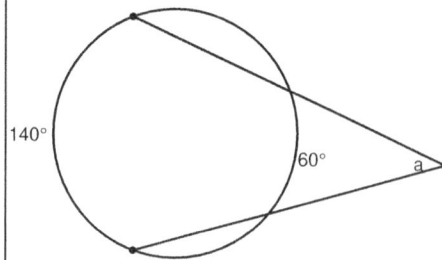

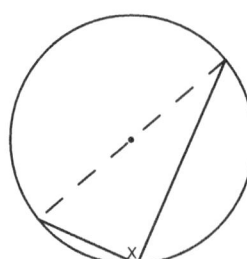

107°

What is the measure of angle a?

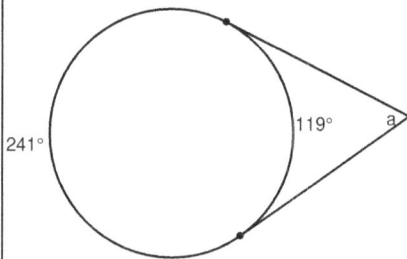

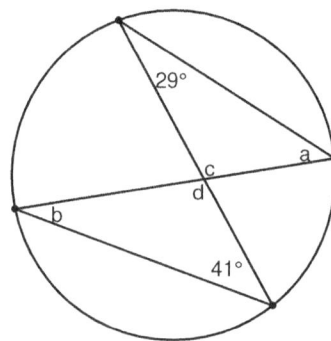

140°

60°

a

What is the measure of angle a?

241°

119°

a

What are the measures of angle a, angle b, angle c and angle d?

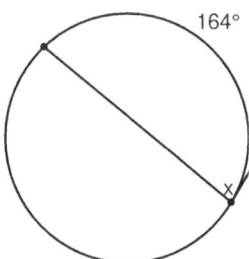

29°

41°

c

d

b

a

What is the measure of angle x?

164°

x

What is the measure of angle x?

x

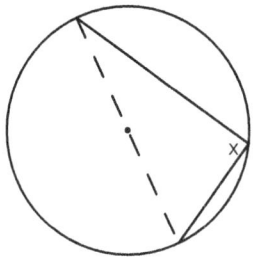

What is the measure of angle x?

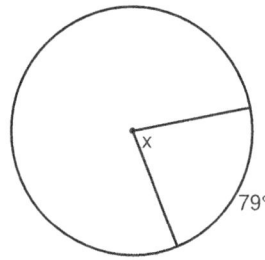

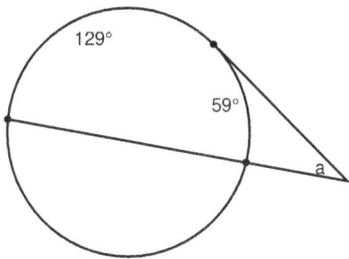

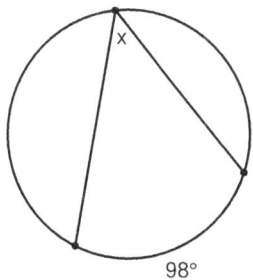

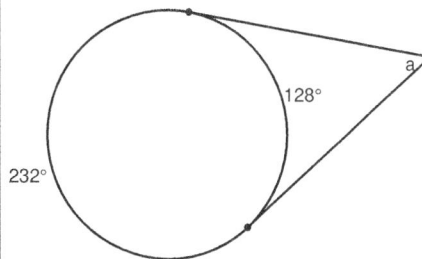

What is the measure of angle x?

79°

What is the measure of angle a?

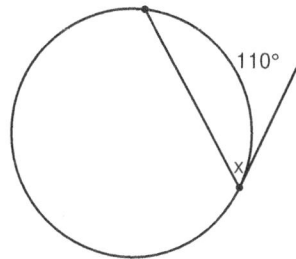

129°

59°

a

What is the measure of angle x?

110°

x

What is the measure of angle x?

x

98°

What is the measure of angle a?

a

128°

232°

Name _____   Date _____

What is the
measure of
angle a?

124°

236°

What is the
measure of
angle a?

54°

138°

a

What is the measure of
angle x?

x

What is the measure of
angle x?

111°

x

What is the
measure of
angle a?

51°

91°

a

What is the measure of
angle x?

x

88°

Solutions for Page 1

Label each pair of lines parallel, perpendicular or intersecting.

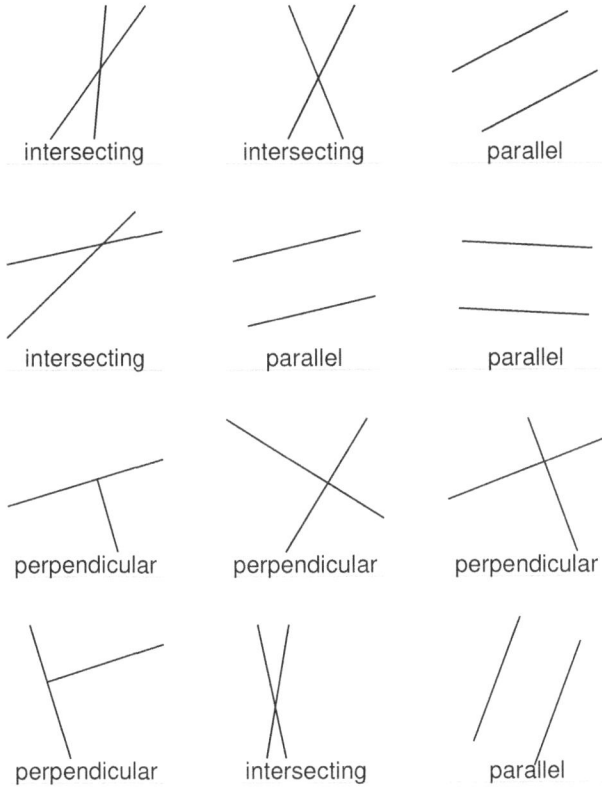

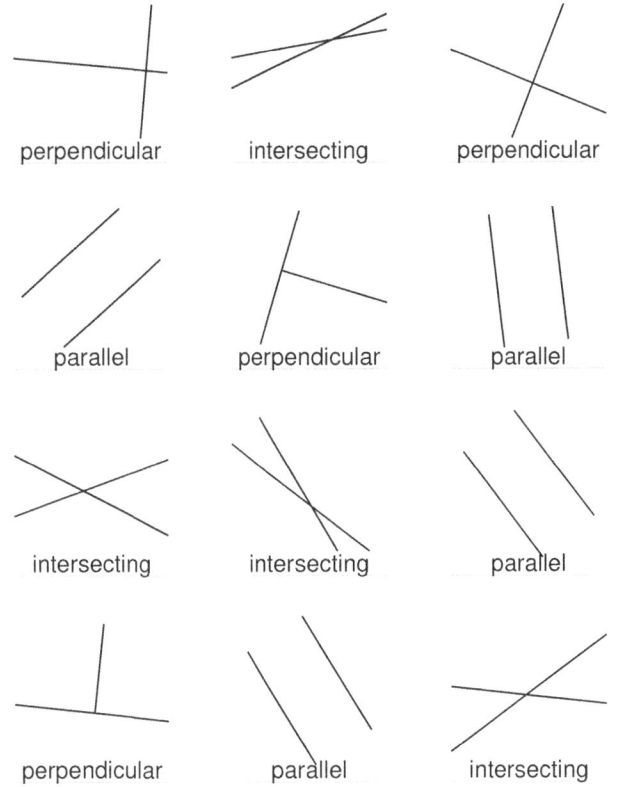

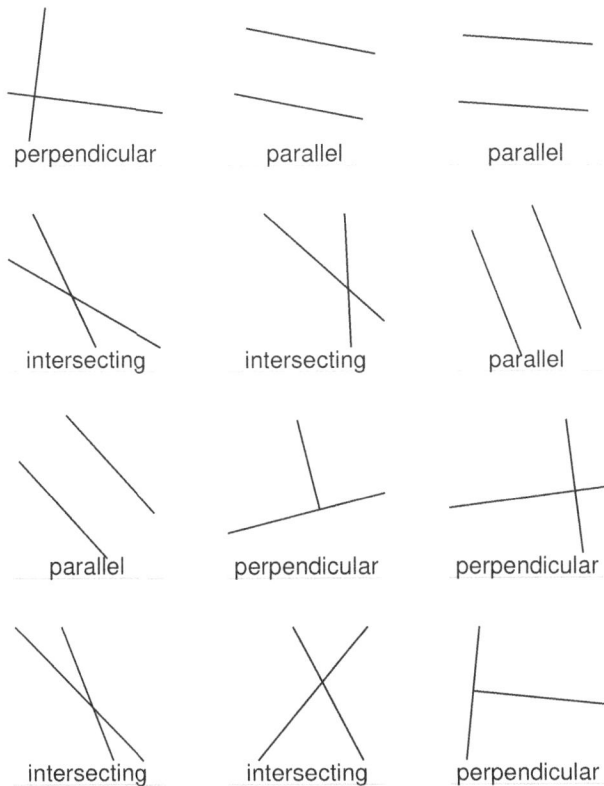

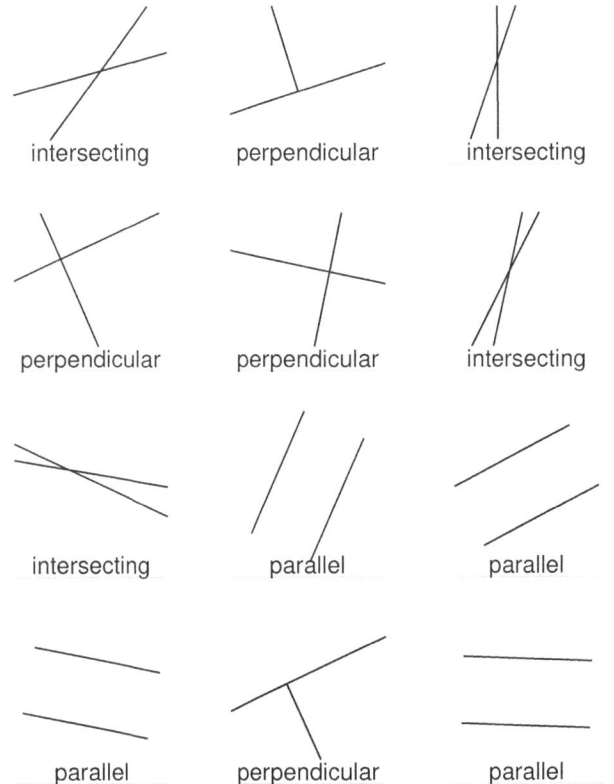

intersecting	intersecting	parallel
intersecting	parallel	parallel
perpendicular	perpendicular	perpendicular
perpendicular	intersecting	parallel

Solutions for Page 2

Label each pair of lines parallel, perpendicular or intersecting.

perpendicular	intersecting	perpendicular
parallel	perpendicular	parallel
intersecting	intersecting	parallel
perpendicular	parallel	intersecting

Solutions for Page 3

Label each pair of lines parallel, perpendicular or intersecting.

perpendicular	parallel	parallel
intersecting	intersecting	parallel
parallel	perpendicular	perpendicular
intersecting	intersecting	perpendicular

Solutions for Page 4

Label each pair of lines parallel, perpendicular or intersecting.

intersecting	perpendicular	intersecting
perpendicular	perpendicular	intersecting
intersecting	parallel	parallel
parallel	perpendicular	parallel

Solutions for Page 5

Label each pair of lines parallel, perpendicular or intersecting.

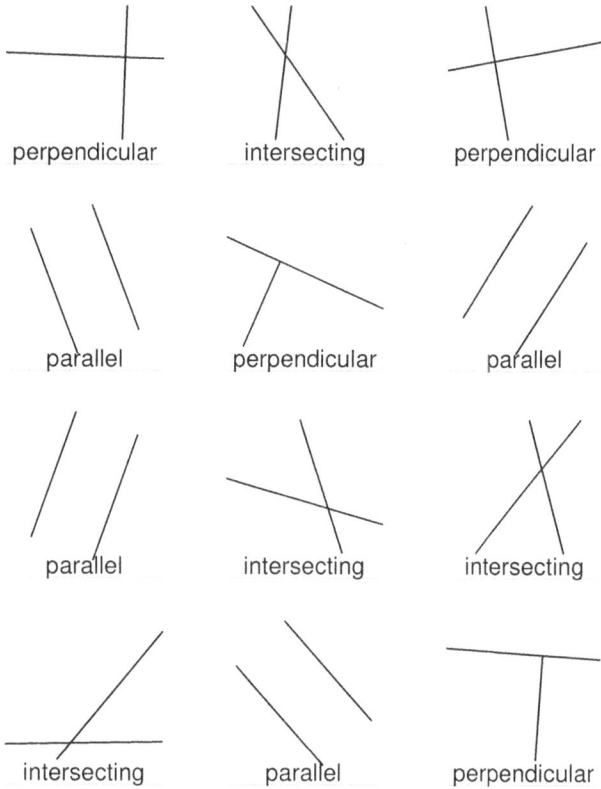

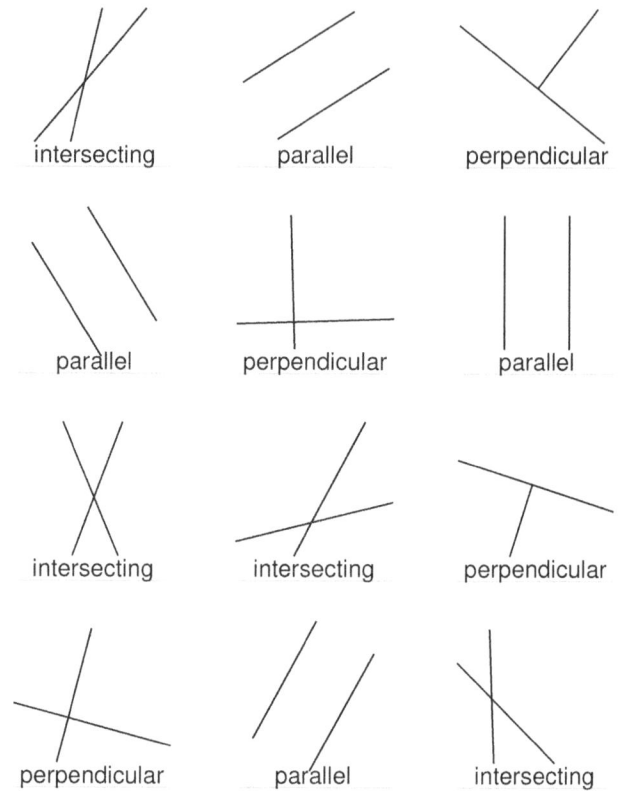

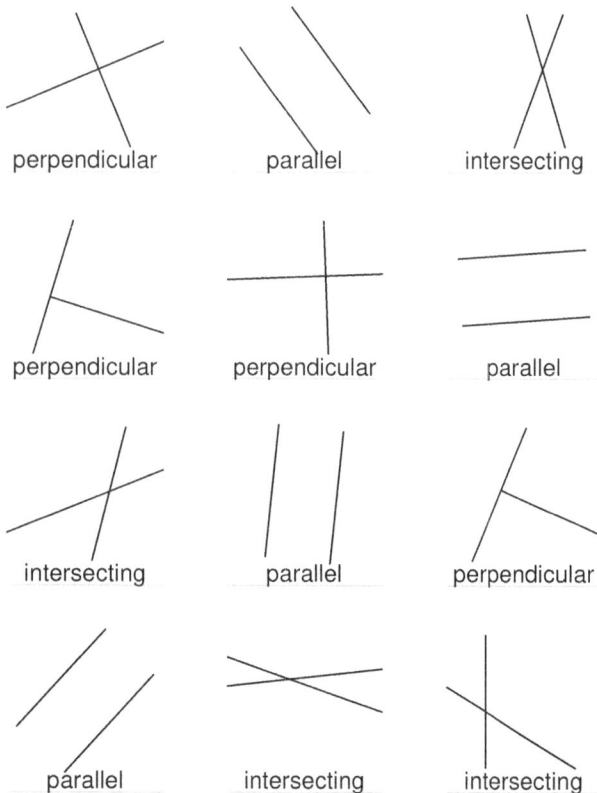

perpendicular   intersecting   perpendicular

parallel   perpendicular   parallel

parallel   intersecting   intersecting

intersecting   parallel   perpendicular

Solutions for Page 6

Label each pair of lines parallel, perpendicular or intersecting.

intersecting   parallel   perpendicular

parallel   perpendicular   parallel

intersecting   intersecting   perpendicular

perpendicular   parallel   intersecting

Solutions for Page 7

Label each pair of lines parallel, perpendicular or intersecting.

perpendicular   parallel   intersecting

perpendicular   perpendicular   parallel

intersecting   parallel   perpendicular

parallel   intersecting   intersecting

Solutions for Page 8

Label each angle acute, obtuse, right or straight.

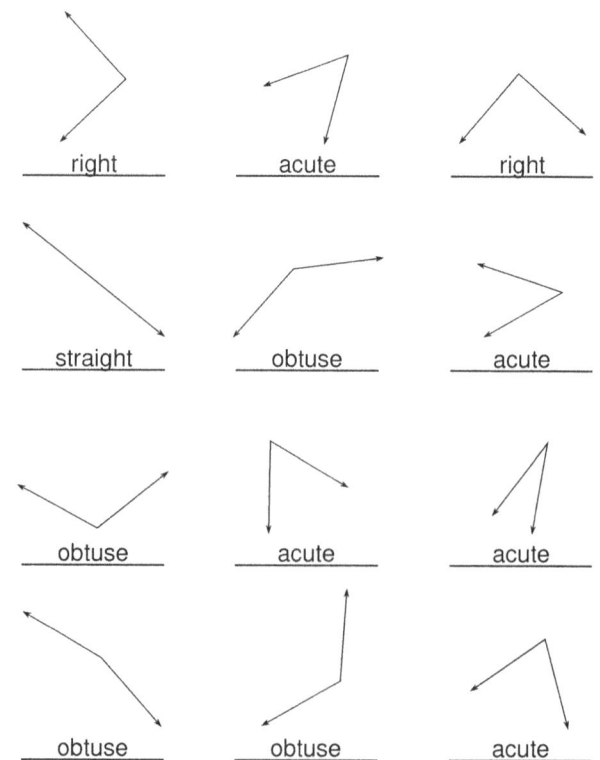

right   acute   right

straight   obtuse   acute

obtuse   acute   acute

obtuse   obtuse   acute

Solutions for Page 9

Label each angle acute, obtuse, right or straight.

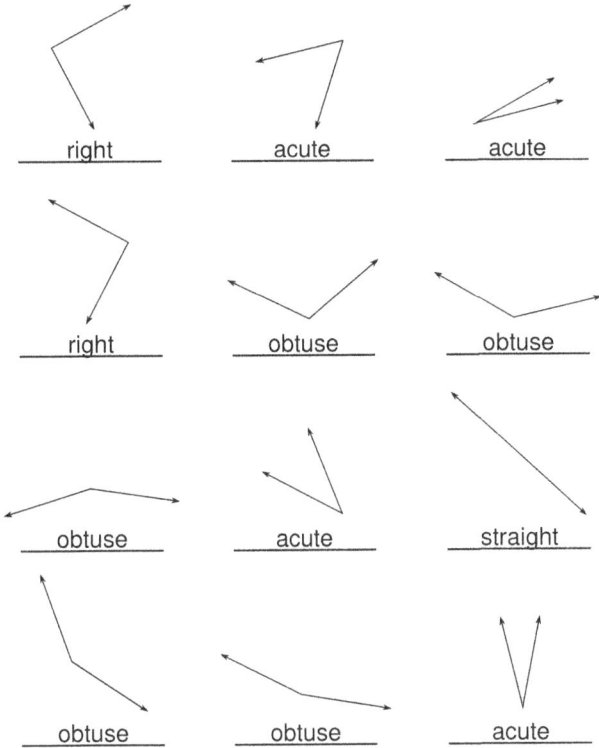

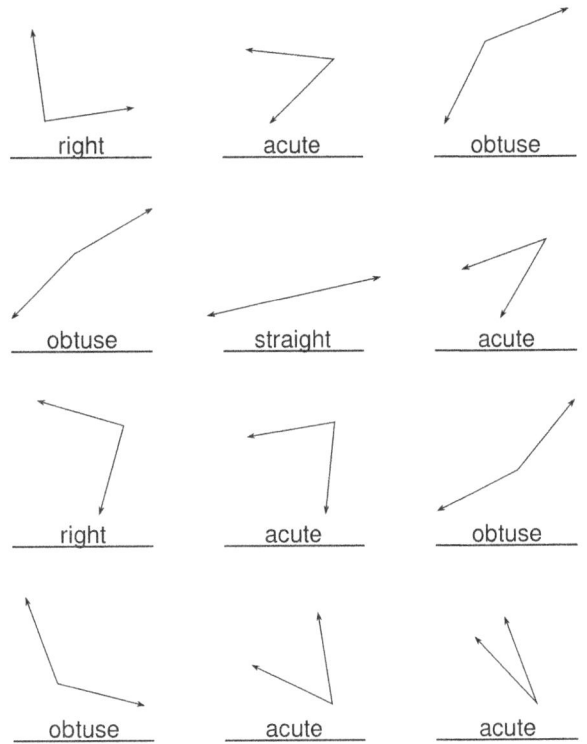

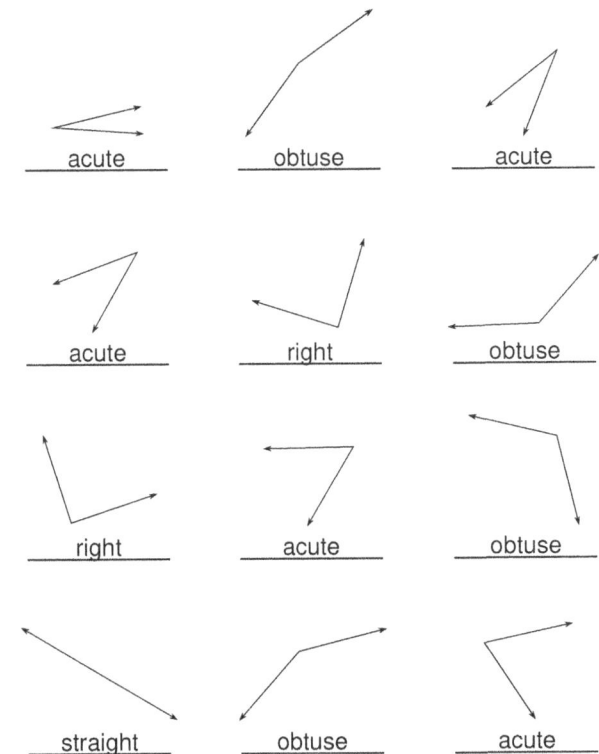

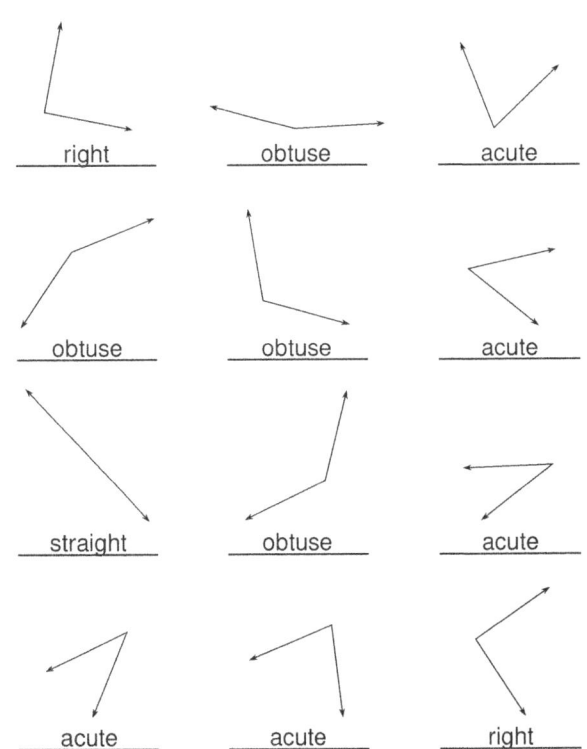

right	acute	acute
right	obtuse	obtuse
obtuse	acute	straight
obtuse	obtuse	acute

Solutions for Page 10

Label each angle acute, obtuse, right or straight.

right	acute	obtuse
obtuse	straight	acute
right	acute	obtuse
obtuse	acute	acute

Solutions for Page 11

Label each angle acute, obtuse, right or straight.

acute	obtuse	acute
acute	right	obtuse
right	acute	obtuse
straight	obtuse	acute

Solutions for Page 12

Label each angle acute, obtuse, right or straight.

right	obtuse	acute
obtuse	obtuse	acute
straight	obtuse	acute
acute	acute	right

Solutions for Page 13

Label each angle acute, obtuse, right or straight.

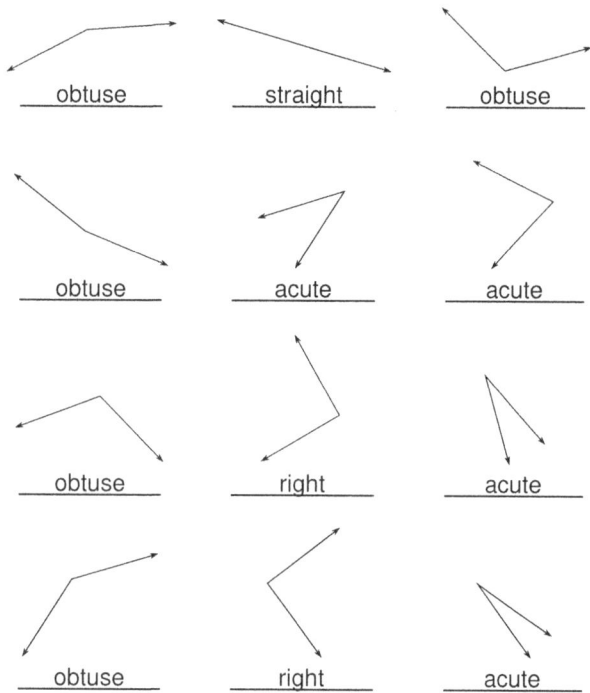

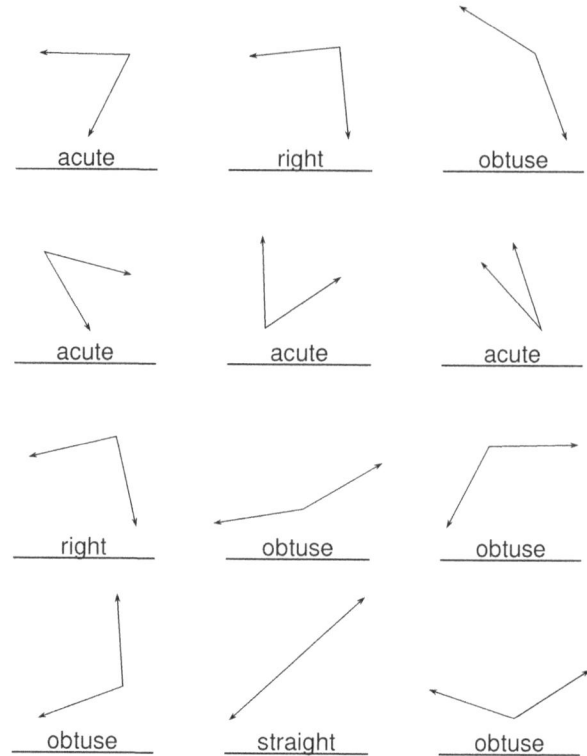

obtuse	straight	obtuse
obtuse	acute	acute
obtuse	right	acute
obtuse	right	acute

Solutions for Page 14

Label each angle acute, obtuse, right or straight.

acute	right	obtuse
acute	acute	acute
right	obtuse	obtuse
obtuse	straight	obtuse

Solutions for Page 15

Label each triangle scalene, isosceles or equilateral *and* acute, obtuse or right.

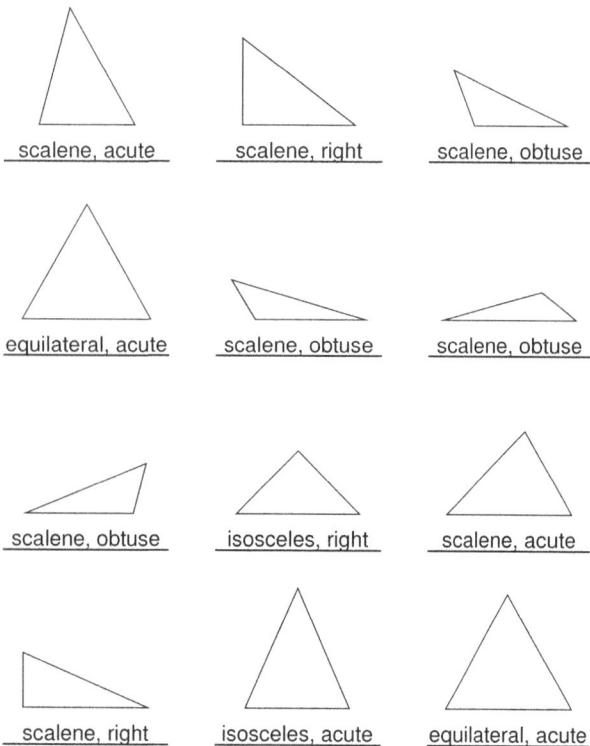

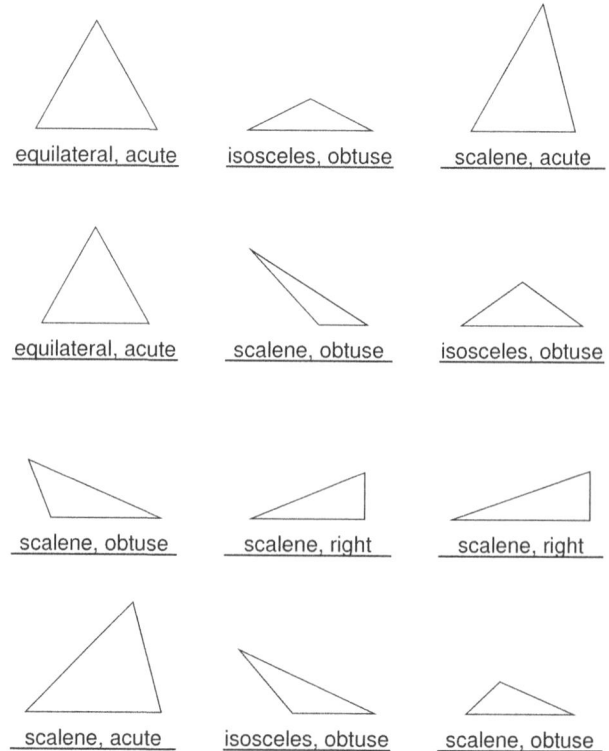

scalene, acute	scalene, right	scalene, obtuse
equilateral, acute	scalene, obtuse	scalene, obtuse
scalene, obtuse	isosceles, right	scalene, acute
scalene, right	isosceles, acute	equilateral, acute

Solutions for Page 16

Label each triangle scalene, isosceles or equilateral *and* acute, obtuse or right.

equilateral, acute	isosceles, obtuse	scalene, acute
equilateral, acute	scalene, obtuse	isosceles, obtuse
scalene, obtuse	scalene, right	scalene, right
scalene, acute	isosceles, obtuse	scalene, obtuse

Solutions for Page 17

Label each triangle scalene, isosceles or equilateral
and acute, obtuse or right.

scalene, acute   scalene, obtuse   isosceles, acute

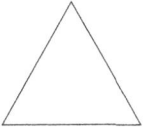

equilateral, acute   scalene, right   isosceles, acute

scalene, obtuse   scalene, right   scalene, obtuse

equilateral, acute   scalene, acute   scalene, obtuse

Solutions for Page 18

Label each triangle scalene, isosceles or equilateral
and acute, obtuse or right.

scalene, acute   scalene, acute   scalene, right

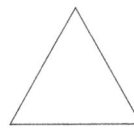

scalene, right   isosceles, obtuse   equilateral, acute

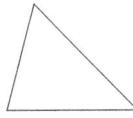

scalene, obtuse   scalene, obtuse   isosceles, obtuse

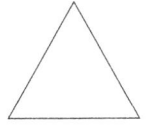

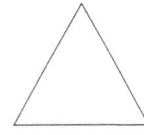

equilateral, acute   isosceles, obtuse   isosceles, obtuse

Solutions for Page 19

Label each triangle scalene, isosceles or equilateral
and acute, obtuse or right.

equilateral, acute   scalene, obtuse   isosceles, obtuse

equilateral, acute   scalene, right   scalene, right

scalene, obtuse   scalene, acute   isosceles, obtuse

scalene, acute   isosceles, obtuse   isosceles, obtuse

Solutions for Page 20

Label each triangle scalene, isosceles or equilateral
and acute, obtuse or right.

isosceles, obtuse   isosceles, obtuse   scalene, acute

equilateral, acute   scalene, acute   scalene, obtuse

isosceles, right   scalene, right   scalene, obtuse

scalene, obtuse   scalene, right   equilateral, acute

Solutions for Page 21

Label each triangle scalene, isosceles or equilateral *and* acute, obtuse or right.

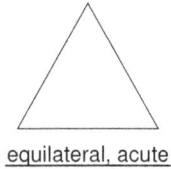

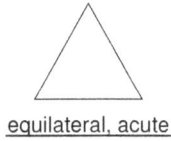

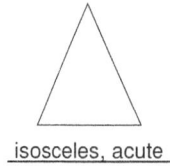

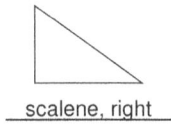

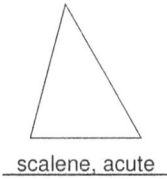

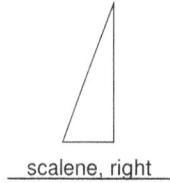

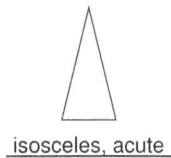

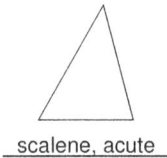

equilateral, acute   scalene, obtuse   isosceles, obtuse

equilateral, acute   scalene, obtuse   isosceles, acute

scalene, right   scalene, acute   scalene, right

isosceles, acute   scalene, acute   scalene, obtuse

Solutions for Page 22

Write the name of each shape.

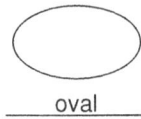

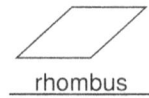

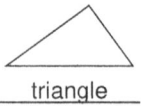

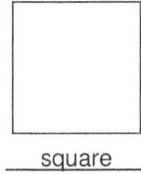

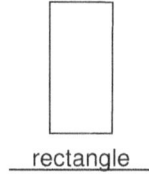

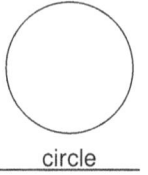

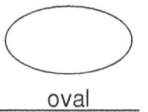

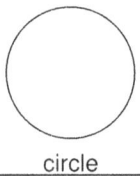

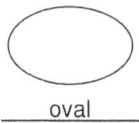

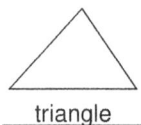

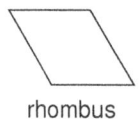

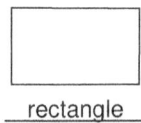

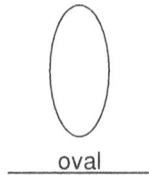

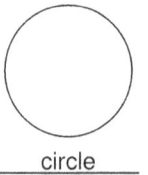

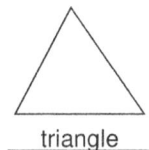

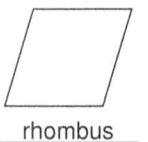

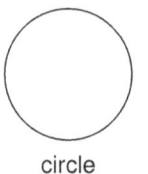

oval   rhombus   triangle

square   rectangle   circle

quadrilateral   trapezoid   parallelogram

trapezoid   parallelogram   oval

Solutions for Page 23

Write the name of each shape.

rhombus   circle   rectangle

quadrilateral   trapezoid   oval

triangle   square   parallelogram

parallelogram   quadrilateral   rhombus

Solutions for Page 24

Write the name of each shape.

square   parallelogram   trapezoid

rectangle   oval   circle

quadrilateral   triangle   rhombus

square   parallelogram   circle

Solutions for Page 25

Write the name of each shape.

rectangle

parallelogram

rhombus

square

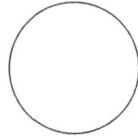

quadrilateral

oval

trapezoid

triangle

circle

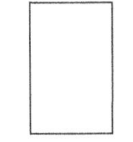

parallelogram

rectangle

square

Solutions for Page 26

Write the name of each shape.

oval

triangle

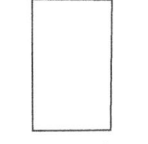

trapezoid

rhombus

circle

rectangle

quadrilateral

square

parallelogram

square

parallelogram

triangle

Solutions for Page 27

Write the name of each shape.

trapezoid

square

circle

quadrilateral

parallelogram

oval

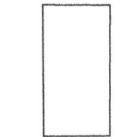

rhombus

rectangle

triangle

circle

triangle

rectangle

Solutions for Page 28

Write the name of each shape.

rectangle

rhombus

parallelogram

oval

circle

trapezoid

quadrilateral

square

triangle

circle

trapezoid

parallelogram

Solutions for Page 29

Write the name of each polygon.

 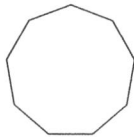 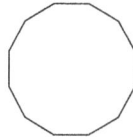

square   nonagon   dodecagon

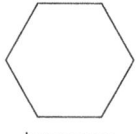 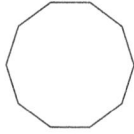 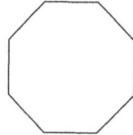

hexagon   decagon   octagon

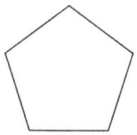 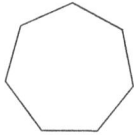 

pentagon   heptagon   square

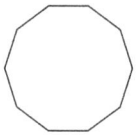 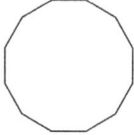 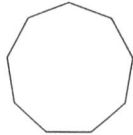

decagon   dodecagon   nonagon

Solutions for Page 30

Write the name of each polygon.

 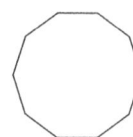 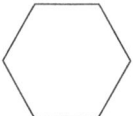

square   decagon   hexagon

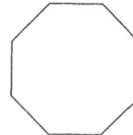 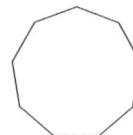 

octagon   nonagon   heptagon

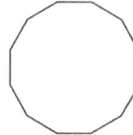 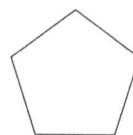 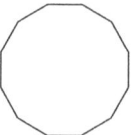

dodecagon   pentagon   dodecagon

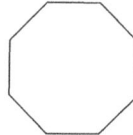 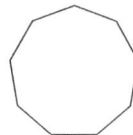 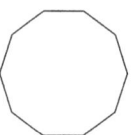

octagon   nonagon   decagon

Solutions for Page 31

Write the name of each polygon.

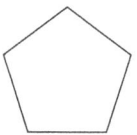 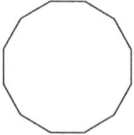 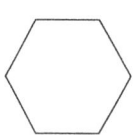

pentagon   dodecagon   hexagon

 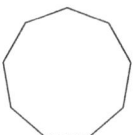 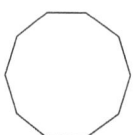

square   nonagon   decagon

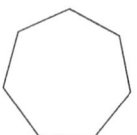 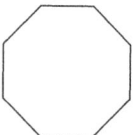 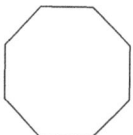

heptagon   octagon   octagon

 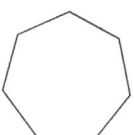 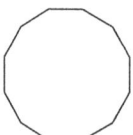

square   heptagon   dodecagon

Solutions for Page 32

Write the name of each polygon.

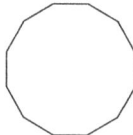 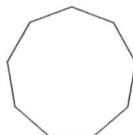 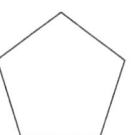

dodecagon   nonagon   pentagon

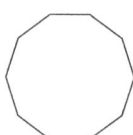  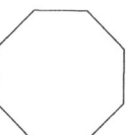

decagon   square   octagon

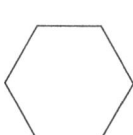 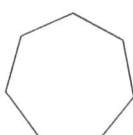 

hexagon   heptagon   square

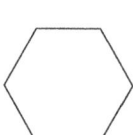 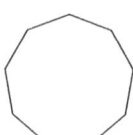 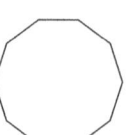

hexagon   nonagon   decagon

Solutions for Page 33

Write the name of each polygon.

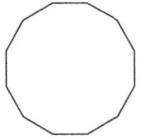 dodecagon

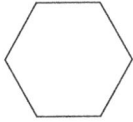 hexagon

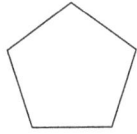 pentagon

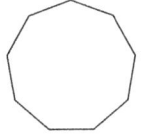 nonagon

 square

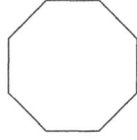 octagon

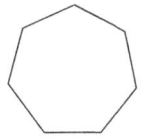 heptagon

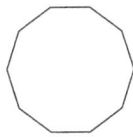 decagon

 square

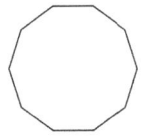 decagon

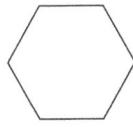 hexagon

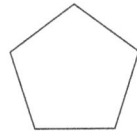 pentagon

Solutions for Page 34

Write the name of each polygon.

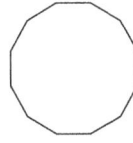 dodecagon

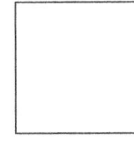 square

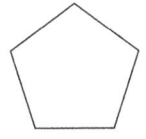 pentagon

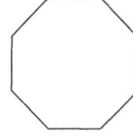 octagon

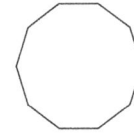 decagon

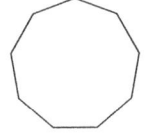 nonagon

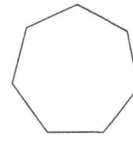 heptagon

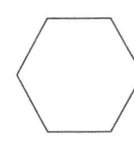 hexagon

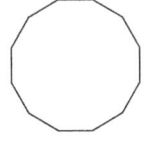 dodecagon

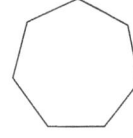 heptagon

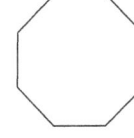 octagon

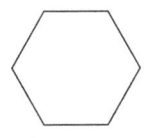 hexagon

Solutions for Page 35

Write the name of each polygon.

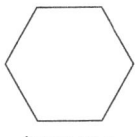 hexagon

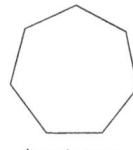 heptagon

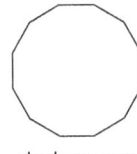 dodecagon

 square

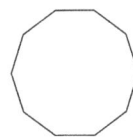 decagon

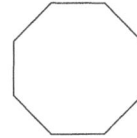 octagon

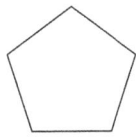 pentagon

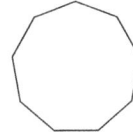 nonagon

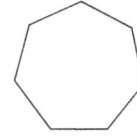 heptagon

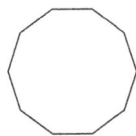 decagon

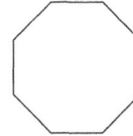 octagon

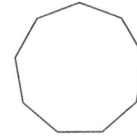 nonagon

Solutions for Page 36

Write the name of each 3-dimensional solid.

cylinder

octahedron

cube

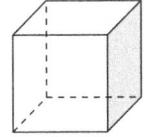 rectangular prism

dodecahedron

sphere

tetrahedron

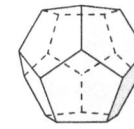 square pyramid

 cone

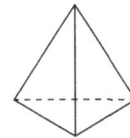 ellipsoid

icosahedron

 triangular prism

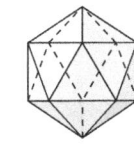

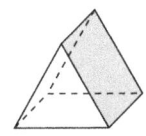

Solutions for Page 37

Write the name of each 3-dimensional solid.

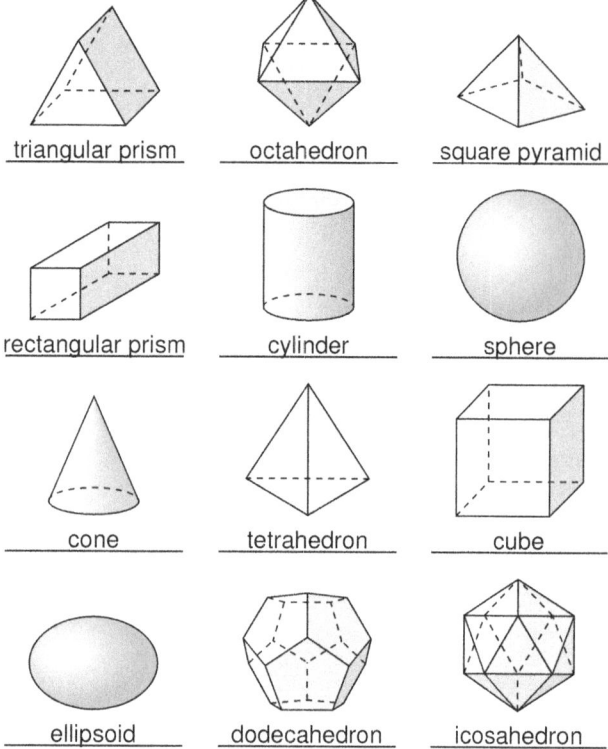

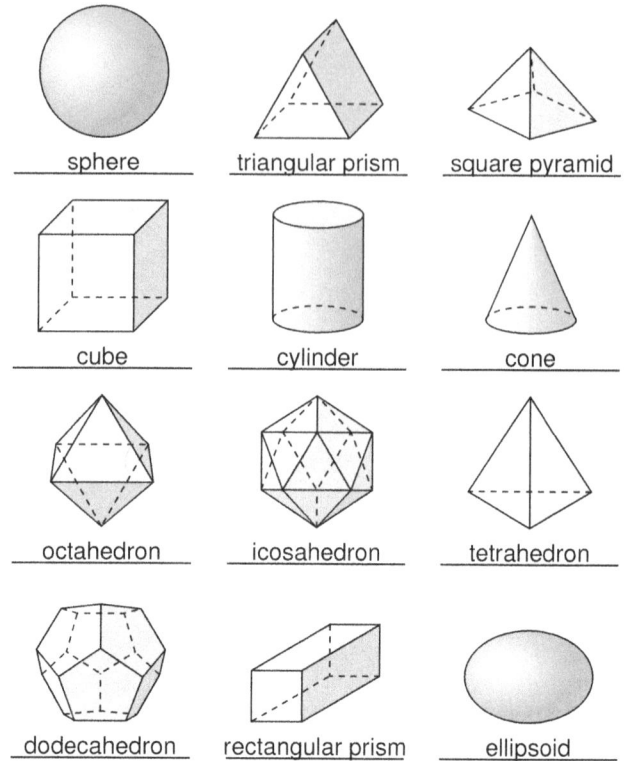

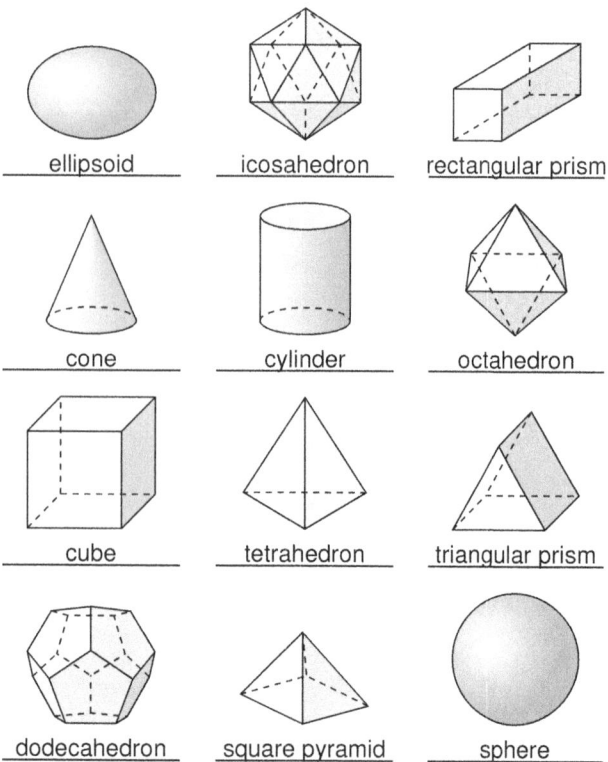

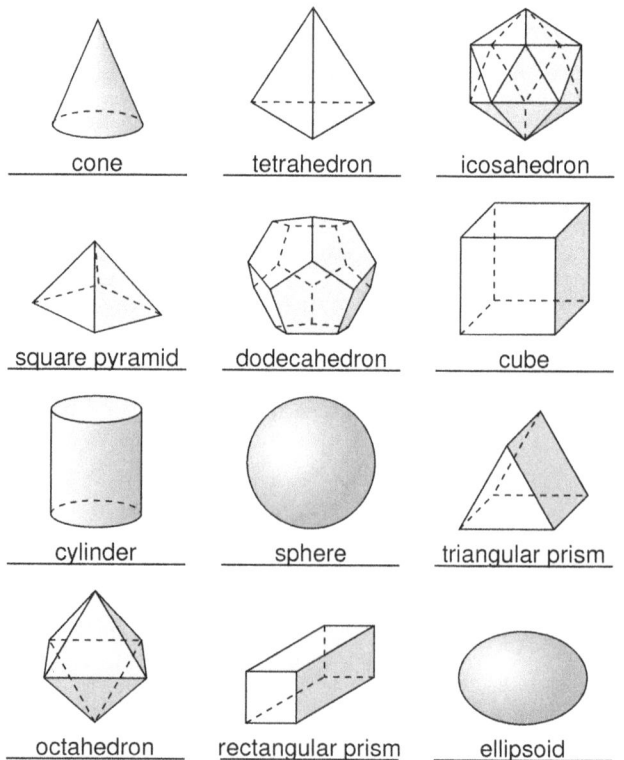

triangular prism	octahedron	square pyramid
rectangular prism	cylinder	sphere
cone	tetrahedron	cube
ellipsoid	dodecahedron	icosahedron

Solutions for Page 38

Write the name of each 3-dimensional solid.

sphere	triangular prism	square pyramid
cube	cylinder	cone
octahedron	icosahedron	tetrahedron
dodecahedron	rectangular prism	ellipsoid

Solutions for Page 39

Write the name of each 3-dimensional solid.

ellipsoid	icosahedron	rectangular prism
cone	cylinder	octahedron
cube	tetrahedron	triangular prism
dodecahedron	square pyramid	sphere

Solutions for Page 40

Write the name of each 3-dimensional solid.

cone	tetrahedron	icosahedron
square pyramid	dodecahedron	cube
cylinder	sphere	triangular prism
octahedron	rectangular prism	ellipsoid

Solutions for Page 41

Write the name of each 3-dimensional solid.

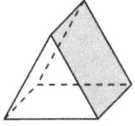
triangular prism

cone

rectangular prism

sphere

octahedron

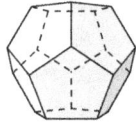
dodecahedron

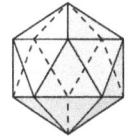
icosahedron

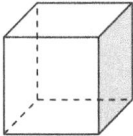
cube

cylinder

square pyramid

ellipsoid

tetrahedron

Solutions for Page 42

Write the name of each 3-dimensional solid.

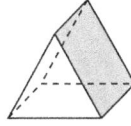
triangular prism

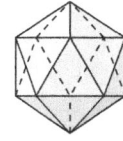
icosahedron

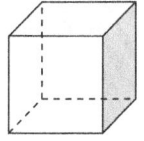
cube

sphere

cylinder

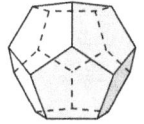
dodecahedron

cone

rectangular prism

square pyramid

ellipsoid

tetrahedron

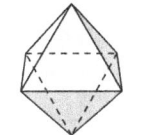
octahedron

Solutions for Page 43

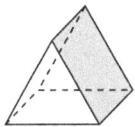

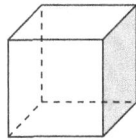

This is a
__Triangular Prism__

It has __5__ faces.
It has __9__ edges.
It has __6__ vertices.

This is a
__Icosahedron__

It has __20__ faces.
It has __30__ edges.
It has __12__ vertices.

This is a
__Cube__

It has __6__ faces.
It has __12__ edges.
It has __8__ vertices.

This is a
__Octahedron__

It has __8__ faces.
It has __12__ edges.
It has __6__ vertices.

This is a
__Square Pyramid__

It has __5__ faces.
It has __8__ edges.
It has __5__ vertices.

This is a
__Tetrahedron__

It has __4__ faces.
It has __6__ edges.
It has __4__ vertices.

Solutions for Page 44

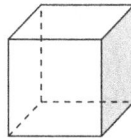

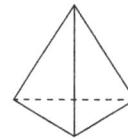

This is a
__Cube__

It has __6__ faces.
It has __12__ edges.
It has __8__ vertices.

This is a
__Tetrahedron__

It has __4__ faces.
It has __6__ edges.
It has __4__ vertices.

This is a
__Square Pyramid__

It has __5__ faces.
It has __8__ edges.
It has __5__ vertices.

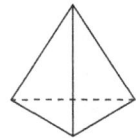

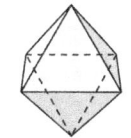

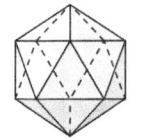

This is a
__Octahedron__

It has __8__ faces.
It has __12__ edges.
It has __6__ vertices.

This is a
__Dodecahedron__

It has __12__ faces.
It has __30__ edges.
It has __20__ vertices.

This is a
__Icosahedron__

It has __20__ faces.
It has __30__ edges.
It has __12__ vertices.

Solutions for Page 45

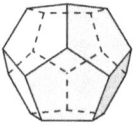

This is a
__Dodecahedron__

It has __12__ faces.

It has __30__ edges.

It has __20__ vertices.

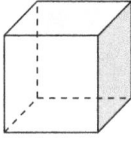

This is a
__Cube__

It has __6__ faces.

It has __12__ edges.

It has __8__ vertices.

This is a
__Octahedron__

It has __8__ faces.

It has __12__ edges.

It has __6__ vertices.

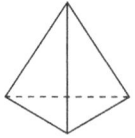

This is a
__Tetrahedron__

It has __4__ faces.

It has __6__ edges.

It has __4__ vertices.

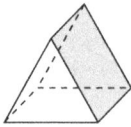

This is a
__Triangular Prism__

It has __5__ faces.

It has __9__ edges.

It has __6__ vertices.

This is a
__Icosahedron__

It has __20__ faces.

It has __30__ edges.

It has __12__ vertices.

Solutions for Page 46

This is a
__Square Pyramid__

It has __5__ faces.

It has __8__ edges.

It has __5__ vertices.

This is a
__Tetrahedron__

It has __4__ faces.

It has __6__ edges.

It has __4__ vertices.

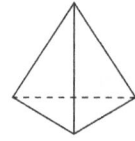

This is a
__Octahedron__

It has __8__ faces.

It has __12__ edges.

It has __6__ vertices.

This is a
__Icosahedron__

It has __20__ faces.

It has __30__ edges.

It has __12__ vertices.

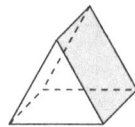

This is a
__Triangular Prism__

It has __5__ faces.

It has __9__ edges.

It has __6__ vertices.

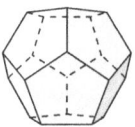

This is a
__Dodecahedron__

It has __12__ faces.

It has __30__ edges.

It has __20__ vertices.

Solutions for Page 47

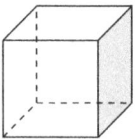

This is a
__Cube__

It has __6__ faces.

It has __12__ edges.

It has __8__ vertices.

This is a
__Octahedron__

It has __8__ faces.

It has __12__ edges.

It has __6__ vertices.

This is a
__Icosahedron__

It has __20__ faces.

It has __30__ edges.

It has __12__ vertices.

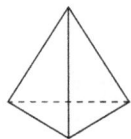

This is a
__Square Pyramid__

It has __5__ faces.

It has __8__ edges.

It has __5__ vertices.

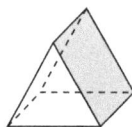

This is a
__Tetrahedron__

It has __4__ faces.

It has __6__ edges.

It has __4__ vertices.

This is a
__Triangular Prism__

It has __5__ faces.

It has __9__ edges.

It has __6__ vertices.

Solutions for Page 48

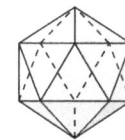

This is a
__Icosahedron__

It has __20__ faces.

It has __30__ edges.

It has __12__ vertices.

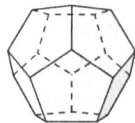

This is a
__Dodecahedron__

It has __12__ faces.

It has __30__ edges.

It has __20__ vertices.

This is a
__Square Pyramid__

It has __5__ faces.

It has __8__ edges.

It has __5__ vertices.

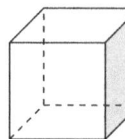

This is a
__Cube__

It has __6__ faces.

It has __12__ edges.

It has __8__ vertices.

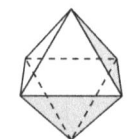

This is a
__Octahedron__

It has __8__ faces.

It has __12__ edges.

It has __6__ vertices.

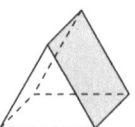

This is a
__Triangular Prism__

It has __5__ faces.

It has __9__ edges.

It has __6__ vertices.

Solutions for Page 49

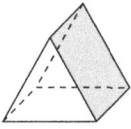

This is a
__Triangular Prism__

It has __5__ faces.

It has __9__ edges.

It has __6__ vertices.

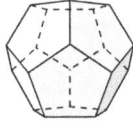

This is a
__Square Pyramid__

It has __5__ faces.

It has __8__ edges.

It has __5__ vertices.

This is a
__Dodecahedron__

It has __12__ faces.

It has __30__ edges.

It has __20__ vertices.

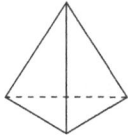

This is a
__Tetrahedron__

It has __4__ faces.

It has __6__ edges.

It has __4__ vertices.

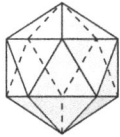

This is a
__Icosahedron__

It has __20__ faces.

It has __30__ edges.

It has __12__ vertices.

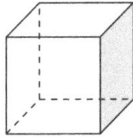

This is a
__Cube__

It has __6__ faces.

It has __12__ edges.

It has __8__ vertices.

Solutions for Page 50

What type of symmetry does each shape have?
Label each shape Reflective, Rotational, Both or None.

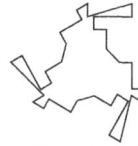

Rotational

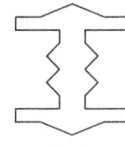

Both

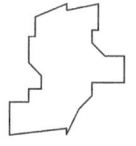

None

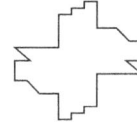

Reflective

Rotational

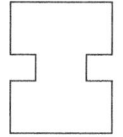

Both

None

Reflective

Rotational

Both

None

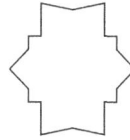

Reflective

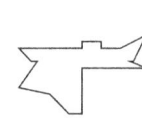

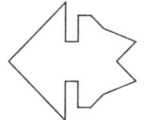

Solutions for Page 51

What type of symmetry does each shape have?
Label each shape Reflective, Rotational, Both or None.

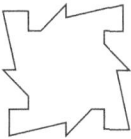

Rotational

Both

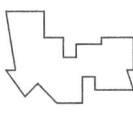

None

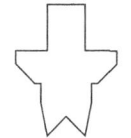

Reflective

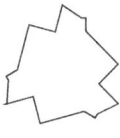

Rotational

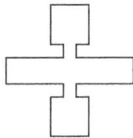

Both

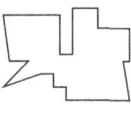

None

Reflective

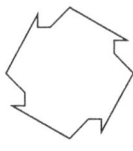

Rotational

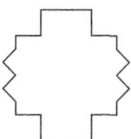

Both

None

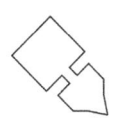

Reflective

Solutions for Page 52

What type of symmetry does each shape have?
Label each shape Reflective, Rotational, Both or None.

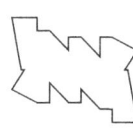

Rotational

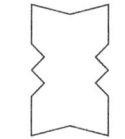

Both

None

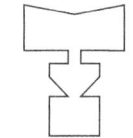

Reflective

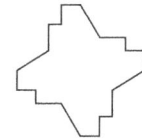

Rotational

Both

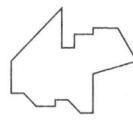

None

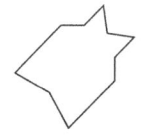

Reflective

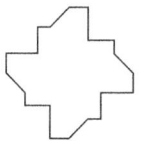

Rotational

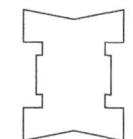

Both

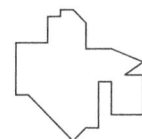

None

Reflective

Solutions for Page 53

What type of symmetry does each shape have?
Label each shape Reflective, Rotational, Both or None.

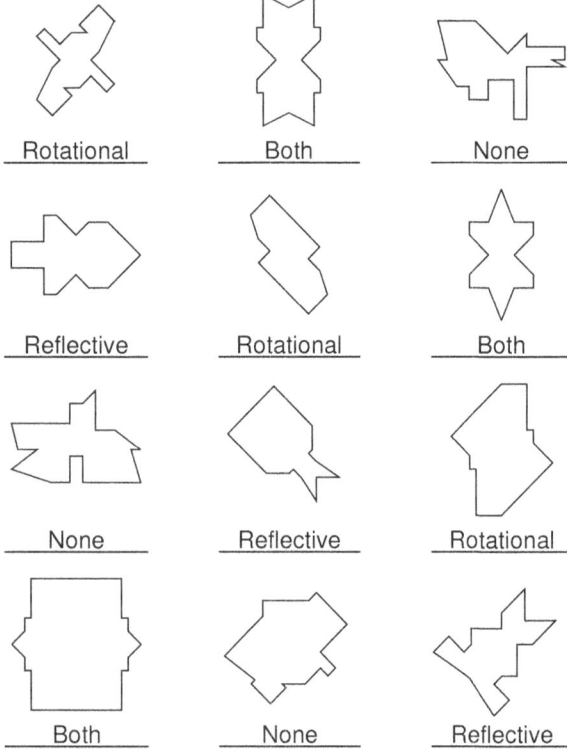

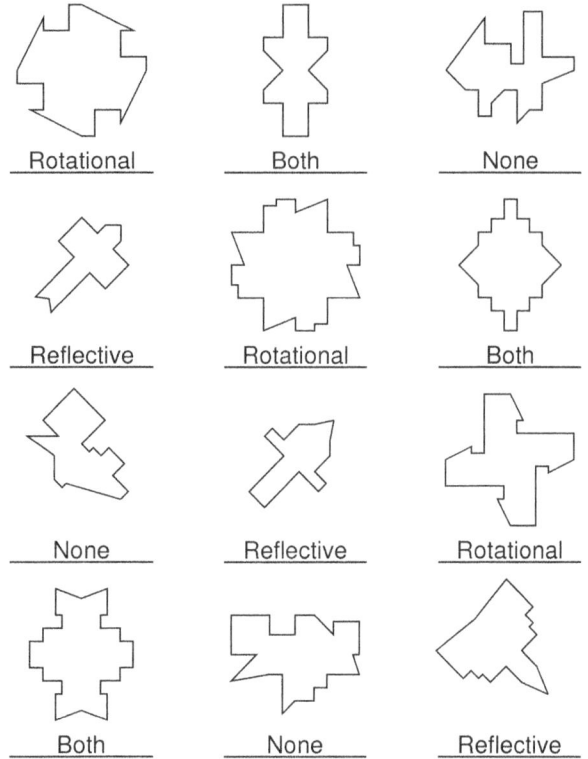

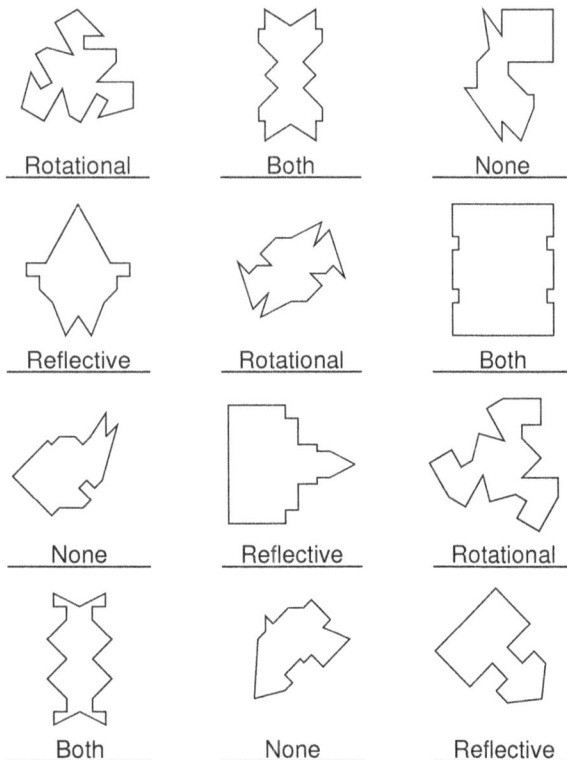

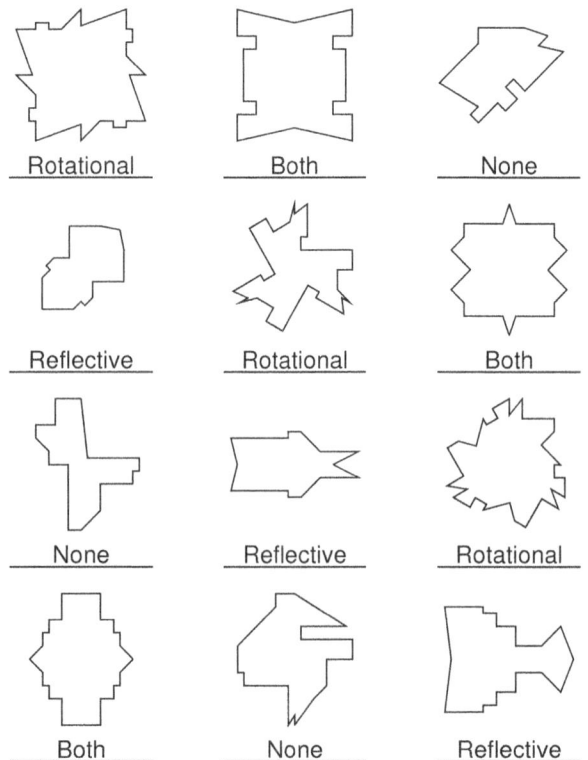

Rotational

Both

None

Reflective

Rotational

Both

None

Reflective

Rotational

Both

None

Reflective

Solutions for Page 54

What type of symmetry does each shape have?
Label each shape Reflective, Rotational, Both or None.

Rotational

Both

None

Reflective

Rotational

Both

None

Reflective

Rotational

Both

None

Reflective

Solutions for Page 55

What type of symmetry does each shape have?
Label each shape Reflective, Rotational, Both or None.

Rotational

Both

None

Reflective

Rotational

Both

None

Reflective

Rotational

Both

None

Reflective

Solutions for Page 56

What type of symmetry does each shape have?
Label each shape Reflective, Rotational, Both or None.

Rotational

Both

None

Reflective

Rotational

Both

None

Reflective

Rotational

Both

None

Reflective

Solutions for Page 57

Draw the line of symmetry for each shape.
Some shapes may have more than one line of symmetry.

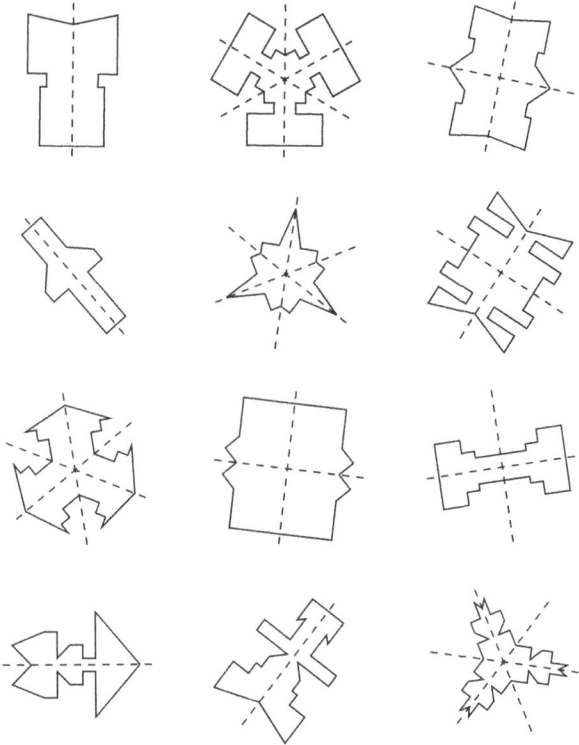

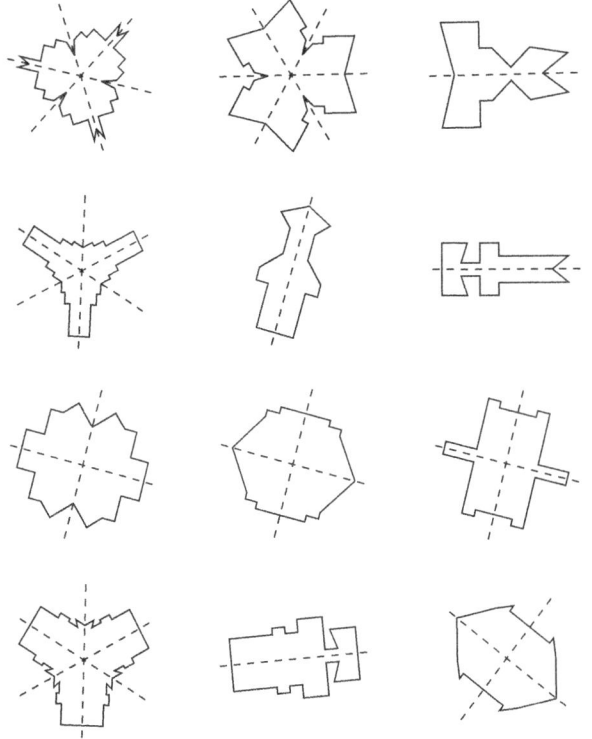

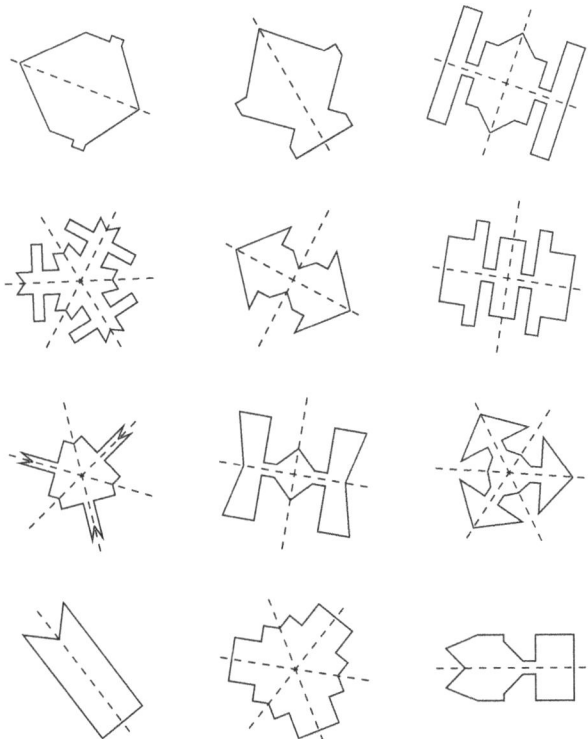

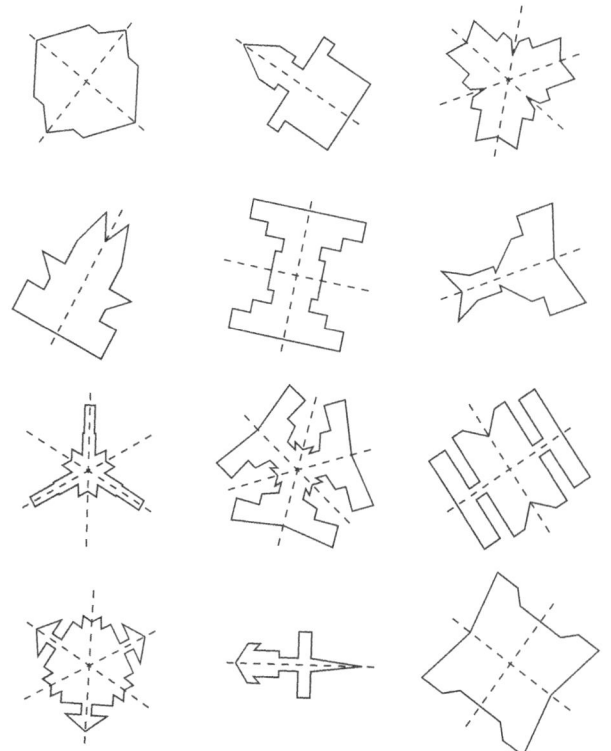

Solutions for Page 58

Draw the line of symmetry for each shape.
Some shapes may have more than one line of symmetry.

Solutions for Page 59

Draw the line of symmetry for each shape.
Some shapes may have more than one line of symmetry.

Solutions for Page 60

Draw the line of symmetry for each shape.
Some shapes may have more than one line of symmetry.

Solutions for Page 61

Draw the line of symmetry for each shape.
Some shapes may have more than one line of symmetry.

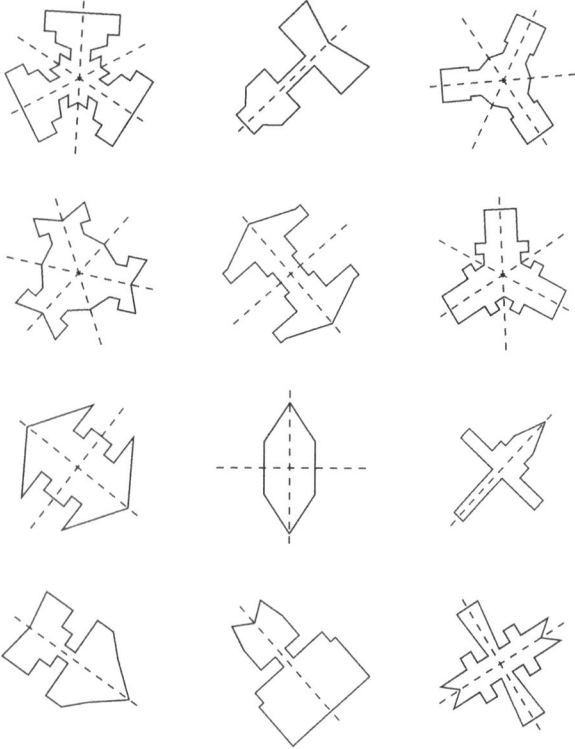

Solutions for Page 62

Draw the line of symmetry for each shape.
Some shapes may have more than one line of symmetry.

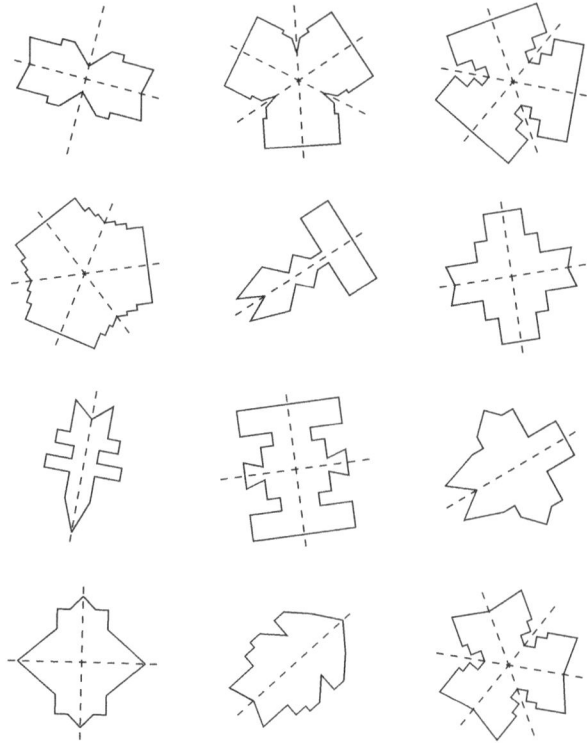

Solutions for Page 63

Draw the line of symmetry for each shape.
Some shapes may have more than one line of symmetry.

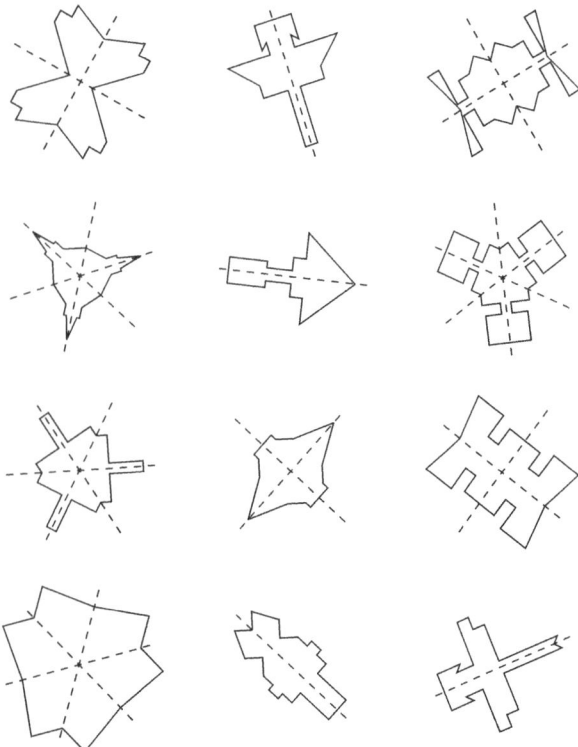

Solutions for Page 64

Draw the reflection of each shape across its line of symmetry.

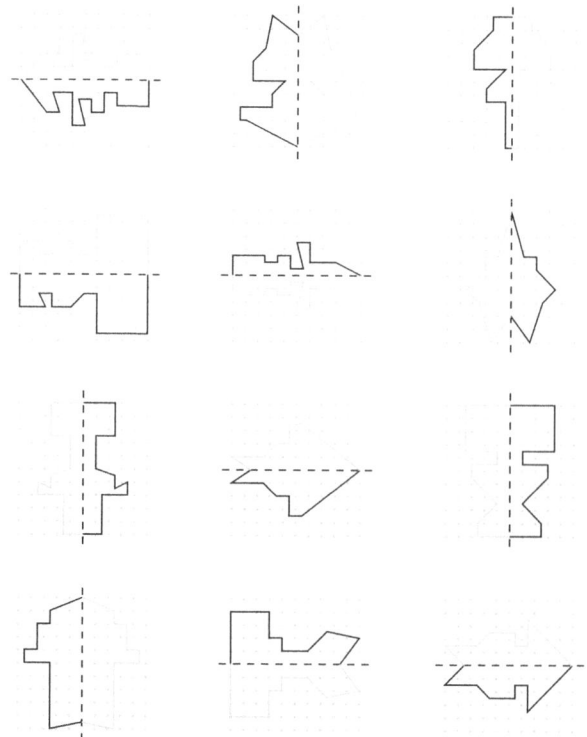

Solutions for Page 65

Draw the reflection of each shape across its line of symmetry.

Solutions for Page 66

Draw the reflection of each shape across its line of symmetry.

Solutions for Page 67

Draw the reflection of each shape across its line of symmetry.

Solutions for Page 68

Draw the reflection of each shape across its line of symmetry.

Solutions for Page 69

Draw the reflection of each shape across its line of symmetry.

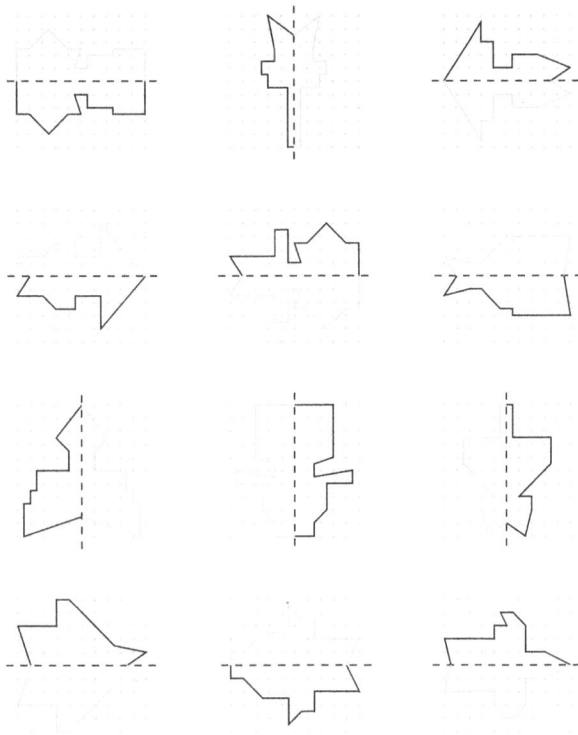

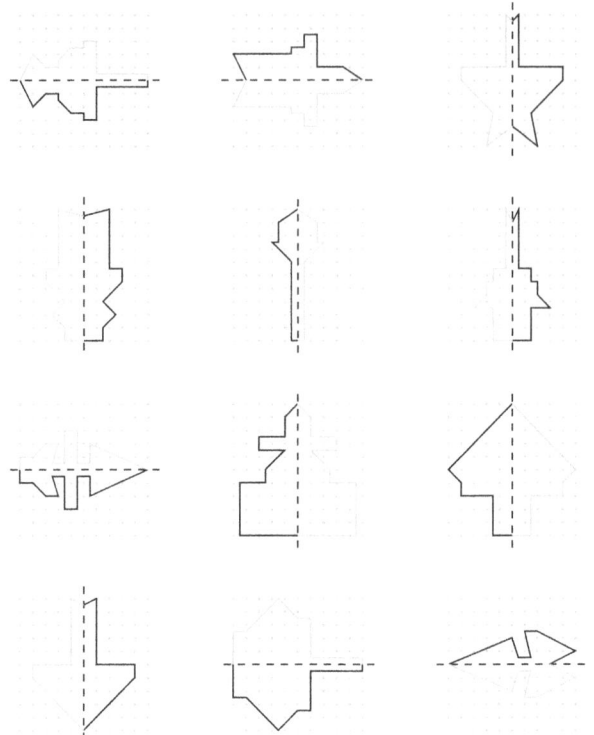

Solutions for Page 70

Draw the reflection of each shape across its line of symmetry.

Solutions for Page 71

Fill in the measures of the unknown angles.

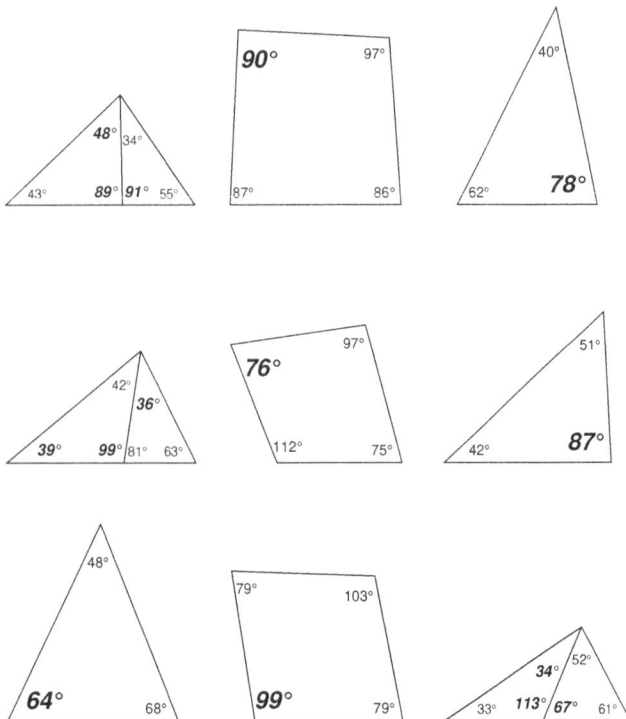

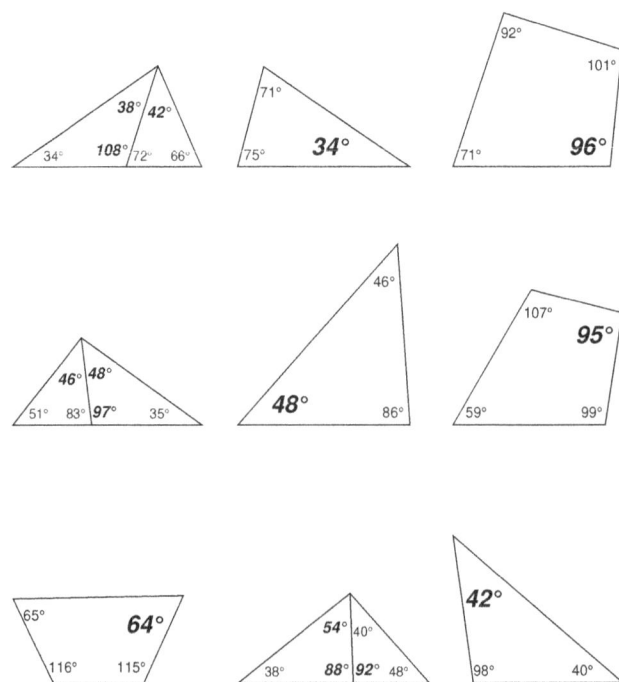

90° 97°

40°

48° 34°

43° **89° 91°** 55°

87° 86°

62° **78°**

42°

36°

39° 99° 81° 63°

76° 97°

112° 75°

51°

42° **87°**

48°

64° 68°

79° 103°

99° 79°

34° 52°

33° **113° 67°** 61°

Solutions for Page 72

Fill in the measures of the unknown angles.

38° 42°

34° 108° 72° 66°

71°

75° **34°**

92°

101°

71° **96°**

46°

46° 48°

51° 83° **97°** 35°

48° 86°

107° **95°**

59° 99°

65° **64°**

116° 115°

54° 40°

38° **88° 92°** 48°

42°

98° 40°

Solutions for Page 73

Fill in the measures of the unknown angles.

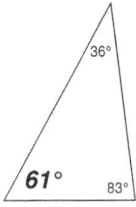

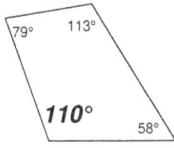

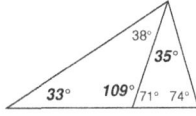

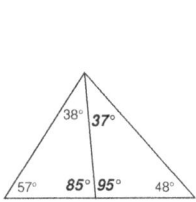

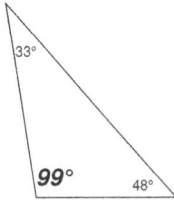

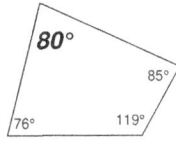

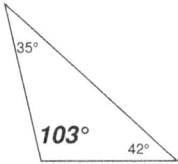

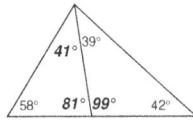

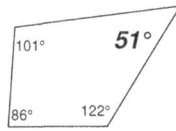

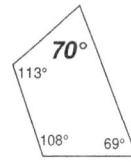

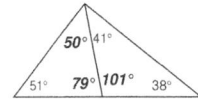

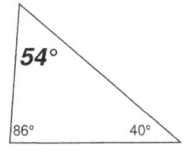

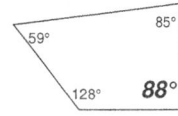

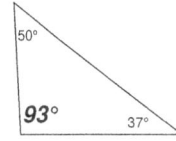

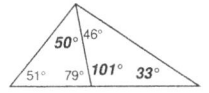

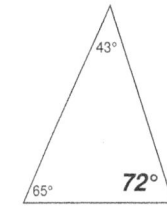

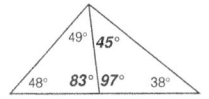

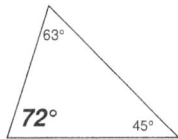

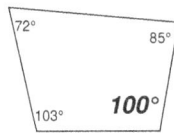

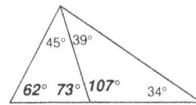

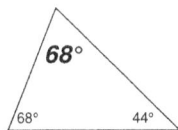

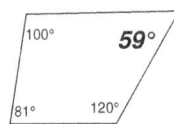

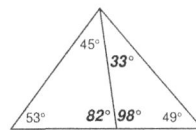

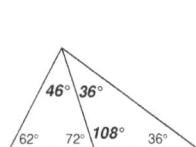

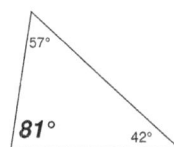

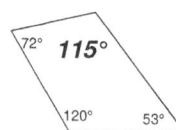

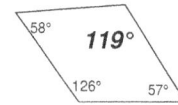

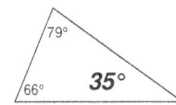

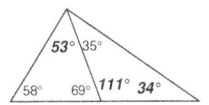

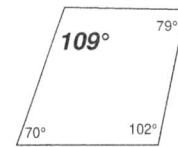

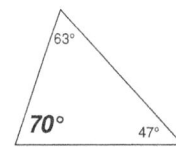

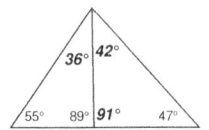

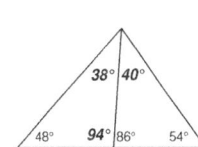

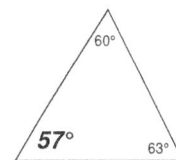

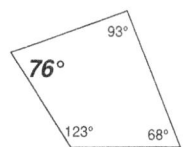

36°
61°
83°

79° 113°
110°
58°

38°
35°
33° 109° 71° 74°

38° 37°
57° 85° 95° 48°

33°
99° 48°

80°
85°
76° 119°

35°
103°
42°

41° 39°
58° 81° 99° 42°

101° 51°
86° 122°

Solutions for Page 74

Fill in the measures of the unknown angles.

70°
113°
108° 69°

50° 41°
51° 79° 101° 38°

54°
86° 40°

59° 85°
128° 88°

50°
93° 37°

50° 46°
51° 79° 101° 33°

56°
112°
100° 92°

43°
65° 72°

49° 45°
48° 83° 97° 38°

Solutions for Page 75

Fill in the measures of the unknown angles.

63°
72° 45°

72° 85°
103° 100°

45° 39°
62° 73° 107° 34°

68°
68° 44°

100° 59°
81° 120°

45° 33°
53° 82° 98° 49°

46° 36°
62° 72° 108° 36°

57°
81° 42°

72° 115°
120° 53°

Solutions for Page 76

Fill in the measures of the unknown angles.

58° 119°
126° 57°

79°
66° 35°

53° 35°
58° 69° 111° 34°

109° 79°
70° 102°

63°
70° 47°

36° 42°
55° 89° 91° 47°

38° 40°
48° 94° 86° 54°

60°
57° 63°

93°
76°
123° 68°

Solutions for Page 77

Fill in the measures of the unknown angles.

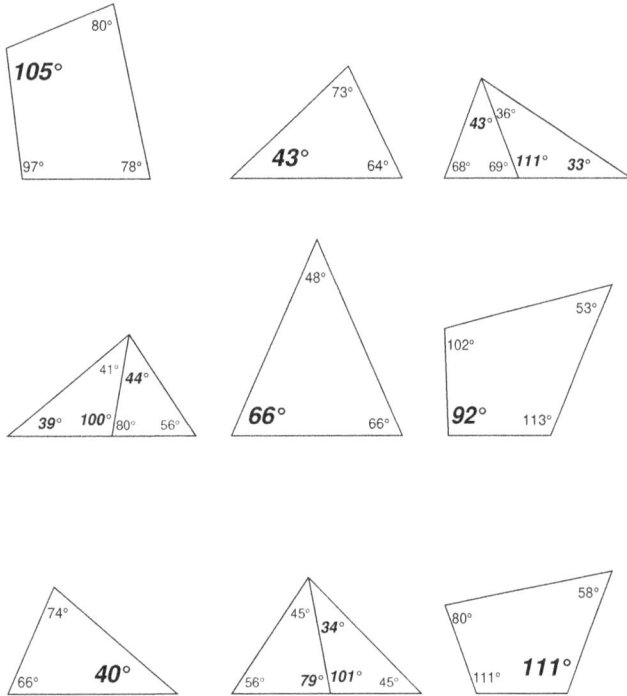

80°
105°
97°   78°

73°
43°   64°

43° 36°
68° 69° **111°** **33°**

41° **44°**
39° **100°** 80° 56°

48°
66°   66°

53°
102°
92°   113°

74°
40°
66°

45° **34°**
56° **79°** 101° 45°

58°
80°
111° **111°**

Solutions for Page 78

Fill in the measures of the unknown angles.
Horizontal lines that appear to be parallel are.

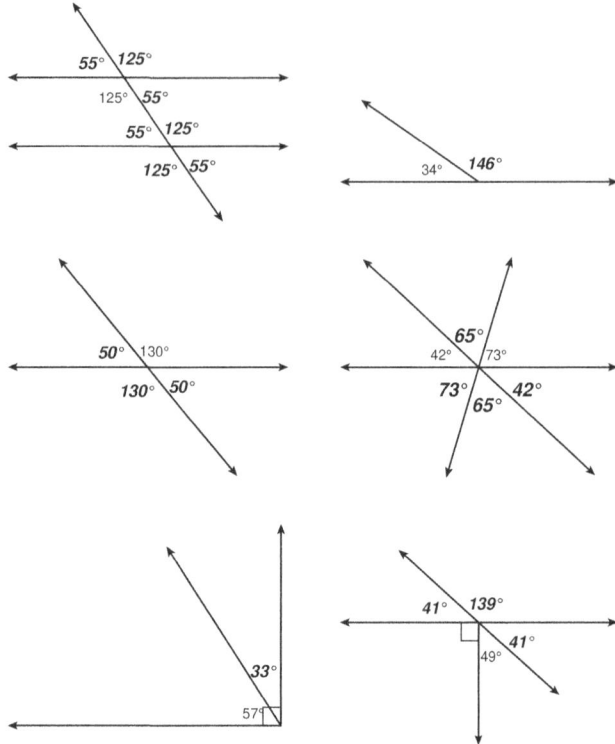

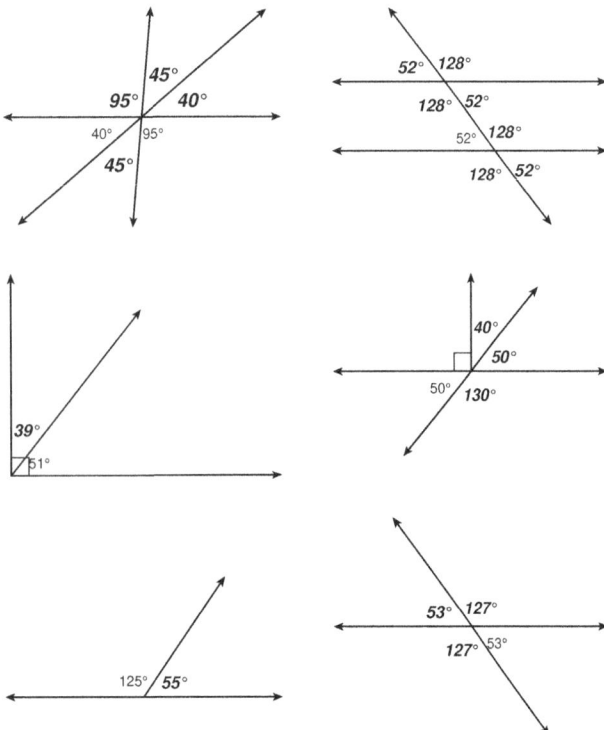

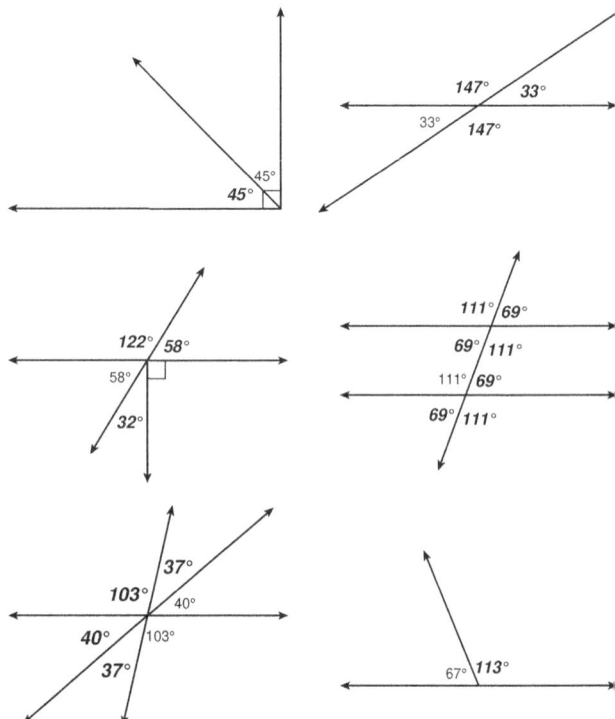

55° 125°
125° **55°**
55° 125°
125° **55°**

34°   **146°**

50° 130°
130° **50°**

65°
42° 73°
73°   **42°**
65°

33°
57°

41° 139°
41°
49°

Solutions for Page 79

Fill in the measures of the unknown angles.
Horizontal lines that appear to be parallel are.

45°
95°   **40°**
40° 95°
45°

52° 128°
128° **52°**
52° **128°**
128° **52°**

39°
51°

40°
50°
50° **130°**

125° **55°**

53° 127°
127° **53°**

Solutions for Page 80

Fill in the measures of the unknown angles.
Horizontal lines that appear to be parallel are.

45°
45°

147° **33°**
33° **147°**

122° **58°**
58°
32°

111° **69°**
69° 111°
111° **69°**
69° 111°

37°
103°
40°
40° 103°
37°

67° **113°**

Solutions for Page 81

Fill in the measures of the unknown angles.
Horizontal lines that appear to be parallel are.

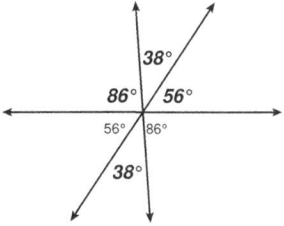

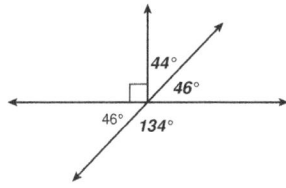

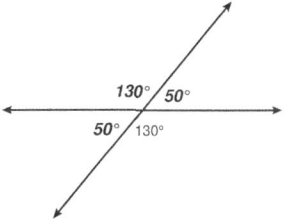

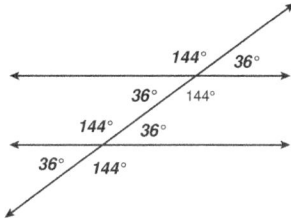

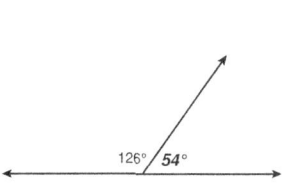

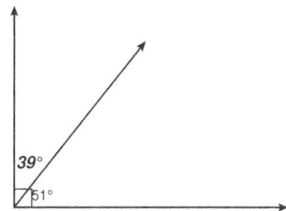

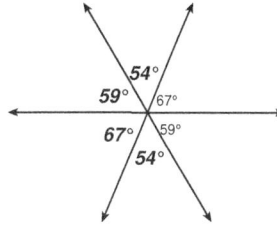

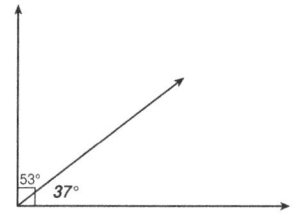

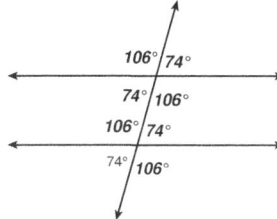

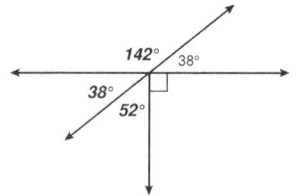

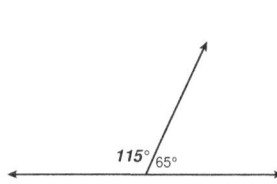

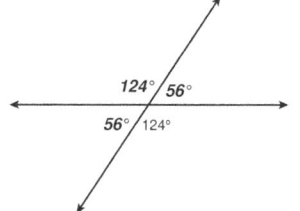

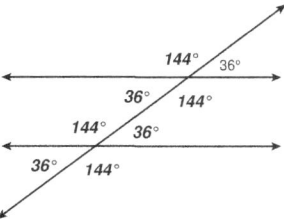

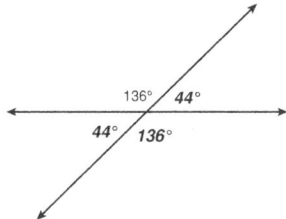

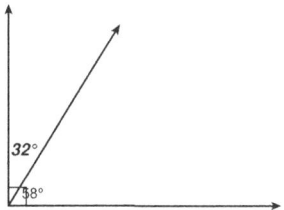

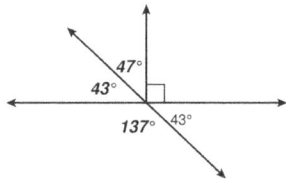

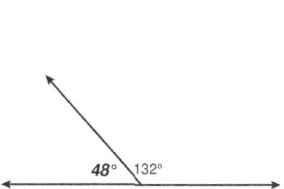

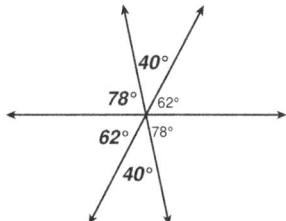

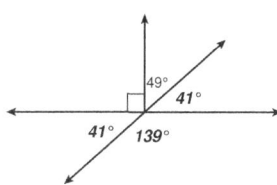

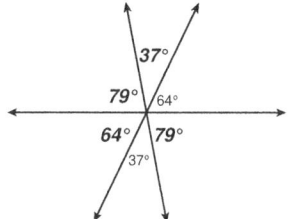

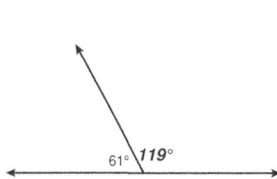

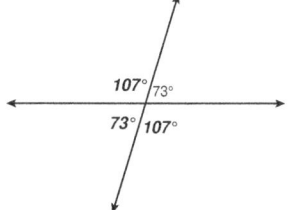

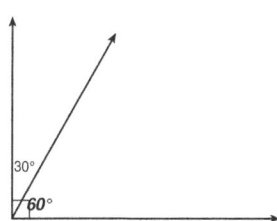

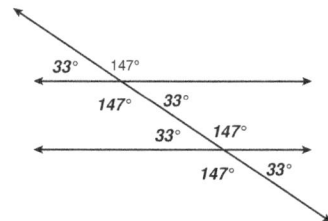

38°
86° 56°
56° 86°
38°

44°
46°
46° 134°

130° 50°
50° 130°

144° 36°
36° 144°
144° 36°
36° 144°

126° 54°

39°
51°

Solutions for Page 82

Fill in the measures of the unknown angles.
Horizontal lines that appear to be parallel are.

54°
59° 67°
67° 59°
54°

53°
37°

106° 74°
74° 106°
106° 74°
74° 106°

142° 38°
38°
52°

115° 65°

124° 56°
56° 124°

Solutions for Page 83

Fill in the measures of the unknown angles.
Horizontal lines that appear to be parallel are.

144° 36°
36° 144°
144° 36°
36° 144°

136° 44°
44° 136°

32°
58°

47°
43°
137° 43°

48° 132°

40°
78° 62°
62° 78°
40°

Solutions for Page 84

Fill in the measures of the unknown angles.
Horizontal lines that appear to be parallel are.

49°
41°
41° 139°

37°
79° 64°
64° 79°
37°

61° 119°

107° 73°
73° 107°

30°
60°

33° 147°
147° 33°
33° 147°
147° 33°

Solutions for Page 85

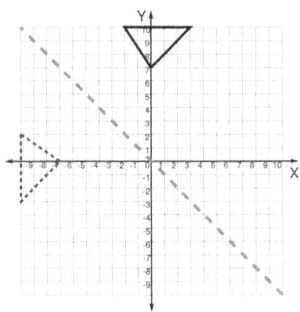

Reflect across y = -x.

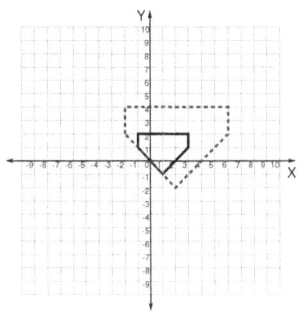

Dilate with a scale factor of 2, centered at the origin.

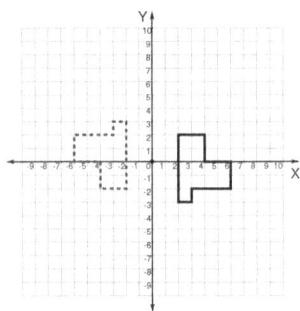

Reflect across (0, 0)

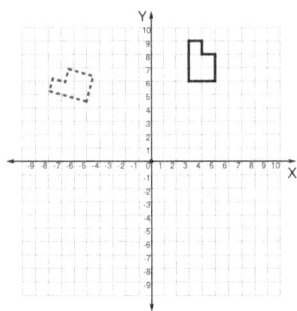

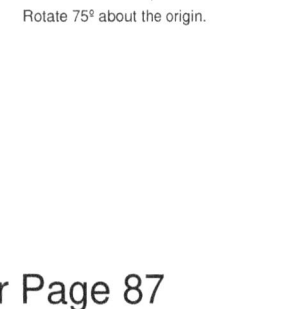

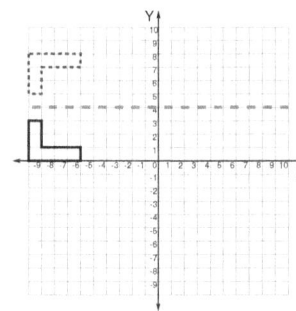

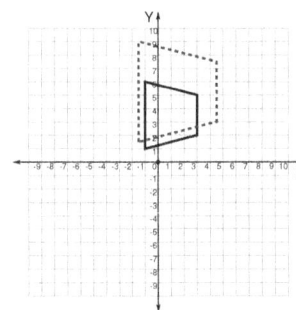

Rotate 75º about the origin.

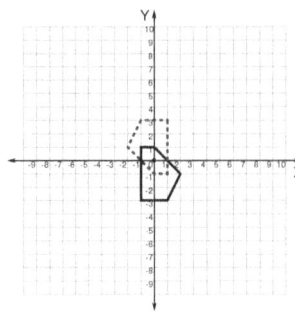

Solutions for Page 86

Rotate 180º about the origin.

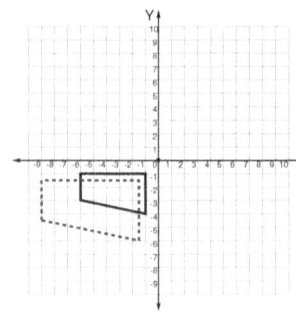

Dilate with a scale factor of 1.5, centered at the origin.

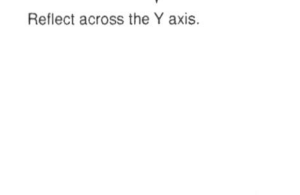

Reflect across (0, 0)

Reflect across y = 4.

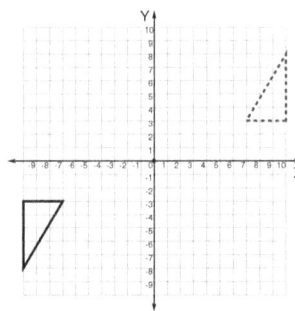

Solutions for Page 87

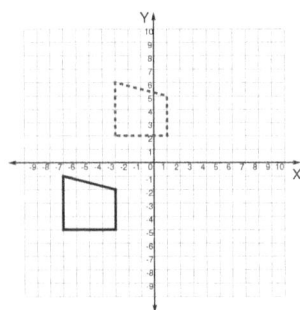

Translate 4 right and 7 up.

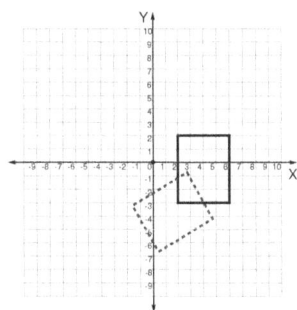

Rotate 60º about the origin.

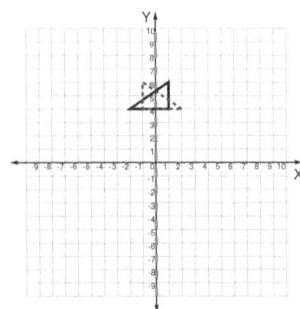

Reflect across the Y axis.

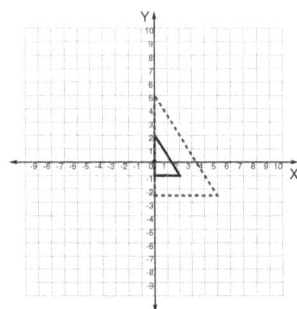

Dilate with a scale factor of 2.5, centered at the origin.

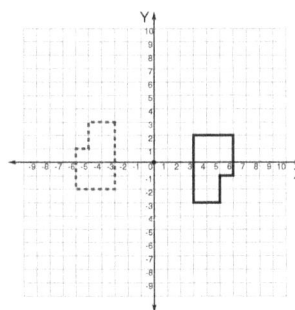

Solutions for Page 88

Reflect across (0, 0)

Dilate with a scale factor of 1.5, centered at the origin.

Reflect across x = 1.

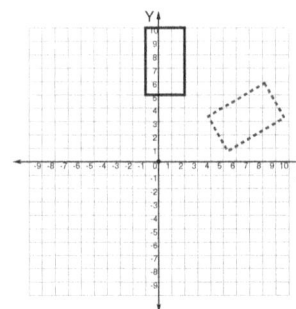

Rotate 60º about the origin.

Solutions for Page 89

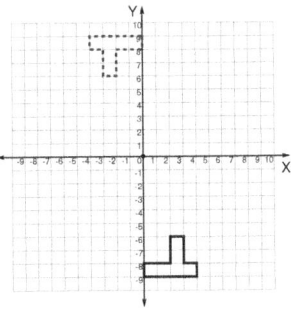

Reflect across (0, 0)

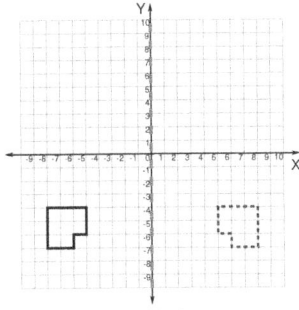

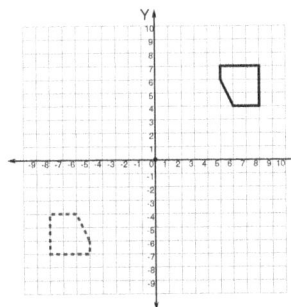

Reflect across the Y axis.

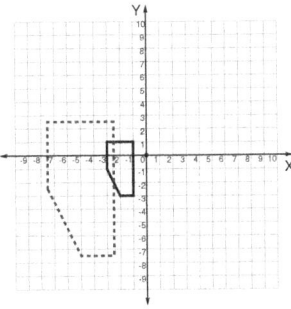

Dilate with a scale factor of 2.5, centered at the origin.

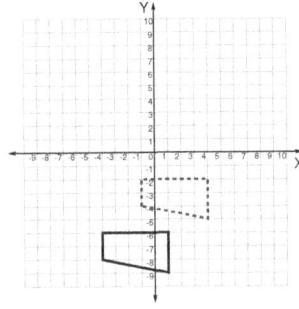

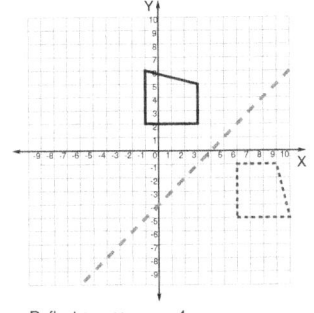

Translate 3 right and 4 up.

Solutions for Page 90

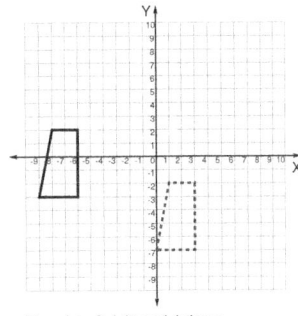

Translate 9 right and 4 down.

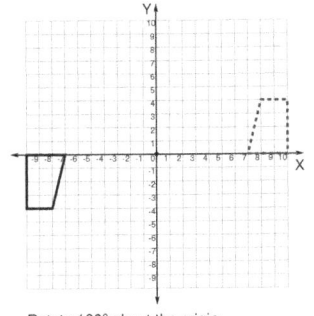

Rotate 180º about the origin.

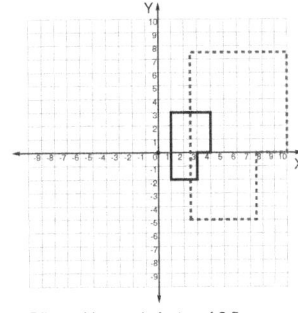

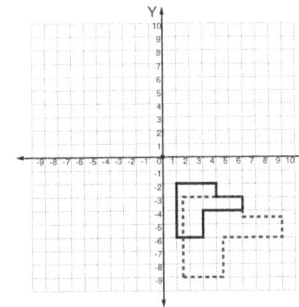

Dilate with a scale factor of 2.5, centered at the origin.

Reflect across y = x - 4.

Solutions for Page 91

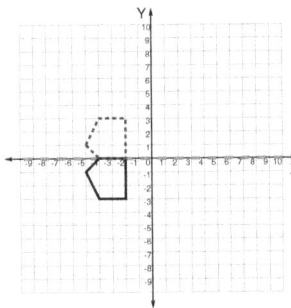

Reflect across the X axis.

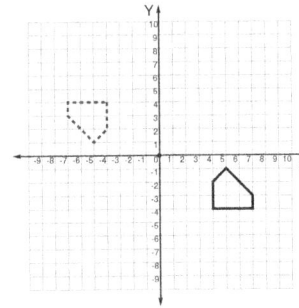

Reflect across (0, 0)

Rotate 180º about the origin.

Dilate with a scale factor of 1.5, centered at the origin.

Solutions for Page 92

What is the measure of angle x?

Angle x measures 156°

What are the measures of angle x and angle y?

$m\angle x = 180 - 109.5$
$m\angle x = 70.5°$

$m\angle y = 180 - 90.5$
$m\angle y = 89.5°$

What is the measure of angle x?

Angle x measures 90°

What is the measure of angle x?

Angle x = 190 / 2
Arc x = 95°

What are the measures of angle a, angle b, angle c and angle d?

$m\angle a = 40°$
$m\angle b = 31°$
$m\angle c = 109°$
$m\angle d = 109°$

What is the measure of angle x?

Angle x = 70 / 2
Arc x = 35°

Solutions for Page 93

What are the measures of angle a, angle b, angle c and angle d?

m∠a = 36°
m∠b = 57°
m∠c = 87°
m∠d = 87°

What is the measure of angle a?

m∠a = (240 - 120) / 2
m∠a = 60°

What are the measures of angle x and angle y?

m∠x = 180 - 102
m∠x = 78°

m∠y = 180 - 83
m∠y = 97°

What is the measure of angle x?

Angle x measures 98°

What is the measure of angle x?

Angle x = 190 / 2
Arc x = 95°

What is the measure of angle a?

m∠a = (124 - 54) / 2
m∠a = 35°

Solutions for Page 94

What is the measure of angle x?

Angle x measures 90°

What is the measure of angle a?

m∠a = (132 - 72) / 2
m∠a = 30°

What are the measures of angle a, angle b, angle c and angle d?

m∠a = 62°
m∠b = 45°
m∠c = 73°
m∠d = 73°

What is the measure of angle x?

Angle x = 78 / 2
Arc x = 39°

What is the measure of angle x?

Angle x measures 70°

What is the measure of angle a?

m∠a = (134 - 52) / 2
m∠a = 41°

Solutions for Page 95

What is the measure of angle a?

m∠a = (134 - 50) / 2
m∠a = 42°

What is the measure of angle x?

Angle x = 192 / 2
Arc x = 96°

What is the measure of angle x?

Angle x = 168 / 2
Arc x = 84°

What are the measures of angle x and angle y?

m∠x = 180 - 112
m∠x = 68°

m∠y = 180 - 82.5
m∠y = 97.5°

What is the measure of angle x?

Angle x measures 90°

What is the measure of angle a?

m∠a = (243 - 117) / 2
m∠a = 63°

Solutions for Page 96

What is the measure of angle x?

Angle x measures 107°

What is the measure of angle a?

m∠a = (140 - 60) / 2
m∠a = 40°

What is the measure of angle a?

m∠a = (241 - 119) / 2
m∠a = 61°

What are the measures of angle a, angle b, angle c and angle d?

m∠a = 41°
m∠b = 29°
m∠c = 110°
m∠d = 110°

What is the measure of angle x?

Angle x = 164 / 2
Arc x = 82°

What is the measure of angle x?

Angle x measures 90°

Solutions for Page 97

What is the measure of angle x?

Angle x measures 90°

What is the measure of angle x?

79°

Angle x measures 79°

What is the measure of angle a?

129°
59°

m∠a = (129 - 59) / 2
m∠a = 35°

What is the measure of angle x?

110°

Angle x = 110 / 2
Arc x = 55°

What is the measure of angle x?

x
98°

Angle x = 98 / 2
Arc x = 49°

What is the measure of angle a?

128°
232°

m∠a = (232 - 128) / 2
m∠a = 52°

Solutions for Page 98

What is the measure of angle a?

124°
236°

m∠a = (236 - 124) / 2
m∠a = 56°

What is the measure of angle a?

54°
138°

m∠a = (138 - 54) / 2
m∠a = 42°

What is the measure of angle x?

x

Angle x measures 90°

What is the measure of angle x?

111°

Angle x measures 111°

What is the measure of angle a?

51°
91°

m∠a = (91 - 51) / 2
m∠a = 20°

What is the measure of angle x?

x
88°

Angle x = 88 / 2
Arc x = 44°

Solutions for Page 99

Solutions for Page 100

Made in the USA
Las Vegas, NV
21 May 2025

22456962R00070